WHAT PEOPLE ARE SAYING ABOUT

FAIRYCRAFT

An in-depth and detailed book about working with *real* fairy witchcraft, Morgan Daimler draws on her own vast wealth of knowledge and experience as well as traditional folklore and ancient myths and legends. Definitely a must for those who wish to find out more about this intriguing pathway.
Rachel Patterson, author of *A Kitchen Witch's World of Magical Food* and *A Kitchen Witch's World of Magical Herbs & Plants*

There are a number of books out there about faeries, and most describe something more akin to Tinker Bell than real faeries. Only a rare few come close to describing the true nature of the Fay and how to work with them. This is one of those rare gems. If you want to understand and work with real faeries this is the book for you.
Stephanie Woodfield, author of *Celtic Lore & Spellcraft of the Dark Goddess: Invoking the Morrigan*

Utterly comprehensive and compulsively readable guide to Fairycraft.
Brendan Howlin, author of *The Handbook of Urban Druidry: Modern Druidry for All*

Fairycraft

Following the Path of Fairy Witchcraft

Fairycraft

Following the Path of Fairy Witchcraft

Morgan Daimler

MOON BOOKS

Winchester, UK
Washington, USA

First published by Moon Books, 2016
Moon Books is an imprint of John Hunt Publishing Ltd., Laurel House, Station Approach,
Alresford, Hants, SO24 9JH, UK
office1@jhpbooks.net
www.johnhuntpublishing.com
www.moon-books.net

For distributor details and how to order please visit the 'Ordering' section on our website.

ISBN: 978 1 78535 051 1
Library of Congress Control Number: 2015958685

A CIP catalogue record for this book is available from the British Library.

Design: Lee Nash

Printed and bound by CPI Group (UK) Ltd, Croydon, CR0 4YY, UK

CONTENTS

This book is dedicated to my children, may it guide them as they seek to find their own way on the Path.

With thanks to everyone who helped me make this book what it is:

Maya for always encouraging me to keep writing.

Caoimhin, Aleja, Erynn, Robert, Niniann, Patty, Ellen, Vyvianne, and Virginia for responding to my question about what people would like to see me include here – I hope I included everything you all mentioned.

The 'Fairy Mafia' of the pine cabin at Temenos – Natalie, Ivy, and Mel – for reminding me to have a sense of humor and to expect the unexpected.

The Fairy Courts

What of the Dark Court?
Storms, and Fire, and rains of blood
sharp thorns on root, leaf, and bud
piercing swords that cut at every end
trees that stand and never bend
rivers endlessly in drought and flood

What of the Blessed Court?
Fierce and shining, bright and good
the Thorn that stands without a wood
brightly burning as a flaming brand
blessing flows throughout the land
when rightly honored and understood

Introduction

Modern paganism includes a dizzying selection of paths and traditions, of which Fairy Witchcraft is but one. Some people may find the combination of neopagan religion and traditional Fairy Faith beliefs ideal; others may decide that it is not the path for them. Indeed, although it is a path with many rewards it is also a difficult one to walk and one that requires a great deal of effort to practice. Above all, it is a religion of risk, not something safe and secure to curl up in like a warm blanket, but rather a tough pair of boots that will take you off the beaten path and into the trackless woods.

Fairy Witchcraft is a way to bring the old Fairy Faith ways and beliefs forward into a modern neopagan context. The Fairy Faith is a belief system that transcends religion and so can be followed within any religion; however, it is uniquely suited to combining with paganism. When a neopagan witch chooses to follow the Fairy Faith and blends the two together, the result is a new system, which I am calling Fairy Witchcraft, that uses elements of the beliefs and practices of both to create a whole. It is a way not just to honor the fairies, but also to connect to them and to the Otherworld on a deeper level.

Fairy Witchcraft as described in this book is the summation of my own personal practices, developed since 1991. It weaves together the different threads that have influenced me: the Irish Fairy Faith, neopagan witchcraft, Druidism, Celtic Reconstructionism, Germanic folk beliefs, and Heathenry. Although this book is intended to offer a complete system of practice, it is also intended to be flexible so that individual practitioners can modify it to fit their own approach. In this way this book is a guide rather than a rulebook.

I choose to call the system contained here Fairy Witchcraft and people who practice it Fairy Witches. However, it is important to understand that these are thoroughly modern terms and are not the words that the older cultures would use. I tend to focus on terms especially from the Irish because Irish culture is probably the main influence on Fairy Witchcraft. The closest modern Irish term for what I am choosing to call a Fairy Witch may be Fairy Doctor. Fairy Doctor is a term that comes from the Fairy Faith, but is very similar in its definition to a Fairy Witch, in that both are used to describe someone who gains knowledge from the fairies and uses that knowledge to help or hinder people. In point of fact the only real difference between the older terms and the modern one I choose to use here is the religious connotations; the older term of Fairy Doctor would apply to people who were at least nominally Catholic, while a Fairy Witch is a polytheist. Of course it may be equally true to say that a Fairy Witch could be called a cailleach or cailleach feasa as well, with the added overtones of ambivalence that Fairy Doctor lacks.

I think it is important for anyone pursuing this path to understand the older terms, their meanings and applications, and the use of the word 'witch' both historically and in this text. I think this helps modern practitioners better understand the roots of the practices and beliefs and the way in which modern Fairy Witches draw on the historic precedents. Much of the witchcraft aspect of Fairy Witchcraft is formed from a particularly Irish and more broadly Celtic understanding of witches and particularly the way that witches interacted with the Fair Folk[1].

In his book *Irish Customs and Beliefs* Kevin Danaher relates an experience he had as a child on holiday in Clare. While exploring he ran across an older woman named Nellie, who he later learned was reputed throughout the area for her herbal cures and willingness to curse anyone who offended her. He describes his thoughts on the experience this way:

> *On the way home that day I couldn't help thinking that the old lady was very like the witch in the story books; the black cat in the hearth*

and the heather besom behind the door were just what a witch should have, and when I heard of her cures and curses my suspicion grew. But I soon found out that the classic figure of the witch cleaving the night air on a broomstick with her cat perched on the pillion was not recognized in local tradition. Old Nellie might be a bean feasa, skilled in cures and in divination, or even an old cailleach who stole the cows' milk disguised as a hare, but not a witch.
(Danaher, 1964, pages 121-122).

Reading Danaher's description helps to show us that in Irish tradition, particularly older tradition, the idea of the witch was divorced from the more popular one most of us grew up with. Witches were not known as evil beings who made pacts with the Devil, flew on brooms, or used their powers to torment their neighbors, but rather as women who had occult knowledge that could be used for good or ill. That is not to say that witches were seen in a good light, because they did have their darker side, being known to work magic on cattle and steal milk (O hOgain, 1995). It is important to note that these are some of the same activities engaged in by the fairies themselves, who also hold an ambivalent place in people's minds. It was only later that the idea of the evil witch as a force working against the community appeared in Ireland and this seems to have been imported from Europe and Scotland (Danaher, 1964). Instead, what we find in Ireland is the idea of different types of magic workers, notably the Fairy Doctors, bean feasa, and cailleach who may all be called witches in English, but who range from benevolent to vexing.

In Fairy Witchcraft we use the term witch in its modern context, as a person who is both pagan and a practitioner of folk magic. In Irish culture the word witch might actually be applied to three different groups of people: caillí[2] (singular cailleach), Fairy Doctors, and mná feasa[3] (singular ban feasa). Although each term has a different nuanced meaning, all of them are sometimes used interchangeably and a single person who gains knowledge from the fairies and works magic may be called by any of these traditional titles or by the English word witch. This fluid understanding of the different labels is shared by the liminal nature of Fairy Witches.

Another thing that shows us the difference between the Irish view of witches and the one found elsewhere is the rarity of witch trials found in Ireland. Ireland had very few witch trials over the centuries and these were usually within settlements of those of non-Irish descent (Danaher, 1964). The last witch trial on record in Ireland occurred in Carrickfergus in 1711 and resulted in a conviction and a sentence of the pillory and a year in prison (Danaher, 1964). This seems to reflect the different attitude with which the Irish approached the subject, compared to the far more rabid witch-hunting that went on in Europe. Perhaps because the beliefs about witches were not as severe or perhaps because the belief in the supernatural and use of magic in folklore was so strong even after Christianization, the Irish witch never created the hysteria in Ireland that was the hallmark of Europe during this period.

What is particularly worth noting though is the connection between Irish and Scottish witches and fairies. The knowledge gained from the fairies can be used to heal or to harm. The witch, or cailleach, knows how to use elfshot[4], and does so in ways that – according to the Scottish witch trial records anyway, which we must look to given the scarcity of Irish witch trials – seem to have been an attempt to use supernatural power where social power was lacking. Often in these trial records we see witches confessing to making deals with or consorting with fairies, going to fairies for knowledge, and going to them to obtain elfshot (Hall, 2005). In the Irish we see witches, like fairies, taking the form of hares in order to steal milk from the cows and this may indicate another connection between the two (O hOgain, 1995).

There is only a slight difference between the words bean feasa and Fairy Doctor and they are often used interchangeably. The qualities of both types of practitioners are skills that should also be nurtured among Fairy Witches so it is worth looking briefly at what each one was known to do. The bean feasa was skilled in divination and was called to find lost objects, find the cause of illnesses and magical afflictions (O Crualaoich, 2005). The fairy doctor, on the other hand, was called when fairy involvement was known or suspected, especially relating to afflictions caused by them, or when witchcraft was suspected, in order to discern the best cure (Wilde, 1991). A slight difference between the two is that the Fairy Doctor would teach others her skills, particularly passing her knowledge on to her children, while the bean feasa never shared what she knew nor performed her magic on front of anyone (Wilde, 1991; Locke, 2013). Following these examples, the Fairy Witch should be skilled in divination and have the ability to find out if the cause of a situation or illness is mundane or magical, especially if it is caused by the Other Crowd, and to locate lost objects. When fairy involvement is known, the Fairy Witch should be able to find a good solution. It is up to each individual to decide whether or not to train others, although it should be noted that Fairy Witchcraft is a mostly solitary path.

It was believed that a bean feasa gained her power after being taken by the Fair Folk or spending time with them; that they taught her occult knowledge and continued to provide her with information and help (O Cualaoich, 2005). Like a bean feasa, a Fairy Witch is someone who deals often with the fairies and gains knowledge from them. The bean feasa helped the community with herbal remedies, divination, and advice especially relating to the fairies; similarly the Fairy Witch should be willing to help people in their community as best they can with the skills they have.

The bean feasa used herbal cures, but not for medicinal purposes; rather her herbal cures were magical in nature (O Craulaoich, 2005). This can be seen in stories that describe the special way or place the herb must be gathered or include geasa[5] around their use. These geis may include the herb being brought to the person in total silence, no one watching as they are prepared or given, or the person receiving the cure not looking backwards upon leaving (O Craulaoich, 2005). These also apply to Fairy Witches who similarly use herbs more for magical than medicinal purposes[6].

Fairy Doctors were more specific in what they did than the bean feasa, focusing on things that seemed to have a supernatural cause, and would be called in to discern if that cause was malignant witchcraft or fairies. The Fairy Doctor was most known for being able to recognize the ill effects of elfshot, the fairy wind, and the evil eye, all of which she could diagnose and then treat with charms or incantations, and less often herbal remedies (Wilde, 1991). Fairy Doctors were also thought to be able to have the spirit sight and so could deal with the Fair Folk and see, for example, if a home had been built on a fairy road or near a fairy door. Fairy Witches who have this ability may use it similarly, but those who do not have it can learn other ways to discern if fairy influence is the cause of problems. It was believed that a person, usually but not always a woman, became a Fairy Doctor after either being away with the fairies or after suffering an illness that brought her near death and so closer to the spirit world (Locke, 2013). For a Fairy Witch, the impetus to follow this path may come from an interest in it, from a natural association with the fairies or from a near death experience or serious illness. The Fairy Doctor used herbs, crystals, chants, charms, and special healing stones to work their cures (Locke, 2013). In the same way, the Fairy Witch uses the same things, which will be discussed in detail later in the book.

From this brief look at the old Irish bean feasa and Fairy Doctor we can see some of the roots of the modern Fairy Witch. Although we may not call ourselves by the older terms anymore, this hopefully shows how each contributes to our practices. A Fairy Witch is someone who has nurtured a relationship with fairy beings, who uses herbs magically, who uses divination, and who can identify and deal with different magical problems, whether they are caused by fairies or other magical people. Studying and understanding these older types of practitioner helps give us guidance on what we should do and how we should approach the practical side of our own witchcraft.

Fairy Witchcraft is largely a solitary practice, something that an individual does alone because it is built on a person's unique connections to the Otherworld and spirits. Although group work is possible in small tight-knit groups or with family members, the majority of the Fairy Witches' practices will end up being done alone and the connections and relationships the Fairy Witch forms with the Gentry will be unique to that person.

Another key thing to understand before going further is what exactly we mean when we say fairy, and that is a difficult topic. Later in the book we will look more closely at several types of fairies that the practitioner is more likely to encounter, but at this point a broad definition is necessary. Many people hear the word 'fairy' and immediately think of small winged children or little garden sprites, but this is not what we mean in Fairy Witchcraft, or at least that is not exclusively what we mean. We use the term to describe a wide array of Otherworldly beings and land spirits, which are not human and may or may not be kindly inclined towards humans. Much like the word 'animal' includes everything from mice to bears, the word 'fairy' includes everything from tiny sprites to monstrous giants, from diminutive pixies to human-sized elves, from hags to water horses.

I don't personally see fairies as elementals, although I know that's a popular view these days. I would define elementals as the embodiment of their element, and hence limited to that element, while fairies are more complex than that. You will see many neopagan books calling them elementals, but for what it's worth it doesn't seem to have been the older folk view in places such as Ireland, but rather to have come from alchemy.

In Fairy Witchcraft we seek to learn as much as we can about the old beliefs and practices and how to incorporate them into our modern lives. This means understanding the old ways and beliefs, which isn't just about reading all the old stories, but also about actually living the old folk ways. This system only has value if it is a living, vital part of your life.

Chapter 1

Beliefs

Far more often [than asking the question 'Is it true?'] they [children] have asked me: 'Was he good? Was he wicked?' That is, they were far more concerned to get the Right side and the Wrong side clear. For that is a question equally important in History and in Faerie.
– J.R.R. Tolkien, *On Fairy-Stories*

A little girl who was at service in the village of Grange, close under the seaward slopes of Ben Bulben, suddenly disappeared one night about three years ago. There was at once great excitement in the neighbourhood, because it was rumoured that the faeries had taken her. A villager was said to have long struggled to hold her from them, but at last they prevailed, and he found nothing in his hands but a broomstick. The local constable was applied to, and he at once instituted a house-to-house search, and at the same time advised the people to burn all the bucalauns (ragweed) on the field she vanished from, because bucalauns are sacred to the faeries. They spent the whole night burning them, the constable repeating spells the while. In the morning the little girl was found, the story goes, wandering in the field. She said the faeries had taken her away a great distance, riding on a faery horse. At last she saw a big river, and the man who had tried to keep her from being carried off was drifting down it—such are the topsy-turvydoms of faery glamour—in a cockleshell. On the way her companions had mentioned the names of several people who were about to die shortly in the village.

Perhaps the constable was right. It is better doubtless to believe much unreason and a little truth than to deny for denial's sake truth and unreason alike, for when we do this we have not even a rush candle to guide our steps, not even a poor sowlth to dance before us on the marsh, and must needs fumble our way into the great emptiness where dwell the misshapen dhouls. And after all, can we come to so great evil if we keep a little fire on our hearths and in our souls, and welcome with open hand whatever of excellent come to warm itself, whether it be man or phantom, and do not say too fiercely, even to the dhouls themselves, 'Be ye gone'? When all is said and done, how do we not know but that our own unreason may be better than another's truth?

– W. B. Yeats, *The Celtic Twilight*, 1893

This story related by William Butler Yeats in one of his books, written over a hundred years ago, fairly concisely sums up the approach we use in Fairy Witchcraft. Much of what we do is what Yeats called 'unreason', things that might be dubbed superstition or practices, which are based in long-standing folk methods whose roots and reasons are lost to time. We do them still not because we can explain rationally exactly how they work, but because we know that they *do* work, and that they have been tested and proved true over many long lifetimes. In the story when the girl disappeared the police officer had every house searched in an effort to find her, but he also burned all the ragwort in the fields to force the Other Crowd to release her, if it was indeed they who had taken her. In the same way the Fairy Witch seeks to use all resources at our disposal – reason and unreason – to effect the outcome we desire.

There are a variety of core beliefs that make Fairy Witchcraft what it is. Some of these beliefs are shared with other groups or traditions, but it is the particular combination of beliefs and practices that make this path unique. It isn't just that we believe in the Fair Folk, but that we actively seek to ally ourselves with them and honor them. It isn't just that we practice witchcraft, but that we practice a historically based folk magic. It isn't just that we celebrate the eight holy days and the moons, but why we celebrate them. Each of these details is important to understand in order to fully embrace this path and live it.

Theology

Fairy Witchcraft is a polytheistic and animistic religion first and foremost, which means that we believe in many individual Gods and also that all things have a spirit. This is a vital difference between Fairy Witchcraft and some other forms of modern neopaganism, which may see the Gods as archetypes or as manifestations of a single Godhead (or Goddess-head as it were). Our Gods are no more or less reflections of an even higher Power than we ourselves are, and as we know them they are unique individuals with personality and presence.

The exact Gods of this path will be discussed in detail later, but the important point at this stage is that the Gods are separate from humanity – not projections of the human mind or dependent on human belief – and have their own personalities and agendas. It might also be noted at this point that our Gods are understood in the context of the Kings and Queens of Fairy, so that there is a very fine line at best between the Gods and the Fair Folk.

As an animistic faith, we believe that all physical things have a spirit, which can with training or an innate gift be perceived and communicated with. This applies to both natural things like animals, plants, stones, and places as well as created things like cars, houses, and swords. These spirits are the same as a human soul, in that as our soul is tied to our body during life, these spirits are tied to the physical thing that they are part of.

The Good People

We also acknowledge a wide array of spirits, for simplicity called fairies, who inhabit a land separate from but connected to ours, which we call Fairyland, or Fairy[7]. These spirits also interact with our world and have the ability to affect us in a variety of ways. The term 'fairy' is used for any spirits that are Otherworldly in nature, but is also used as a catch-all to describe animistic spirits and land spirits. Entire books have been written about fairies because of the complexity of the subject and any Fairy Witch should make a serious study of this subject. In a later chapter we will take a closer look at fairies and discuss in-depth several of the types that we are more likely to encounter, but some general things that should be mentioned here:

- It is almost impossible to generalize about fairies as there are always exceptions to any rule about them. Everything said here, or in any book, about fairies should be understood as being the most widely held beliefs or common truths, but will still sometimes be contradicted.
- Because fairies can influence our lives for good or ill it is important that anyone whose practice focuses on them make a strong effort to have a proper relationship with them.
- For simplicity's sake we often choose to divide the Good Folk into two groups – the good fairies and the bad fairies. This should never be taken as a hard and fast division, but rather as a general guideline. A so-called good fairy is just as capable of doing us harm as a bad fairy is of doing us good, should they be motivated to. Also there is fluidity even with an individual fairy in which grouping they may belong to. People do tend to like the division of the Fey by courts – Seelie and Unseelie, or Light and Dark – but that shouldn't be understood as a rigid division so much as a general guideline.
- The Fey Folk have a very different understanding of morality and etiquette than we do, and they do not grade on a curve or excuse our ignorance. In dealing with them you must be prepared to learn their ways, rather than expecting them to understand yours.
- Time moves differently in the Otherworld, so that what is a day here may be a year there, or a day there may be a lifetime here.

Personal Power

As much as it is a religion, Fairy Witchcraft is also a magical practice and the two are intrinsically related. The practice of folk magic is a main part of this type of witchcraft and inherent to that is the idea of the witch's personal power. The concept of personal power is an important one in Fairy Witchcraft because the witch's ability to successfully influence things with magic is rooted entirely in the strength of the witch's will. Your belief in your own power is part of what fuels that power and in doing anything magically you must have full confidence in yourself. Any spell you undertake should be done with the total belief that it will succeed and any spirits that you deal with must be approached with the confidence that you can deal with them. As part of this it is important that the witch be utterly honest in her speech, because this will reinforce the strength of her will. If you only ever speak the truth then when you speak in a magical context your words have more weight.

Death and Rebirth

The Fairy Witchcraft view of death and the afterlife is a thoroughly Celtic one, reinforced with some Heathenry. We know from Roman and Greek sources that the Celts believed that the soul was immortal and that after dying in this world it was reborn into the Otherworld for a certain amount of time before being reborn here again (Freeman, 2000). Caesar mentions in his work *The Gallic Wars* that the great courage the Celts had in battle came from this belief, because they did not fear death, but saw it as merely a transition into another life. They believed this so strongly in fact that people could write an I.O.U. promising to repay debts in the next life.

From this we know that the soul is eternal and lives on after death, but what we do not know for sure is where exactly it goes. In Irish belief we have stories of islands in the west, of Tech Duinn, the house of Donn, and of people who went among the fairies. We also have stories of wandering souls and ghosts of people who remain earthbound. Every witch should decide for themselves where exactly the dead go between lives; there is no right or wrong answer. Personally, I look to the older Irish myths and stories for guidance.

Several different Irish myths discuss the topic of the immortal soul including the story of Tuan mac Cairill in the *Yellow Book of Lecan*. In this story Tuan mac Cairill tells the tale of Ireland from the beginning, which he has witnessed throughout his various lives in various forms: a man, a stag, a wild boar, an eagle, a salmon, a man again. This seems to hint at a belief in the continuity of the soul during the rebirth process, something we also see in the story of the Two Pigkeepers, who go through a variety of transformations as different animals, and in the tale of Etain who also is reborn in a variety of forms.

We can also look to Norse beliefs for guidance. This tells us that some dead become mound dwellers; their souls going into the land. In *Eyrbyggja Saga* after Thorolfr's son drowns it is believed he goes into a hill on his father's land where he is welcomed with feasting (*Eyrbyggja Saga,* 1972). In *Gisli Saga,* a man who is called a friend of Freyr dies and is buried in a mound and it is said that no frost will form on the hill because Freyr does not want frost to come between them (Our Troth, 2006). In the *Voluspa,* Odin goes to get the prophecy from an ancient seer in a mound and, indeed, the entire process of outsitting (utisetta) is based on the idea of contacting spirits within grave mounds. Additionally it has been suggested that some alfar are the male dead of a family as the disir are the female dead (Our Troth, 2006). Speaking of disir, it is entirely possible for a woman, after death, to become a disir, or idis, that is a specific type of spirit that watches over her family line (Our Troth, 2006).

Reincarnation is also an old Heathen belief. Specifically it is believed that a soul might be reborn within a family line and that naming a child after a deceased ancestor can mean the rebirth of that ancestor in the child (Ellis Davidson, 1968). In some cases a child might be born with similar marks or the appearance of a deceased family member, which could indicate a soul relationship (Our Troth, 2006). I have also heard it said, although I can't place the reference at the moment, that it was considered bad luck to name a child after a living relative for this reason.

It is clear that there are a wide array of possible places for a soul to go after death. As individuals we do not seem to have much real control over where we might go when we die, so I honestly don't see the point in worrying much about it. Live a good honorable life while you are here and worry about the afterlife when you get there.

Positive Qualities in Yourself

One of the basic ways to begin connecting to the Otherworld is to focus on creating or increasing certain qualities within yourself. There are seven qualities, in particular, to nurture for good relations with the Other Crowd: hospitality, generosity, kindness, compassion, courage, politeness, and adventure-someness. These are all qualities we see exemplified in folklore and myths as the things that draw the blessings of the Good Neighbors to people and earn their appreciation and respect. We might choose to call them virtues. It follows then, quite logically, that if you want to be the sort of witch whose practice is centered on the Gentry then you need to manifest these same qualities in yourself.

Hospitality: Hospitality has long been an essential quality that people were expected to show. This includes welcoming those who come to your space and sharing what you have with guests. This quality is about both being a good host and being a good guest and hinges on the idea of having a welcoming attitude in life.

Generosity: A related aspect is generosity. We should freely give what we have to those in need or those who have less. This doesn't mean giving away what we ourselves need, necessarily, but sharing what we have an excess of. Generosity is also more than just generosity with material things or money; we can be generous with our time, our knowledge, and our abilities as well.

Kindness: Kindness often comes down to treating others as we would like to be treated. It is about an attitude that is friendly and considerate of others. Kindness extends to all living things and within the animist world view of Fairy Witchcraft to non-living things as well. We should strive to be gentle and considerate to the beings around us, whether or not they are human, although as with the quality of generosity this doesn't mean kindness to excess. We should be kind, but not to a point where we allow ourselves to be taken advantage of or hurt.

Compassion: Compassion is an essential quality in humans in general, it is what lets us be sympathetic and concerned for the suffering of others. Compassion is what moves us to act in ways that are helpful to those who are suffering.

Courage: In Fairy Witchcraft courage is defined as the ability to face fear and keep going; this is an essential quality in either witchcraft or the Fairy Faith.

Politeness: This may seem an odd virtue, but in dealing with Otherworldly spirits, good manners are absolutely vital.

Adventuresomeness: There's a saying 'fortune favors the bold' and that certainly holds true when dealing with the Otherworld. Although caution and a willingness to deal with the consequences of any action are also important, the Fey Folk have always seemed to respect and be drawn to people who take chances.

The Fetch/Guide

Everyone has a spirit double, sometimes called a fetch[8]. In Fairy Witchcraft this spirit is an essential spiritual guide. The fetch is, in truth, not a separate being, but a part of the witch's spirit, which can appear immaterially in either human or animal form; in the Norse this is called the fylgja (Lecouteux, 1992). The fetch or fylgja can appear as a literal double of the person, but usually appears as the opposite gender of the witch and can communicate with them as an independent being, able to give guidance and bring luck. There is some blurring, however, between the witch's own soul here and the realm of fairy, and perhaps we might venture to say that just as some believe the soul is reborn in the Otherworld after death before being born again here, the fetch is that part of ourselves which is most strongly tied to the Otherworld. In some stories the fetch/fylgja is directly connected to the person's destiny and may send an animal to lead the person to them in order to guide the person into the fulfillment of their potential (Lecouteux, 1992).

Fate

Many cultures have a concept of destiny or a person's purpose in life. We tend to call this idea fate, from the Latin 'fatum', which means 'that which was spoken', and our understanding of fate is something predestined or predetermined, which cannot be changed. This concept is illustrated in Greek tragedies such as Oedipus, where even a person aware of their fate is unable to change it, but rather usually causes it in trying to avoid it. In Fairy Witchcraft our concept of fate is influenced by two things: the Anglo-Saxon concepts of orlog and wyrd and the Irish concept of dán. These cultural concepts shape how we approach the idea of fate and see it as relating to our religion and magical practices.

Wyrd is an Anglo-Saxon word and means, roughly, 'to come to pass' or 'becoming'; related to this is the concept of orlog, meaning 'from the law'. These two terms work together to form a concept similar to fate. As I learned it, orlog is what we inherit at birth from our family and also represents all of our own past actions. In this sense orlog is fixed and unchangeable. Orlog isn't something that only affects people, but rather is a universal principle that influences all beings including the Gods and spirits. As Bauschatz says in his book *The Well and the Tree*: *'This past includes the actions of all beings who exist within the enclosing branches of Yggdrasil: men, gods, giants, elves, etc.'* (Bauschatz, 1982).

Along with this is wyrd, the fate that we create with our own choices, the reactions that we have to the events in our lives. Wyrd is an active principle, where orlog is fixed. Every action we take is based on our wyrd and orlog and further creates the wyrd we are then living with. We shape our wyrd by our choices, but our wyrd creates orlog, which in turn directs our lives. Some people argue that orlg and wyrd are the same concept, and that may be so, I just find that it is easier to grasp them as separate but interlinked concepts. I like to think of them like a river, where wyrd is the water flowing and orlog is the riverbed that shapes and is shaped by the water. Free will is an important aspect of wyrd, as we always have choices on how to act within the circumstances we find ourselves in.

Dán is an Irish word that translates as 'fate' – and also as gift, offering, craft, calling, and poem (O Donaill, 1977). It is a complex term, but is often understood as the fate or destiny that a person is born with. There is a saying that goes, *'A man won't drown whose dán is to hang'*, that illustrates this idea that dán is inexorable and inescapable. Dán is our destiny and it is also the gifts and abilities we have to reach that destiny.

In Fairy Witchcraft we see these two concepts interwoven. Fate is something that is both fixed and fluid, because we have certain things in our lives that are predestined, but we also have much that is influenced by free will. When we do magic it is important to understand the role of fate in people's lives and that while some things can be influenced other things cannot. Over time, a Fairy Witch learns to read the patterns of orlog and understand the influence of dán, and their choices are guided by this understanding.

Fate is often personified: in Greece we see the Moreia (the Fates) who create the 'thread' of a person's fate, measure it, and cut it at death, in the Norse cultures we see the Norns who tend the Well of Wyrd from which fate comes. The Norns are complex beings who are both deities, particularly the more well-known triple Norns, and also not-Gods that resemble what we might categorize as fairies, usually referred to as norns (lower case n). The lesser norns can bless or curse children at birth by influencing their fate. A Fairy Witch may choose to honor the beings who personify fate, or may at points interact with them; for example they can be called on to bless a newborn child.

Karma

Karma is an enormously popular concept in neopaganism, but it is not a major one in Fairy Witchcraft, where the focus is more on fate and the ways we influence our fate with our choices and actions. This is not the same as the idea that what we do comes back to us with the same energy or intent we had, but rather is based in believing that all actions and inactions have consequences. However, if we were to look at the concept of karma, it would be the traditional Eastern view of it, which is very similar to the idea of orlog.

The term karma is from Sanskrit and means 'action' and is a concept found in both Hinduism and Buddhism. Effectively karma is a neutral principle, the result of the sum total of our actions in this life and previous incarnations. Karma is what directs the circumstances under which we will next reincarnate. We can affect our own karma by choosing the actions we take, because all action inherently creates karma, but karma works on a cosmic scale. I like to think of karma as something like painting; each and every color choice and brush stroke, i.e. action, affects the end result. If we compare this to our discussion on fate we can see the obvious parallels with orlog and wyrd.

Divination

Another important aspect of Fairy Witchcraft is divination, but it is up to each individual witch to find the method that works best for them. At this point there are an almost endless number of possible methods available for people to choose from, but the most popular are probably tarot, ogham, runes, and general scrying. There is no one preferred method, only the way that works best for you as an individual. I'd recommend if you are new to divination trying out a variety of different methods to find the one that you like best.

Directionality and Movement

I've become somewhat infamous in my local community for my reaction to things in open rituals or groups being passed around counter-clockwise, although in recent years I have gotten a bit better about it. I realize that without any intent behind it, it's probably harmless, but it has been drilled into me for so long that movement with the sun (clockwise) is for blessing and movement against the sun (counter clockwise) is for cursing that my reaction is reflexive. Although it is amusing to my friends, this illustrates a key belief in Fairy Witchcraft.

The idea that the direction of your movement creates certain types of energy is deeply rooted in Celtic culture. Direction could be used to bless or curse, and the way that a person approached a place or another person could indicate their intentions for good or ill. In Fairy Witchcraft this concept permeates everything from rituals to magic work, and even daily life, where we can use movement to nurture blessing when we cook, for example.

In folk belief, clockwise movement is always seen as drawing positive energy[9]; blessing activities are done in a sun-wise motion and in older days a warrior would approach a fort walking clockwise to indicate peaceful intentions (McNeill, 1956). In contrast moving counterclockwise creates negative energies, or perhaps more properly undoes positive ones. All baneful actions are done against the sun and historically a warrior with bad intentions would approach a place counter-clockwise to indicate that they were an enemy (McNeill, 1956). Sacred spaces were always circumambulated three times before being entered as McNeill tells us in her book *The Silver Bough*:

> *...expectant mothers went thrice round a church to ensure a safe delivery; fire was carried thrice round an infant before baptism to save it from the fate of a changeling; at a wedding, the company went thrice round the house before entering; sick persons thrice circulated a holy well before drinking the healing water; boats putting out to sea thrice rowed about sunwise in order to ensure a safe passage or a good catch; even coffins were carried thus to the grave.*
> (McNeill, 1956).

A Midwinter house blessing in the *Carmina Gadelica* is accomplished by chanting while walking clockwise around the home, and likewise a home may be cursed by walking around it counterclockwise while reciting a malediction. It is not only the words that matter, but the actions and the direction of the actions, and the way we move directly influences the energy we create.

We also see related concepts of positivity with the right-hand side and south, and negativity with the left-hand side and north (O hOgain, 1999). This idea is rooted in the way that physical orientation expands outward: when facing the rising sun a person's right hand is to the south-side, both then being associated with positive energy while the left hand is to the north making both associated with going against the sun and the negative (O hOgain, 1999). Even the words for these things in

Irish relate to these concepts: *'In Irish the word deas and its derivatives are used in the sense of both 'south' and 'fortunate', whereas the word tuath and its derivatives are used to mean both 'north' and 'dangerous'.'* (O Donaill, 1977). The old Irish words for male and female witch – tuaithech and bantuaithech – are both strongly connected to the concepts of north and counterclockwise.

In short, it is a deeply ingrained idea in the Irish and Scottish tradition that certain directions have associations and that to move in a direction – with or against the sun – is significant. Go with the sun to bring luck and blessing, whether it is walking around a sacred place, creating sacred space, or stirring your food as you cook. And when you need to curse someone or undo what has been set in place, you go the other way. Positive magic is done by turning or circling to the right, while cursing and destructive magic involves turning to the left.

Ethics

Ethics in Fairy Witchcraft, as with so many things fairy, are tricky, and may best be described as situational ethics, where there are few hard and fast rules, but rather the situation dictates the correct moral response. Generally speaking, a person should strive to be kind, take responsibility for their own actions, be generous, compassionate, brave, and honest because these are qualities fairies respect. However, in some cases it is also good to be clever even if that involves deception, if you can pull off being tricky in an honest way, because fairies also admire people who can outsmart their adversaries. Magic in Fairycraft is applied to all aspects of life from healing and blessing to binding and hexing. Protective magics, divination, and undoing others' baneful work is also done. There is nothing in Fairy Witchcraft prohibiting harming others, particularly in defense of those who are weaker or to avenge genuine wrongs done against you, but caution is always needed when such action is being contemplated. Any harm, whether it is punching someone in the face or cursing them, should be seen as irreversible and taken very seriously indeed. If you are not willing to take responsibility for your action, whether those actions are physical or magical, and its consequences than you should not do it. That said, respect yourself and be willing to stand up for you and yours and what you know is right – just accept that you bear the responsibility for the results.

In any dealings with the Otherworld it is essential to be completely honorable; fairies expect that a debt will be repaid and oaths will be kept. They abhor liars; however, they admire cleverness and deception is an art form in the fairy world view, where it is entirely possible using semantics to lie by telling nothing but the absolute truth. Fairies love beauty and this includes beauty of spirit; therefore they love people who are generous, kind, helpful, and compassionate. However, they themselves are also beings of unmixed passions, as Yeats would say, who love or hate completely and react to anything in ways we consider extreme. Those they approve of are often rewarded with extreme generosity while those who anger them are punished in ways that seem excessive or even cruel to us. Although they do admire determination in us, it is unwise to try to imitate this behavior ourselves as the negative end of the spectrum tends to typify the things fairies themselves dislike in us. In other words, trying to act like you might believe a fairy would act in anger is more likely to anger them than win their approval.

It can be difficult for us to understand the fairy people and the Fairy Gods when their behavior seems unethical to us, because there are many aspects of their nature we will never be able to fully understand. What we can know though is what they expect of us and what behavior they want to see from us, and that is what we should strive to do. Living an honorable life and being generous and honest is important for anyone following this path.

One question that often comes up in relation to practicing Fairy Witchcraft when a person begins doing spells for others, is whether it is ethical to charge money. In this case we can look at the historic precedents of the Irish bean feasa and Fairy Doctors. It is said in many sources that neither the bean feasa nor Fairy Doctor would take money for their charms or spells, but would accept gifts afterwards; money could be taken though for herbal cures (Wilde, 1991). Fairy Doctors were known to be paid in barter, especially food and drink (Locke, 2013). It should be kept in mind though that the gifting after a cure was a requirement more than a suggestion; Biddy Early, one of the most well-known Irish witches, was said to make enough in her curing work that none of her husbands had to work for a living. In modern Fairy Witchcraft it is up to each individual practitioner to decide whether or not to charge for their services. However, barter should always be an acceptable payment. I have personal had great success with the barter system and find it very satisfying to exchange my time and effort for the products of other people's time and effort, but I also think that we should not be afraid to put a price on our experience.

Symbols

The Fairy Star

Many faiths have a symbol that represents them – for Wiccans it's the pentacle, for Heathens the Thor's Hammer, for many Druids it's the triskele. Although the older Fairy Faith has no unifying symbol, in Fairy Witchcraft it's the fairy star or septogram[10]. This seven-pointed star is used much as other religious symbols are, to represent personal faith in that path and also as a sign of protection, blessing, and connection.

The fairy star, as with most things of Fairy, has layers of symbolism to it. Each point, so I was told, represents one of seven permanent gates into the world of Fairy (as opposed to the innumerable temporary ones). Each point is also symbolic of seven qualities to nurture for good relations with the Other Crowd: hospitality, generosity, kindness, compassion, courage, politeness, and adventuresomeness. In addition each represents one of the seven directions: north, east, south, west, above, below, and center.

The seven-pointed star is also used in other systems and groups for different purposes, so one cannot assume that a person wearing one, or otherwise using the symbol, necessarily follows Fairy Witchcraft. However, those who do may choose to use this symbol in much the same way that Wiccans and some witches use the pentacle, which is what I have been doing with it for about 15 years or so now. It can be worn or drawn on objects for protection, for example, or traced over items, people, or places for blessing.

The Living and Dying Tree

Another symbol used in Fairy Witchcraft is that of the Living and Dying Tree. This tree is something of Fairy and appears healthy and flourishing on one side and dead and rotting on the other, being simultaneously both. It represents the timelessness of Fairy, the liminality and the perpetual state of both growth and decay that encompasses all things. It is a representation of balance between the positive and negative. The Living and Dying Tree can be used on the Fairy Witch's altar as a symbol of the magic and contradictions of Fairy. It can also be used as a meditation tool, as a focal point, in order to better understand the mystery of Fairy Witchcraft.

Modern Experience

The more you connect to the Otherworld and the Other Crowd the more strange and unexplainable things are bound to happen to you. I have had a tiny, opalescent shell appear in with a bag of herbs, I've seen a feather fall down in front of me from above inside a room with no possible source for it, I've had a pendant that I left as an offering at a State Park show up 10 years later on the floor in front of my altar inside my house. You'll have things happen to you that no one else will believe and other things that you won't be able to tell anyone about. In ceremonial magic and witchcraft there is something called the witches' pyramid or the four pillars, originally credited to Eliphas Levi: 'scire, velle, audere, tacere' – 'to know, to will, to dare, to be silent'. There are very specific ways that this is applied in other traditions, but in Fairy witchcraft we might say:

To know: To know the old ways, old beliefs, and old practices. To know the Good Neighbors, what they expect and how to safely deal with them. To know how to protect yourself against those things that won't be reasoned with.

To will: To will is to be connected to your own personal power. It is the strength to stand in our own will and not allow ourselves to be moved. It is understanding the depth of power that our will has.

To dare: To dare is to be willing to take risks, to embrace possibilities. Take chances, and know when the risk is worth the reward. Dare to be bold, and brave, and step into the unknown.

To be silent: To be silent is to know when not to speak. Sometimes it is better to dare to speak and other times it is better to be silent, and you must be able to judge between the two. With fairy experiences, some things are not meant to be shared.

Chapter 2

Gods

Let us be silent, that we may hear the whispers of the gods.
– Ralph Waldo Emerson

When humans first came to Ireland they fought a great war with the Gods and spirits for the right to live there. After the battles were done and humans had taken the land the Gods went to live with the spirits in the sí, the fairy mounds. But people found that it was not that easy or simple to push the Old Gods out – the cows would not give milk and the crops would not grow without the good will of the people of the sí. So the leaders of the sons of men went to the Gods, in particular to the Dagda, a king of the Tuatha Dé Danann in Ireland, and a very powerful God. They went to the Dagda and asked what needed to be done to preserve the crops and milk and the Dagda told them that he would give them his friendship and that the Gods and spirits would let the cows and crops flourish if people agreed to give back some of the produce when it was harvested. And so it has been since then that people offer some milk and some bread to the Gods and people of the sí in appreciation for the blessing that allows the harvest to be brought in.
– Modern re-telling of The Taking of the Sidhe

Fairy Witchcraft is a polytheistic religion, meaning we acknowledge the Gods as unique individual beings. This also means a couple other things that are important to understand: we acknowledge the existence of a multitude of Gods, but we do not worship every God we acknowledge, and a practitioner has a choice of who they do worship. This first part can be challenging for people, because it means we acknowledge Gods we may not like or may find appalling in some way, but we believe that we cannot affirm the reality of our own Gods without acknowledging the reality of other people's Gods as well. The important thing is to understand that while we believe that the Gods and spirits of other religions and traditions exist and have power, we do not believe that we have any obligation to worship them. If I am visiting a new place or am in a ritual that honors a deity I don't worship, I may acknowledge that deity to be polite, but that doesn't change that my own Gods are my own. I can be respectful while visiting a Catholic church, Jewish temple, Wiccan circle and so on without worshipping the deities invoked there. The second aspect of this is that any Fairy Witch has a choice in who they worship; Fairy Witchcraft is not a tradition with a set pantheon, although we do also have our own specific Gods. It is generally best to honor a deity that has a known association with the Fey, and usually these can be found in any pantheon.

A short list includes:

Freyr (Norse): Said to be the 'owner' of Ljiossalfheim, the home of the light elves

Odin (Norse): Associated with the Wild Hunt, who some sources say include the Fey (the Wild Hunt will be discussed in depth in the next chapter)

Frau Holle (German): Associated with the Hiddenfolk

Frau Perchta (German): Associated with a type of Fey called the perchten

Hecate (Roman/Italian): In later periods called the Queen of Fairies

Nicneven (Scottish): Goddess of witches and a Fairy Queen

Gwynn ap Nudd: Welsh God of the Underworld/Otherworld and King of the Fairies

The Tuatha De Danann: All of the Irish Gods are associated with the fairies because it is said the Gods went into the fairy hills when humans came to Ireland

Polytheism is a key theology in Fairy Witchcraft and it is one that needs to be fully understood by anyone seeking to follow this path. The Gods are real and as such they have their own personalities as well as agency, which means they can and will directly influence things. And that is a blade that cuts both ways; yes they can act in helpful ways that benefit us, but they can also act in ways that are harmful. They are Gods after all and have personalities that include both good and bad; there is no such thing as an all-benevolent deity who only ever hands out candy and kisses. If we look at the mythology of well-known Gods of any pantheon we will see that this is true, and while the liminal Gods of Fairy Witchcraft do not have the established mythology of other pantheons, they share this balanced nature. Sometimes you will get smacked because you deserve it or because a smack is the most helpful thing in that moment. Or quite frankly because you've done something that you deserve getting smacked over. Gods have expectations of us, especially where we have promised certain things, whether that's regular worship or a specific item, and if we blow those duties off there will be repercussions. If responsibility isn't taken for your actions, then a divine smack upside the head is an option, and the liminal Gods, being as close as they are to the fairies, are very strict about holding us to our word and enforcing consequences if we act dishonorably.

It's also important to remember that all deities deserve our respect, if only because they are deities and we are not. There are Gods I do not or will not worship, but I still respect them, because they are Gods. Just because I choose not to honor them doesn't lessen their power or ability to affect me – although who I do honor may influence the latter. I never forget that a deity I don't like or want to have anything to do with can still influence my life, especially if I give them the opportunity to or a reason. So polite respect and strong allies are essential, and knowing how to respectfully say no without offending a deity. Remember that if the Gods you like, who bless your life, are real and have agency then it follows the Gods you don't like also are real and have agency, since our likes or dislikes have nothing to do with their existence, or for that matter their abilities. It's important to ask yourself what you believe about the Gods. Do you think the Gods can affect your life for good and bad? Do you think they have personality? What do those things mean to you? Are the Gods just abstract concepts to you, or do you – can you – see them as actual beings? These are vital questions to ask in deciding if Fairy Witchcraft is the right path for you.

As Terry Pratchett said in his book *Witches Abroad*: '*Most witches don't believe in gods. They know that the gods exist, of course. They even deal with them occasionally. But they don't believe in them. They know them too well. It would be like believing in the postman.*'

Part of this knowing comes from direct experience, something that will be different for every witch. We each connect to and experience the Gods differently, and one of the reasons that Fairy Witchcraft is usually a solitary path is that it is difficult to truly share or even explain these experiences, even though we often have an urge to share them. It is always hard to describe the numinous and so often after such an experience we find ourselves questioning and rationalizing away what we felt. This makes sharing these moments far more difficult, but there have also been times when the presence of the Gods created noticeable, tangible effects that were witnessed by many people and these are harder to rationalize away.

I have been in rituals where the presence of the Gods was like a physical weight hanging in the air, where it became harder to breathe and move simply because they were there. I have felt indescribably small when the Gods come into a space and fill it, and once, when I'd inadvertently offended a deity, I felt like a bug under someone's shoe about to be crushed. I have been filled with terror and awe in the presence of the Irish Goddess Nemain (who still scares me) and overcome by calm in a terrifying situation when Flidais was with me. All of these experiences are precious, and all were profound for me, but they are and can only be deeply personal. Even with poetry I cannot truly convey what it felt like, nor convince anyone else that what I experienced actually occurred.

In contrast, I have personally experienced moments when the presence of the Gods was physically perceptible, if only in small ways. While attending a public Imbolc ritual I and several other people noticed a candle on the altar burning out; it smoked briefly as it burned down then extinguished itself. Several minutes later as the group was singing a chant to Brighid that candle relit itself, the light flaring briefly and then burning steadily for the duration of the chant. At a ritual to the Morrigan when the Goddess was invoked the temperature dropped so much that people could see their breath in the air and the temperature stayed down for more than five minutes before rising again. Several friends witnessed a broken string of lights, which was unplugged, lighting up and remaining lit during a ritual after Odin was invoked into the space. These little moments represent a few examples of times when the presence of the Gods was tangible and evident to groups of people, many of whom are not usually mystically inclined.

We are often in the presence of the Gods, both in and out of ritual. It is up to us to be aware of their presence and willing to acknowledge it. We can choose to cherish these moments of connection, or we can rationalize them away, strip them of their numinous beauty. Better, I think, to appreciate the little moments of connection, the glimpses into the mystic, the times when we feel the Gods reaching back towards us, rather than to reject them. It is up to us to decide.

The Liminal Gods

Fairy Witchcraft honors many Gods, including any that are historically connected to the fairies. If you personally honor deities within one particular pantheon there is no need to go outside that pantheon, rather look within it for the God or Goddess who acts as the intermediary for that culture between the Gods and the fairies. This is important because of the role that honoring the fairies plays, and the need to have a connection between the different spirits that we honor.

Beyond the more well-known Gods from common pantheons, Fairy Witchcraft also honors certain liminal beings as Gods; whether they actually are Gods in the traditional sense or are powerful beings – Kings and Queens of Fairy – I do not know, but they have the power to interact and respond as Gods. These liminal Gods that I personally honor appear in pairs, and seem to both balance and complement each other. However, it is entirely possible that a witch might connect only to Fairy God or Goddess alone, or to a single-gendered pair or even to an androgynous or binary-gendered fairy deity. Within the realm of Fairy the possibilities are really quite diverse and it is better to connect to the deities that come to you than to try to force a connection that isn't there, if the deities who come to you are appealing.

There are two main pairs of liminal Gods that I personally honor: the Lady of the Greenwood and the Lord of the Wildwood, and the Hunter and the Queen of the Wind. These titles are indicative of the characteristics of the Gods they describe. These deities may have names as well as titles, but I find there is more power in calling them by the titles, and so that is what I use.

The liminal Gods are not like other deities – they have no millennia of myths and stories behind them, no layers of theology, no nuanced understandings. They are both primal and wild and the only way to truly understand them is to experience them directly. They are of Fairy. I can share my experiences of them with other people, but each individual will find their own interactions and perceptions unique. Worshipping the liminal Gods is based in trusting your intuition and letting yourself be aware of their presence, preferences, and personalities. You must learn to let them speak to you, and to listen and let the messages you receive shape your practice. That said, there are some general things about them that can help you connect to them.

The liminal Gods are deities of the transitional space between wild and tame, between safety and danger, between our world and Fairy. They are not Gods of the mundane. They are the essence of Fairy, of enchantment, even as they are the heart of our reality. They exist in ordinary moments and in magic. They are urban and wild as much as they are in the wild woods and calm moments. They are immortal, endless, and relentless. They are eternal and fleeting, constant and ever changing. They are unspeakably beautiful and horrifyingly ugly. They are gentle; they are cruel. They are all of these things at all times.

You do not have to seek out these liminal Gods in some distant place or some mystic realm, because they are here. They form the heart of Fairy Witchcraft, the connection between the Gods of known pantheons and the Fairy Folk and other spirits; the tie between pagan religion and the Fairy Faith. Speak to them under the boundless sky, in the thick woods, and at the edge of the shore. Listen for their voices in dreams, synchronicity, and omens. Offer to them, pray to them, and be open to their blessings and guidance.

To connect to and honor these Fairy Witchcraft Gods you have only to reach out to them. Be open to your own intuition and inspiration, and understand that the faces that these Gods show to you will be unique to you; it is unlikely that two people will perceive the liminal Gods exactly the same way. For some they may be the elaborate and fanciful Kings and Queens of Fairy – for others they may appear as primal and wild beings. They may wear crowns of precious metal and jewels or they may be crowned with horns and antlers. As with other Fairy beings they are shapeshifters and masters of glamour so they will appear as they choose to appear and as they wish for you to see them.

Theirs is not an easy path to follow because it means letting go of the civilized expectations we hold with other Gods. It is a path through the trackless forests and the untouched wilds both within and without. It puts aside logic and rational thought and embraces instinct and emotion. And once you are on their path you cannot help but be changed by it. And once you are on their path there is no turning back from it.

Fairy Gods

There are four main Gods in Fairy Witchcraft who are regularly honored, but there are also other Fairy Gods as well. As you walk your own path you may find that different Fairy Gods call to than the ones mentioned here, and that is normal, it's the way that Fairy speaks to each of us. Generally though these main Gods will be the ones most easily reached and related to and so they are the ones that will be discussed.

The Lady of the Greenwood is a Goddess of potential, growth, healing, and ultimately life. She nurtures and comforts as well as guides and inspires those who follow her, and her energy is boundless fertility, sexuality, and beginnings. She is every budding flower seeking the light, each fruit ripening in the sun and the joy that pulses in our veins when we embrace that which makes us feel most alive. She is often surrounded by green, sometimes clothed in it, sometimes with every growing thing touching her bursting into leaf and flower. She is also often accompanied by different animals, particularly deer, hounds, cows, bears, and rabbits. Her special bird is the wren and her tree is the rowan. Roses are her flowers. I often see her as a woman in her prime, full figured and smiling, with light brown hair. She is the soul of the forest and its Queen, the Queen of the Greenwood, the quintessential Fairy Forest.

The Lord of the Wildwood is a God of the physical. He is physical prowess and good health, a spirit of movement and action that embodies the will to live, to overcome, to win. He is the nurturing masculine element that guards and protects, but is also the sense of adventure that drives exploration and takes risks. He can be seen in every father protecting his young, in the urge to reproduce, the lust for life that drives us, and in the fullness of completion. He is a guardian of the wild wood, and a protector of the life within it. He appears clad in shades of brown, from the light tan of tree bark to the rich deep brown of fresh turned earth. His animals are the horse, stag, bull, mouse, and fox. His birds are the bluejay, pheasant, and sparrow. His tree is the oak and his special plant is the foxglove. I see him as a man with dark brown hair, clean shaven, carrying a staff hung with many charms, with a look of mischief on his face. He is the spirit of everything that lives in the Fairy wood, its King, and he rejoices in lives well lived.

The Queen of the Wind is a Goddess of the deep dark time of winter, of renewal, introspection, and enchantment. She is the balance between death and life that creates harmony. A Goddess of magic, she is a seer who knows all fates without judgment and therefore is a deity of divination. She is death and rebirth, the cold earth holding the sleeping seed and giving rest to the bodies of the dead. She is the spirit of the wind carrying ice and snow that kills and the wind that brings the warmth of spring that thaws and renews. She appears clad in white, her hair black and shifting in the wind that accompanies her. Her touch is rest, and peace, and relief, as well as magic and new beginnings. Her animals are the white hind, the skunk, and cat. Her birds are the crow and the owl. Her tree is the birch and her special herbs are the nightshade and the bluebell. She appears to me as a stately woman, strong and beautiful, her hair always moving, clad in white and carrying a sword. She is the spirit of timelessness that exists between the worlds, the essence of the liminal spaces of that which was, and is, and may yet be.

The Hunter is a God of planning, tactics, and wisdom. He is the psychopomp who guides the newly dead into the next world and carries new souls into this world to be born. He is the blade separating life from death and the energy planting each new soul in the womb. Within him is the heart of every warrior, beating fiercely, the shrewdness of each predator seeking a meal, the ruthlessness and determination to make the hard choices and see them through the tough times. The Hunter is the guardian of every living thing in the darkness of winter, and also the one who will bring death or grant life. His colors are black and grey, his animals are the wolf, boar, weasel, and porcupine. His birds are the hawk and goose. His tree is the yew and his plants are the fern and dandelion. When I see him he appears as a well grown man, blond and bearded, strong and enduring. He carries a bow, which is always strung, and a quiver of dark arrows. He is the timeless moment that is always now: the instant before the arrow strikes, the moment when first it hits, and the blood flowing afterwards; he is all of these things at once and always.

The four main Fairy Gods divide the year in half, with each pair ruling for six months out of the year. The light half of the year, from Bealtaine to Samhain, is ruled by the Lady of the Greenwood and Lord of the Wildwood, who are also honored at the full moon each month. The dark half of the year, from Samhain to Bealtaine, is ruled by the Queen of the Wind and the Hunter, and they are also honored at the dark moons. Each exists within the other half, of course, and can be called on and prayed to at any time, but they are strongest during the times when they rule.

I mention these four to start because they represent the most basic connection between the Fairy Witch and the Otherworld and are the first beings one needs to connect to. Some might understand the liminal Gods as the Kings and Queens of Fairy, while others might understand them through the names certain cultures called them by. I chose not to name them, but to refer to them only by title because I was concerned that using specific names would distract people from seeking to connect to and experience them directly. There is also an ambiguous quality to these Gods that is an important part of what they are which is preserved by keeping their exact identity obscure.

So, we have talked about the Lady of the Greenwood, Lord of the Wildwood, the Hunter, and the Queen of the Wind. Who are some of the other liminal Gods? Actually they are many, diverse, and varied; it is entirely possible that you might connect to one that is unknown to me so I can only offer my own experiences as a rough guide. To find the liminal Gods, the Gods of Fairy, one must be open to the possibility of them, be willing to listen for them in dreams and visions, and to slowly build the connections to them that lead to experience. Remember though that all liminal Gods contain both shadow and light within themselves and that they are all directly part of Fairy in ways that other traditional Gods are not. Here are some of the other ones that I am familiar with – you may or may not find these as well to connect to them, or find entirely different ones unknown to me.

Another pair I have encountered is the White Lady and the Storm Lord. The White Lady appears as a tall, fair woman dressed in white accompanied by white animals, usually a deer or rabbit. The White Lady is a Goddess of life and death, a protector of children (human or otherwise), and a psychopomp who leads the newly dead to the Otherworld, much as the Hunter also does. She is also a guide for the living, both spiritually and literally as the Queen of lonely wild places. It is she who you would want to pray to if you were lost, spiritually or geographically. She is the special Goddess of witches who seek her wisdom, guidance, and protection. She is both the gentle mother and the fierce spirit of the wilderness beyond human experience. Her animal is the swan and her special herb is flax. The Storm Lord rides the storm clouds and is heard in thunder and seen in lightning. He appears riding a dark grey horse, driving the clouds before him. He is a God of swift death and destruction, of strife and battle, but also of fertility, growth, change, wisdom, and rebirth. He is the force that clears the old to make way for the new; a God of the dead he also cares for the souls of the dead in the Otherworld. In my experience, while he is related to storms and destruction in our world, his home in the Otherworld, where at least some of the dead go, is a place of peace and rest. His animal is the raven and his herb is mistletoe.

The White Lady and Storm Lord form a pair. Together they may be honored at the Midwinter Solstice in particular. In my experience they have a strong connection to the Wild Hunt (which we will discuss later in depth).

Another pair that I have encountered, particularly at the seashore, is the Queen of the Tides and King of the Waves. The Queen of the Tides is the spirit of the ocean, and like the ocean she is vast and mercurial, beautiful and ferocious, a source of abundance and illusions. Her mood changes quickly, yet she is always constant. Primal and ancient, she is very wise, but she speaks in riddles and can be hard to understand. She is merciless and unforgiving, but also generous with her gifts and blessings. She is a Goddess of healing and health, who rules over the tides of the body as well as those of the ocean. The King of the Waves is the God of the living sea, that which is always in motion and always changing. He is boundless joy and utter despair, ruler of a realm where nothing is exactly as it seems. He is a traveler's God, a God of change and movement, whose journey never ends and who sees opportunity and a lesson in every moment. He is also a God of magic and enchantment.

The Queen of the Tides and King of the Waves are a pair and may be honored at Midsummer.

It is alright, by the way, to honor any of these Gods alone, without their partner, so for example if you want to set up a healing shrine to the Queen of the Tides you do not have to include the King of the Waves, although there is an important balance offered by honoring both together. The Kings and Queens – Lords and Ladies – balance each other in vital ways and especially on holidays and for deeper workings it is safer to include that balance.

Beyond the Fairy Gods

The liminal Gods are arguably the most important for the Fairy Witch to honor, but there are several named Gods and greater spirits who may or may not be Gods that should also be considered and, if not honored, at least acknowledged. The first of these is Donn who is the Irish God of the dead – or at least the first person to die in Ireland. Donn is also said to be a Lord of Fairy. The other are the Matronae, primal ancestral mother spirits. Both of these straddle the fine line between the dead and the Fey – and we may say perhaps between the Gods as well putting them in three different liminal categories.

Donn and the House of the Dead

> *The wind concentrated upon the ship where Donn the king was, and Donn was drowned at the Sandhills; whence Tech Duinn derives its name.*
> – *Lebor Gabala Erenn*, volume 5

Donn is the keeper of the dead, where the ancestors go when first they die. Some people say the dead stay in his house always, others that Tech Duinn (Donn's House) is only a stopping place on the way to another destination. In Fairy Witchcraft we believe that the newly dead go to Donn's House when they first transition, but may then go on to different Otherworldly locations.

There is some debate about whether the Irish have a God of the dead, but if they do it's generally agreed that it would be Donn, a king of the Milesians who died at sea when the sons of Mil were trying to take Ireland. In this sense Donn is the first ancestor, the first person to die in the land of the Gods (Ireland) before it was taken by people. The place where he died, off the southwest coast of Ireland, was called Tech Duinn. Tech Duinn became equated in folklore with the Otherworldly land of the dead and Donn with a primal ancestor and underworld God (Jones, 2004). In the Death Tale of Conaire, Donn is explicitly called the King of the Dead and a 9th century text has Donn claiming that all who die will go to him and his house (O hOgain, 2006).

According to Miranda Green, Donn's name means 'Dark One'; however, looking up the Old Irish we see a variety of meanings for the word donn including brown, noble, poet, stolen property, pregnant, and ale (Green, 1997; eDIL, n.d.). The dictionary also defines Donn as, *'Probably the God of the dead or the ancestral father to whom all are called at their death'* (eDIL, n.d.). Both Green and Jones compare Donn to the Roman Dis Pater, who Caesar said the Gauls believed they descended from; as Donn was seen to be an ancestor of the Gaels and also a deity of the land of the dead, this comparison seems valid. Green goes further in saying that Donn is likely also Da Derga, who appears according to her as a death God in the story of Da Derga's Hostel (Green, 1997). O hOgain relates the name to the concept of darkness and the realm of the dead (O hOgain, 2006).

There are a variety of explanations for why Donn died. I have heard some Irish pagans say that it is because he insulted Eriu, one of the main sovereignty Goddesses of Ireland, when the Milesians were negotiating with her. Others say Eriu only predicted his doom, but did not cause it (Berresford Ellis, 1987). The actual text from one redaction says:

> *Then Donn son of Mil said: 'I shall put, said he, under the edge of javelin and sword all that are in the island now, only let land be reached. The wind concentrated upon the ship where Donn the king was, and Donn was drowned at the Sandhills; whence Tech Duinn derives its name.'*
> (Macalister, 1956)

I tend to read this myself and believe that it was his threat to kill all living things in Ireland that led to the sea and air turning against him and causing his death before his ship could land. However, in another version from the *Metrical Dindshenchas* he was a voluntary sacrifice:

> *The house of Donn, what origin? Not difficult. When the sons of Mil came from the west to Ireland, their Druid said to them, 'A man must go up that mast', said he, 'and then chant his best Druidic chants on the Tuatha De, this will rout the battle on them, and after that time this will be our land forever: and the man will die who casts the spell.'*
>
> *They set a casting of lots on them, and it was cast to Donn to go to the sail. Afterwards it was done thus, and Donn moved to the sail, and chanted Druidic spells against them, and returned down after, and said: 'I swear by the Gods', said he, 'we will be without granting justice or recompense to you henceforth.'*
>
> *They chanted also from the land Druidic spells against them in response. Then they cursed Donn and afterwards the Tuatha De brought a shaking-sickness immediately on the ship.*
>
> *Said Amergin, 'Donn shall die', said he, 'and not lucky his keeping on account of taking back the illness. If we carry Donn to the land, the sickness will be in Ireland forever.'*
>
> *Said Donn, 'Take my body', said he, 'to one of the islands, and my people will give blessing on me forever.'*
>
> *Afterwards through the spell casting of the Druids a storm was brought on them, and the ship of Donn was sunk.*
>
> *'Take his body there to that high rock yonder', said Amergin: it will be called Tech Duinn. 'His people will go to that place there', said Amergin.*
>
> *And for that burden the souls of sinners visit Tech Duinn before they go to Hell, according to the heathens, indeed, to give their blessings on the soul of Donn. Nevertheless righteous souls, that is penitent men, they see it from a distance, and do not take a detour*

> *there. That is then the opinion of the heathens. So it is called Tech Duinn.*

Comparing the two we can see that the *Lebor Gabala Erenn* version has a very different tone – Donn is an aggressor who not only wants to conquer Ireland, but also to kill everything there; because of his bloodlust the wind itself rises up against him and capsizes his ship and he along with several others are drowned. In the *Metrical Dindshenchas* version on the other hand we are told that Donn was chosen by throwing lots to sacrifice himself in order to break the power of the Tuatha De Danann so that the Sons of Mil could succeed in their invasion. Because of this he was cursed by the Tuatha De and died, but his burial on a 'high rock' on an island created a blessing or perhaps we should say created a situation where the souls of the newly dead were obligated to go to Donn's House and bless him. Even the obviously Christianized aspects at the end of the story are telling in that they reveal the pagan belief that the dead were required to 'visit' Tech Duinn before moving on elsewhere; even the so-called 'righteous men' (one may assume Christian souls) had to see it, if not go into it. The *Metrical Dindshenchas* version strongly supports a view of Donn as a God of the dead, and his house as a place where souls go after death.

Folklore tells us that Tech Duinn is a place where the dead go, but not necessarily their final destination. Some believe that the house of Donn is where the dead go before moving on to the Otherworld (Berresford Ellis, 1987). This is the view held within Fairy Witchcraft. In the 8th to 10th centuries Tech Duinn was seen as an assembly place of the dead, and a place that the dead both went to and left from (O hOgain, 2006). Besides Tech Duinn (present day Bull Rock, County Cork) Donn is also connected to Cnoc Firinne in county Limerick and Dumhcha in county Clare.

The Donn of Cnoc Firinne had strong aspects of a lord of the aos sí, being called Donn Firinne and said to kidnap people into his hill who had been thought to have died (O hOgain, 2006). Like many other Irish deities, belief in Donn seems to have survived conversion to Christianity by shifting him from God to Good Neighbor, albeit a very powerful one. In County Clare, Donn was Donn na Duimhche, Donn of the Dune, and was believed to ride out as a fairy horseman with his army (O hOgain, 2006).

Donn may or may not always have been seen as a deity, but he certainly seems to have been understood as one from at least the 8th century onward, until his shift into an Otherworldly horseman. Throughout his shifting mythology though he has always been related to death and the dead, both as the Lord of the 'house' where the dead go and also as a primordial ancestor of the people. He also has a strong association to the sea, the drowned, and to horses.

In Fairy Witchcraft we acknowledge and honor Donn – even if you choose not to worship him – as both Lord of the Fairies and as Lord of the Dead. I tend to call him most often either the Dark One or the Keeper of the House of the Dead, and envision him as a stoic looking dark haired man, obviously a warrior. There is a stillness and a contemplative air to Donn that is unnerving, but I believe it is important to show him respect as the one who's house offers hospitality to the dead, including the ancestors. I keep a place for him on my ancestor altar.

The Matronae

Another specific type of deity that we honor in Fairy Witchcraft besides Donn are the Matronae. These Goddesses also occupy a liminal space between ancestors and deities, and may be honored either as primal female ancestors or as Goddesses. Different witches will relate to them in different ways.

The Matronae, whose name simply means 'Mothers' in Latin, are found in Celtic (specifically Gaulish), Roman, and Germanic sources (Lendering, 2013). These Goddesses are known from more than 80 inscriptions on images found from France to Germany and through northern Italy, and can be found on hundreds of votive altars (Evans, 2005). The Matronae are usually depicted as three seated women holding symbols of abundance, including fruit, animals, infants, and cornucopias, as well as items like small pieces of cloth, basins, and spindles; the women wear long skirts and have one breast bare, possibly symbolizing a nursing mother (Evans, 2005; Green, 1992). Often the figures on the sides are shown wearing wide hats and sitting next to trees while the central figure has loose hair; in one case the inscription was accompanied by an image of a tree, a snake, and a goat (Lendering, 2013; Green, 1992). Images also depict the Matronae being worshiped by women and by soldiers and being offered fruit and bread (Green, 1992). Although it's difficult to know with certainty what the Matronae were worshiped for, most scholars surmise that they were related to fertility, abundance, healing, and protection. Many Matronae had distinctive names relating to the area they were in or people who worshiped them so it is also possible that they represented communal maternal ancestors, an idea supported by inscriptions naming them 'matres paternae', which may be translated as ancestral mothers (Lendering, 2013). It is also possible that the Matronae were examples of cults of genus locii[11] expressed in a set form, although Ross suggests that they are reflexes of tribal mother Goddesses (Green, 1992; Ross, 1970). In specific locations, the Matronae also had specific associations: the Matres Comedovae and the Matres Griselicae were associated with healing and specific healing springs, for example (Green, 1992).

I tend to relate to the Matronae as the Great Mothers, the Deae Matres, the ultimate ancestral mothers of us all. To me they are both ancestors and deities; they are a force that ultimately connects all humanity together back at the beginnings and that connects us to the land as a source of basic life sustaining nourishment. I use three images of Paleolithic female figures to represent them on my altar and pray to them for protection of my home and family as well as abundance. I also pray to them for peace within my home and for healing, particularly of my children. I offer them fruit, honey, and bread, and celebrate them especially on the night before the Winter Solstice.

Modern Experience

One of the difficult things in connecting to the liminal Gods is simply learning to trust our own intuition. And while it's true that we should not get in the habit of asking for too much confirmation – too many signs and omens to reassure us that we are on the right path – because there can be an addictive quality to such things, it is sometimes necessary to ask for confirmation that we aren't just making everything up whole cloth. I went through something like this when I was trying to first understand the liminal Gods and how they related to each other.

I was working on setting up my altar to honor the first two that had come to me – the Lady of the Greenwood and Lord of the Wildwood – but I started to second-guess everything. The more uncertain I became the more sure I was that it was all wrong, even that the deities themselves were not as I was perceiving them and were not comfortable being honored together. I had spent several hours one night on this, arranging and re-arranging my altar, before giving up and going to bed.

When I got up the next morning and went to light some incense and a candle, as was my custom each morning, I found a very unexpected sight. Stretched between the two images I was using to represent the liminal Gods on my altar was a perfect, intricate spider web. There was no spider to be found anywhere; being a bit arachnophobic I checked very thoroughly. Obviously even though I couldn't find a spider there could still have been a logical explanation, but under the circumstances I chose to take the inexplicable web – something that has never happened before or since – as an omen that I was going in the right direction. It was subtle indication to me that the connection I was seeing between these things had something deeper to it.

And sometimes, in personal practice, that subtle confirmation is enough.

Chapter 3

Fairy Etiquette and Protections

Faeries – Seelie, Unseelie – either way, don't piss them off or they will mess you up.
– M. Daimler

The Fairies' Revenge

The fairies have a great objection to the fairy raths, where they meet at night, being built upon by mortal man. A farmer called Johnstone, having plenty of money, bought some land, and chose a beautiful green spot to build a house on, the very spot the fairies loved best.

The neighbours warned him that it was a fairy rath; but he laughed and never minded (for he was from the north), and looked at such things as mere old-wives' tales. So he built the house and made it beautiful to live in; and no people in the country were so well off as the Johnstones so that the people said the farmer must have found a pot of gold in the fairy rath.

But the fairies were all the time plotting how they could punish the farmer for taking away their dancing ground, and for cutting down the hawthorn bush where they held their revels when the moon was full. And one day when the cows were milking, a little old woman in a blue cloak came to Mrs Johnstone and asked her for a porringer of milk.

'Go away,' said the mistress of the house, 'you shall have no milk from me. I'll have no tramps coming about my place.' And she told the farm servants to chase her away.

Some time after, the best and finest of the cows sickened and gave no milk, and lost her horns and teeth and finally died.

Then one day as Mrs Johnstone was sitting spinning flax in the parlour, the same little woman in the blue cloak suddenly stood before her.

'Your maids are baking cakes in the kitchen,' she said; 'give me some off the griddle to carry away with me.'

'Go out of this,' cried the farmer's wife, angrily; 'you are a wicked old wretch, and have poisoned my best cow.' And she bade the farm servants drive her off with sticks.

Now the Johnstones had one only child; a beautiful bright boy, as strong as a young colt, and as full of life and merriment. But soon after this he began to grow queer and strange, and was disturbed in his sleep; for he said the fairies came round him at night and pinched and beat him, and some sat on his chest and he could neither breathe nor move. And they told him they would never leave him in peace unless he promised to give them a supper every night of a griddle cake and a porringer of milk. So to soothe the child the mother had these things laid every night on a table beside his bed, and in the morning they were gone.

But still the child pined away, and his eyes got a strange, wild look, as if he saw nothing near or around him, only something far, far away that troubled his spirit. And when they asked him what ailed him, he said the fairies carried him away to the hills every night, where he danced and danced with them till the morning, when they brought him back and laid him again in his bed.

At last the farmer and his wife were at their wits' end from grief and despair, for the child was pining away before their eyes, and they could do nothing for him to help him. One night he cried out in great agony: 'Mother! mother! send for the priest to take away the fairies, for they are killing me; they are here on my chest, crushing me to death,' and his eyes were wild with terror.

Now the farmer and his wife believed in no fairies, and in no priest, but to soothe the child they did as he asked and sent for the priest, who prayed over him and sprinkled him with holy water.

The poor little fellow seemed calmer as the priest prayed, and he said the fairies were leaving him and going away, and then he sank into a quiet sleep. But when he woke in the morning he told his parents that he had a beautiful dream and was walking in a lovely garden with the angels; and he knew it was heaven, and that he would be there before night, for the angels told him they would come for him.

Then they watched by the sick child all through the night, for they saw the fever was still on him, but hoped a change would come before morning; for he now slept quite calmly with a smile on his lips.

But just as the clock struck midnight, he awoke and sat up, and when his mother put her arms round him weeping, he whispered to her:'The angels are here, mother,' and then he sank back, and so died.

Now after this calamity the farmer never held up his head. He ceased to mind his farm, and the crops went to ruin and the cattle died, and finally before a year and a day were over he was laid in the grave by the side of his little son; and the land passed into other hands, and as no one would live in the house it was pulled down. No one, either, would plant on the rath; so the grass grew again all over it, green amid beautiful, and the fairies danced there once more in the moonlight as they used to do in the old time, free and happy; and thus the evil spell was broken for evermore.

But the people would have nothing to do with the childless mother, so she went away back to her own people, a brokenhearted, miserable woman – a warning to all who would arouse the vengeance of the fairies by interfering with their ancient rights and possessions and privileges.

– Lady Wilde, *Ancient Legends, Mystic Charms, and Superstitions of Ireland*, 1887

Before we get into looking at some of the specific types of fairies you may deal with, let's look at some basic fairy etiquette and protections. Dealing with the different fairies and spirits is the backbone of Fairy Witchcraft and so understanding how to do that safely is essential. This means knowing how to avoid problems and how to handle them when they can't be avoided.

In Fairy Witchcraft it is absolutely vital that a practitioner have a strong grounding in the traditional folklore and myths of the fairies. The main focus of most Fairy Witches tends to be Celtic and to a lesser degree Norse material. However, the fairylore of any culture is entirely acceptable as long as you make an effort to learn as much as you can about it. Part of the reason that this is so important is that dealing with the Other Crowd is a tricky thing; their culture is truly foreign from our own and it is dangerous to interact with them without understanding this. The more you study the old fairy stories the better you will come to grasp the rules and manners that exist in Fairy, and you will start to see the patterns between the fairies in one culture and another.

Euphemisms

Although in this text and more broadly in Fairy Witchcraft we do call them fairies, it is usually considered unwise to do so. Rather, euphemisms are used in order to ensure that if their attention is drawn it is drawn in a positive way. These euphemisms include: Fair Folk, Gentry, Good Neighbors, Good People, Other Crowd, Hidden People, Hidden Folk, Mother's Blessing, and People of Peace. We also sometimes use culture specific terms like aos sí, daoine sí, alfar, and huldufolk. When speaking out loud about them it is better to use a euphemism, but for the purpose of this book I am using the more familiar terms, most often fairy, for clarity. It's good to try to remember though not to call them fairies when you can avoid it.

Thanks Versus Gratitude

Speaking of things to avoid, as strange as this sounds to most people, you should try never to say thank you to any being of fairy[12], although you must always remember to show proper gratitude. There are several ideas behind why you shouldn't say thank you, and I suspect that there is no one correct answer. Rather I think that different Otherworldly beings may have a problem with it for different reasons. One theory is that saying thank you is dismissive, and implies that you feel superior to the spirit. Another says that saying thank you acknowledges a debt between you and the fairy, and it is never wise to be in debt to the Fey, especially when the debt is an open-ended one. Whether saying thank you offends them because it is dismissive or is dangerous because it puts you in their debt, you should try not to do it. Instead pay back any help, blessing, or gifts with gifts. I carry around a small pouch full of little items for this purpose. You can also offer any food or drink you have with you as a thank-you gift. Fairies abhor people who are greedy or stingy so it is important to show proper gratitude to them. Instead of saying thank you, you may choose to say 'I appreciate' or 'I am grateful for' to express the same sentiment.

Honesty

Fairies are utterly honest and expect the same from us; they tend to react very badly to being lied to. Because of this one should never lie to a spirit or fairy, either tell the truth or stay silent if being honest would be unwise. There is also the option of being honest, but misleading. However, that needs to be done with caution because while cleverness is respected if done well it will get you into trouble if it doesn't work. As a witch it is also very important to be honest, so that our will and words have potency because what we say aloud has power. When we speak the truth it gives our words more weight in magic, whereas someone who lies will not have that same strength in their word. Our word, and its power, is a key aspect of magic in Fairy Witchcraft and it is important to be honest in all aspects of your spoken word.

Keep in mind though that although honesty is expected, the Fey can deceive us with great skill without ever saying anything that isn't true. They are masters of semantics and very skilled at manipulating with words. Caution must be taken when interacting with spirits not to assume that what they say has a simple or straightforward meaning.

Although honesty is a prized virtue, you must also keep in mind that discretion is important. Many of your experiences with the Other Crowd will be things that you should not share or talk about as the Fey often punish those who speak too freely of receiving blessing from them or interacting with them.

Behavior

Beings of the Otherworld also often display behavior that seems to us to contradict our expectations. In folklore we see fairy wives of mortal men laughing at funerals and crying on happy occasions, for example. When dealing with Otherworldly beings it is essential to keep in mind that we cannot expect them to react in the same ways human beings would. Fairies also tend to experience emotions in a pure form, unlike we do, embracing any feeling completely and without ambivalence (Yeats, 1962). Indeed William Butler Yeats calls them the 'Untiring Ones' and says it is this purity of feeling that keeps them ever young (Yeats, 1962). Whether that is so or not it does seem to be true that the Fey Folk experience emotions intensely and without reserve[13]. It is best to anticipate strong reactions, good or bad, from any of the Other Crowd you interact with.

Oaths and Geasa

At some point as a Fairy Witch you may feel the need or desire to make an oath; this should be seen as a very grave undertaking. Sometimes people will promise to focus on a certain thing, skill, or working with a spirit for a certain amount of time, for example, or to give a certain offering, go to a certain place, accomplish a specific goal, or achieve something. A person might also pledge themselves to a specific deity, temporarily or permanently, or to make offerings to specific spirits regularly. These can all be excellent ways to nurture a closer relationship with Fairy and its inhabitants, and to create friendships with specific spirits, but you must be careful never to promise anything you cannot actually give. This means not making promises on the spur of the moment, but giving serious thought to any promise first and assessing your own ability to fulfill it. The consequences of failing to fulfill an oath include weakening the power of your word, losing luck or angering the spirits you are dealing with, or being forced to pay a forfeit.

In some rare cases we may also be asked to make promises or have prohibitions – called geasa in the Irish – put on us. If a fairy asks something from you or asks you to make a promise to them do not rush to give your word, but take some serious time to think about it. Once given it can't be taken back and failure to keep one's word is really not an option, but just because we are asked to make a promise, doesn't mean we must do so. And remember it is always a good idea to ask why the promise is being asked for and what the benefit to you will be. In many cases negotiation is possible and beneficial.

Geasa on the other hand are a bit more complicated and have more weight to them because they are backed by magic. A geis (geasa is the plural) is the Irish term for a ritual taboo that binds a person either to do or not to do something. I have a geis not to eat horse meat, for example, which was put on me when I became a priestess of the Irish Goddess Macha. It is uncommon, but not impossible, that in your practice you may end up being given a geis by one of the Powers you work with. These ritual taboos must be taken extremely seriously because to break one is to lose one's luck and usually results in death.

The Otherworld

Connecting to and experiencing the Otherworld are important in Fairy Witchcraft so you should have at least a basic knowledge of what that world is and how it works compared to ours. There are, of course, many different Otherworlds, but the main ones that we interact with are those that are the homes of the fairy beings and elves. Generally speaking these will end up being the ones related to the culture you personally work with, so in my case I mostly deal with the Irish and occasionally Norse Otherworlds. However, you may find if you connect mostly to a different culture that your experience of the Otherworlds will be very different from what I am about to describe – that is perfectly fine.

Things in the Otherworld are often the inverse of our world. When it is spring here it is fall there, and it is not uncommon to find yourself experiencing seasons out of sync with our own. In the Irish story *The Adventures of Nera,* the main character Nera ventures into a sí on Samhain and then is sent back to his king and queen; as a token that he had actually been in the Otherworld he is given some spring flowers to bring back (*Echtra Nera,* n.d.). When we look at the liminal Gods, who we honor in our practice, we will see that this pattern holds true: the Gods who hold sway in our world during the light half of the year then return to the Otherworld during its light half, and vice versa for the Gods of the dark half of the year. So the Lady of the Greenwood and Lord of the Wildwood are eternal rulers of summer, following that energy from the Otherworld into our world and back again, while the Queen of the Wind and Hunter rule the winter, endlessly, in the same pattern.

If you use spiritual practices such as journeywork or guided meditations that bring you to the Otherworld there are some general rules to keep in mind. Although magic is a stronger force there than here the laws of physics and such as we understand them do still apply. If you jump off a cliff you will fall – and if you don't then wherever you are it isn't Fairy. You can be injured and there are things that want to hurt you. Unlike most people's experiences of our world, humans aren't the top of the food chain in Fairy and most Fairy beings aren't that impressed with us, especially when we are visiting in their home. Speaking of that, as visitors always be sure to be a good guest. When in the Irish Otherworld it is a bad idea to eat or drink anything, and if its offered to you find a way to very politely decline; on the other hand if in one of the Norse Fairy worlds – ljiossalfheim or svartalfheim, for example – it is acceptable to take food and drink and is worse to refuse it than accept it. Should you be in a Fairy world that is not Norse or Celtic try to learn the expected customs first or ask your fetch to accompany you and help guide you.

Protections Against Fairies

> *The [midwives] to this Day put Bread, the Bible, or a piece of Iron, in Women's Beds when travailing, to save them from being thus stolen; and they commonly report, that all uncouth, unknown Wights are terrified by nothing earthly so much as by cold Iron.*
> – Robert Kirk

> *There was Evan Thomas, who, travelling by night over Bedwellty Mountain, towards the valley of Ebwy Fawr, where his house and estate were, saw the Gwyllion on each side of him, some of them dancing around him in fantastic fashion. He also heard the sound of a bugle-horn winding in the air, and there seemed to be invisible hunters riding by. He then began to be afraid, but recollected his having heard that any person seeing Gwyllion may drive them away by drawing out a knife. So he drew out his knife, and the fairies vanished directly.*
> – Wirt Sikes, 1880

Although the main point of Fairy Witchcraft is to encourage friendship and alliances with the Other Crowd this should not be attempted unless a person knows how to protect themselves and their property against unwanted or malicious fairy attentions. Some kinds of Fey mean us harm and others may not dislike us in general, but can be upset or aggravated into acting against us.

Just as one shouldn't try to handle anything dangerous without knowing how to do so safely, one shouldn't start mucking around with Fairy unless you know how to protect yourself if you need to. Generally speaking if you offend the Good Neighbors the best strategy is an immediate apology and offering.

Historically when the Good People are upset with a person they are capable of a variety of dangerous responses. The most well known are probably bad luck, illnesses, and madness. Bad luck can manifest in a variety of ways, but is fairly self-explanatory; nothing will work out in your favor and as in the old definition of 'Murphy's luck', anything that can go wrong will wrong. Illnesses associated with angry Fair Folk are diverse, but include everything from sudden cramping and pain to wasting illnesses, jaundice, and flu-like symptoms. The madness brought by the Fey may be expressed by crushing depression, frenzy, or a loss of connection to consensual reality. In some cases if they are angered enough they may also directly physically assault someone[14].

Turning a person's luck if they have angered the Good People can be a difficult thing, which is part of why it's best to avoid angering them to begin with. It has happened that people have come to me over the years after causing some offense though and needing advice on how to fix it and I have found that a quick apology and copious offerings of cream, honey, and bread or cookies works. Mind you these are for fairly minor offenses like disturbing a fairy ring. The greater the injury done to them the more extreme the response will be and the more effort has to go into apologizing for it.

Treating illnesses caused by the Good Neighbors is a complex subject in its own right. I can really only touch on it here but for those interested I recommend reading Karen Louise Jolly's book *Popular Religion in Late Saxon England: Elf Charms in Context.* Basically Fey-illnesses were usually treated with a combination of herbal cures and magical charms. The most common herbs used in these remedies, which may be used as protection against fairies in general, are lupines, betony, fennel, and leeks, with garlic, pennyroyal and rue being used slightly less often (Jolly, 1996). These would be administered either in a salve, drink, or used as a fumigant, although I do not recommend using any herbs without thoroughly investigating their safety for yourself. Many examples of such herbal remedies can be found in the 9th century Old English text *Bald's Leech Book*. For my own purposes I am most inclined to use these herbs either combined as an incense blend or carried in a charm pouch, rather than consumed in any way.

Madness is another thing that can be caused by angry Fair Folk. In the Irish to sleep on a fairy mound might result in madness. In Norse cultures the huldufolk – hidden folk – could be offended by the desecration of their land, either through construction or if a person urinated[15] on it, and might respond by driving the offender mad. It was a very old belief, particularly in Norse, German, and Anglo-Saxon areas, that elves had the ability to cause nightmares and influence a person's mind (Grimm, 1982). In Anglo-Saxon this is called 'aelf-siden', which means the influence of elves; in Icelandic the term alfsida or alfseidhr means an elf-charm, but is understood as similar to the Anglo-Saxon in meaning (Tichy, 2010). In the older belief aelfsiden seems to have been understood as a kind of spirit possession and is usually discussed alongside demonic possession in the older texts (Jolly, 1996). It is marked by fevers, shaking, and changes in personality (Jolly, 1996). While the Good People quite clearly have physical bodies, in many stories they can also travel without form and seem to be able to go from substantial to insubstantial and back again. Grimm tells us that elves have the ability to enter through the knotholes in doors and can influence people as a breath or wind, but also relates a story of an elf-woman who entered a home through a knothole in a door, married the family's son, gave him four sturdy children, then left just as she'd arrived (Grimm, 1982). In the Irish the fairy-wind can cause illness or madness. Those driven mad by the Good People are often called fairy-touched. It is said that there is power in the eyes of the Gentry and they can enchant a person with a glance, so one defense may be to avoid looking them directly in the eyes. As with illnesses caused by the Fey, madness caused by them is often cured with herbs and charms, if it can be cured at all. Two main methods of curing those being aelfsiden are smoking the aelf out and pricking (Jolly, 1996).

Fairies and Iron

First of all it's best to remember that fairy is a general term, like animal, that applies to a wide array of beings. There is no single protection that will work against all fairies all the time, indeed different types of fairies often have very specific things that can be used to protect against them, which is why knowing your fairylore is so important. However, there are a few things that can be generalized out because they are known to work against a larger percentage of fairies.

Iron is recommended as a superlative protection against fairies, and can take the form of a horseshoe hung up over the door, a knife or pair of scissors[16] under the mattress, or an iron nail in the pocket. In my experience 80-plus percent of fairies can't bear the touch of iron – the others though have no problem with it, and those would include mine faeries, forge spirits, and some house spirits; basically any fairy that would naturally exist or dwell near iron or iron ore. Also any of the aos sí connected to smithing don't seem to be bothered by iron.

True forged iron is hard to come by these days and although it is the best protection, steel will also work in a pinch. Steel, of course, is almost entirely iron with only a small amount of other material added, so it will still have a very similar effect. Your best bet is to find real iron though if you can. Generally the type of item isn't as important as the material in this case, so anything made of iron that you can procure can be used for protective purposes.

Why iron? The truth is no one knows for sure, but there are many theories. There is one good argument that the Irish Gods, the Tuatha De Danann, used bronze and part of why the Gaels drove them out was the Gaels' use of iron, and that this in turn developed into the fairies' aversion to iron, although it seems unlikely that smith Gods would be averse to any metal. Some also argue in the same vein that as humans developed iron we drove the fairy beings out of our world because they could not handle the refined metal. Some also argue that it was the process of forging itself that endowed iron with a magical quality that granted it the ability to protect from fairy enchantments; it is worth noting that there is a deep and longstanding belief that blacksmiths have magical abilities and knowledge. In the end of course no one really knows why, but it is a ubiquitously recommended protection in Celtic folklore.

Now my personal theory – and this is purely my theory – is that it gets back to the strong grounding nature of iron versus the inherently magical nature of fairies. Iron draws and grounds magical energy. Fairies by their nature not only use this same energy, but also often seem to be made up of it, particularly if you go by how Robert Kirk describes them:

> *Said to be of a middle Nature betwixt Man and Angel, as were Daemons thought to be of old; intelligent fluidious Spirits, and light changeable Bodies, (like those called Astral) somewhat of the Nature of a condensed Cloud.*
> (Kirk, 1893)

I don't believe all fairies are 'astral' as he describes them, but certainly they all rely heavily on magic, which iron interferes with and dispels, which may be enough reason for them to avoid it.

There are several ways to use iron to protect your home from fairies, if it's needed. In Celtic tradition you could hang a horseshoe, points up, over your doorway, which would also act to bless the home and draw luck to you. For protection against fairies you can also place an iron knife or scissors in a strategic place. Knives in general are believed to have protective qualities, whether they are of iron or steel, and the presence of a knife or drawing a knife from a sheath is said to drive fairies off (Wirt, 1880). For those practicing Fairy Witchcraft, although it is best to have a ritual blade that is non-ferrous it is a good idea to have a second knife of iron to use for protection and in work that involves exorcising spirits or banishing fairies from spaces.

Another method found in Germanic and Norse traditions is to hammer an iron nail into a post near the doorway or alternatively part of the door frame. Additionally it is said to be an effective protection to draw a circle using an iron nail or knife around what you want to protect (Gundarsson, 2007). A more modern, but still useful, method is the use of iron water. Fill a small spray bottle with water and add iron filings, iron dust, or a piece of iron, and allow it to sit for a few days. The water can be sprayed into a room or around the home as needed.

As always keep in mind that the use of iron will not affect all fairies, as some – including mine fairies and house fairies – are not bothered by it. In the Norse culture, iron is a defense against the alfar, but not against some of the more dangerous spirits including etins (Gundarsson, 2007). For those that are sensitive to it, though, it is a superlative protection. For this reason those who seek to work with fairies must be very cautious about using this metal, as it will drive away most fairies. One should never, for example, cut a plant to be harvested for magical purposes with an iron knife as this will drive away the plant's spirit. However, in some cases it may be necessary to know how to rid an area of disruptive or dangerous spirits, so it is important to understand the uses of iron.

Other Protections

Iron is not your only option to protect yourself from fairy influence or from those Otherworldly beings who might harm you. A variety of methods and objects can be used to break fairy enchantments besides iron, and these include hag stones, four-leaf clover, salt, turning clothing inside out, and bells.

Although not as widely recommended as iron, salt also has protective qualities. Salt was used with fire and water to bless pastures, salt was sprinkled on cows who had just calved to protect them from fairy influence, and salt was used to protect butter from the influence of fairies and witches (McNeill, 1962). Salt is said to symbolize eternity and carrying it is a strong protection (Briggs, 1976). The idea of using salt by sprinkling it around yourself, often in a circle, is one that has entered pop culture thanks to movies like Hocus Pocus and television shows like Supernatural, but the core idea behind this is rooted in older folklore; salt is used in purification and so it is believed that impure – or as the Scottish might say unsainly – beings cannot be around it.

The main power of the four-leaf clover against the Fey Folk is its ability to dispel their glamour (Briggs, 1976). Because glamour and enchantment are some of the main powers that are used to mislead people; by making them think a handful of leaves are a fistful of gold coins, perhaps, or that a dreary cave is a palace, the Fair Folk can control people to their own benefit and the person's misfortune. The four-leaf clover gives some power back to the human by taking away this advantage.

Bells, specifically the ringing of bells, are also said to put malicious spirits to flight. Most references to this specify church bells; however, folklore makes it clear that any kind of bell, including those worn by Morris Men, and those attached to livestock, will have the same effect (Briggs, 1976). I was always told, although I could not say where I learned this, that the ringing of bells will have no effect on most spirits, but only certain types that are most inclined towards causing us harm. For those spirits, the sound of bells is piercing and very painful.

Certain herbs are protection against fairies as well, and these include St. John's wort, broom, daisy, red verbena, broom, and rowan berries, although it is also said that some of the aos sidhe live off rowan berries (Briggs, 1976; McNeill, 1962). The color red itself seems to have a warding effect against some fairies[17], which can be seen in its use not only with certain herbs and berries, but also in the combination of rowan twigs and red thread, or rowan, amber, and red thread, to protect against baneful magic. Amber is another protection against the Fey, and is often used to protect babies and children. Sulfur is also a protection against fairies, particularly those of the Norse tradition (Gundarsson, 2007).

When outdoors, if you find yourself in danger from anything Fey, one method to protect yourself is to cross running water. It is best if the water you cross is south-running, as anything moving southwards, like anything moving sunwise, has positive and blessing qualities. This method of protection is also said to work against ghosts and malignant spirits (Wilde, 1887). Although leaping running water is a good method if caught outdoors, don't forget that some beings, like the Kelpie, make their homes in water and will not be stopped by it (Briggs, 1976).

St John's Wort

St John's wort is a well-known herb with a long magical history. It grows in Europe and can now be found in the United States, often by the side of the road. The plant's yellow flowers bloom in the summer and the plant itself grows up to about 3ft tall. For medicinal purposes prepared tinctures, teas, and supplements of St John's wort can be purchased or grown although for traditional magic charms the plant should be found wild. As with most Celtic herbal magic, the plant is most powerful when found at a specific time, in this case on the day of a full moon, at noon in bright sun (Wilde, 1991).

Magically, St John's wort is said to protect against fairy enchantments, and grant luck, prosperity, and blessing. In Irish tradition St John's wort is one of the seven herbs that cannot be affected by anything supernatural (Wilde, 1991). In Scottish tradition it should be gathered with the right hand, dried with the left, and kept to ensure prosperity (Carmichael, 1900).

If you are fortunate enough to come across St John's wort growing wild, this charm may be recited while it is gathered. Finding it, reciting this, and keeping the herb is believed to bring luck and prosperity, and of course it is a protective herb against the Fey.

St. John's Wort Charm 168

Saint John's wort, Saint John's wort,
I envy whoever has you,
I will pluck you with my right hand,
I will preserve you with my left hand,
Whoever finds you in the cattle fold,
Shall never be without prosperity.
(Daimler, 2010)

Modern Experience

Now I live in the northeast United States, but as it happens I have a fairy thorn in my yard. That's a bit of a story of its own, but suffice to say that I'm certain it is, and we have left offerings to the aos si there for many years now.

Last summer my husband was doing yard work and damaged the tree. He came inside and told me that he had accidentally taken a palm sized chunk of bark off of the trunk. I immediately told him to go out and apologize and leave an offering at the tree, because the Fair Folk are notorious for punishing those who damage fairy thorns. I was so worried about that I went out myself and left some cookies and poured out some honey, because I was afraid of the consequences to the household luck and to my husband. Unfortunately, he decided since I had done this there was no need for him to do anything.

A week went by, and then around 7am one morning I heard a tremendous crash. Grabbing my young son I ran out and found my husband's car impaled by an enormous branch, which had plunged down like a spear from an oak tree. The branch had gone through the car and broken, so that part of it still jutted up while the rest lay on the ground next to the vehicle. Glass, bark, leaves, and splintered wood lay everywhere.

I was grateful that my husband hadn't been in the car. I was thinking that after living in that neighborhood for more than 30 years nothing like that had ever happened before. I was immediately suspicious that it wasn't a simple accident, that on a morning with no wind, no storm, no reason for the branch to fall – and no logic for it to have fallen on the car and not straight down to the ground next to the driveway – there was something Fey afoot. It looked for all the world as if a giant hand had thrown the 15-plus foot branch like a spear through the vehicle.

I ran back inside and woke my husband, asking him if he'd made the offering I'd told him to, to the Good People after the incident with the tree. No, he told me, he hadn't, because he thought what I had done was enough. Up he got from bed and out I made him go to make an offering right then, before anything else could happen.

And I can say that he won't ever make that mistake again...

Chapter 4

The Other Crowd and Ancestors

Gin ye ca' me imp or elf,
I rede ye look weel to yourself;
Gin ye ca' me fairy,
I'll work ye muckle tarrie;
Gind guid neibour ye ca' me,
Then guid neibour I will be;
But gin ye ca' me seelie wicht,
I'll be your freend baith day and nicht.
(Chambers, 1842)

(If you call me imp or elf,
I counsel you, look well to yourself;
If you call me fairy,
I'll work you great misery;
If you good neighbor call me
Then good neighbor I will be;
But if you call me Seelie wight[18]
I'll be your friend both day and night)

A Story

Some people say that there are good fairies and there are bad fairies, and that the good ones will always do us good and the bad will always do us ill. And this is true in its own way, although it's also true that we should never anger even the good ones because they won't hesitate to do us harm if they feel we deserve it. And generally the bad ones are dangerous and should be avoided, but nothing with Fairy is ever entirely one way or another and any rule has exceptions....

Once long ago in Scotland there was a Kelpie, a kind of trickster spirit, a Water Horse, who could assume the form of a man or dog or even goat some say. Kelpies were often feared because they were known to trick people into riding on their backs only to rush into the lake the Kelpie lived in and drown the person before devouring them. This Kelpie though fell in love with a mortal girl who lived near his aquatic home and he could do her no harm. Instead he came to her in the form of a handsome young man, and courted her. She didn't know him for what he really was and over time fell in love with him.

Eventually the two were married and came to live in a small house together. The Kelpie continued to hide his nature from his wife and the years passed in happiness for the couple. The mortal woman bore her husband a child and he loved his small family with all his heart. But although he could have the form of a mortal man he was a Fairy creature at heart and he could not entirely suppress his true nature. Sometimes when he could not bear keeping his foreign shape and when the sound of the wind on the water overwhelmed him he would sneak away from his little family and run along the shoreline as a sleek dark horse.

One day when he had gone out early to run like this his wife went looking for him and saw the dark horse shift into the shape of her handsome husband. Realizing he was a Kelpie, she abandoned her child where she stood and fled in terror. The Kelpie tried to stop her but, knowing that his pursuit was only frightening her more, he returned instead to the spot where their young child sat on the ground crying for his mother. The Kelpie held the child, offering what comfort he could as he watched for any sign of his wife returning.

Still deeply in love with his mortal wife, he remained in the little house and raised their child, waiting futilely for her to return.

– Modern re-telling of traditional Scottish folktale

When many people talk about religion the discussion centers on deity: are the Gods real? Do they have agency? Can and will they adversely affect people? In Chapter 2 we looked at this question from a Fairy Witchcraft point of view, but the Gods are not the only beings that are honored in our tradition. We need the conversation to include all the Powers – are our ancestors real and do they affect people? Spirits of place? Spirits of the Otherworld? Because, you see, if we are going to ask ourselves these questions about deity, then it follows we should ask them as well about the other spirits. If we believe the Gods are real in the sense of beings that do exist in any way beyond the human mind, and that those beings affect us in concrete tangible ways, then isn't that also true of all supernatural beings? Many people may be willing to at least tentatively accept the reality of the Gods, but have a harder time with the lesser spirits, those beings separate from and more powerful than humans, beings who can and will interact with and shape our lives if they choose to. In Fairy Witchcraft we acknowledge and honor a variety of such spirits including: ancestral spirits, land spirits, and Otherworldly spirits.

What is true of the reality and agency of the Gods is also true of the reality and agency of other spirits. As an animist I firmly believe that the world is full of spirits of all kinds and that these spirits are everywhere. They are real, whether or not they are corporeal, whether or not they are significant to our lives. There are disembodied human spirits, ancestral spirits, spirits of place, house spirits, and Otherworldly spirits of an enormously wide variety. All have agency and personality, and each will have the ability to affect us to varying degrees. To what degree can range from nearly-as-much-as-the-Gods to barely noticeable, and I tend to use this range of influence, of power, to decide what a spirit is and where it ranks in my worship. A powerful enough Good Neighbor is little different from a God, which is in fact where the Gods of Fairy Witchcraft came from, because if it's as powerful as a God and able to influence me like a God, then for all intents and purposes it's a God. However, even those spirits that are clearly not deities can still help or harm us and are still important. Our house spirit is an important part of our home and should be given respect and offered to and, if treated well, will help to nurture a happy environment and give the home luck. Our ancestors can and will protect us and are worth remembering and honoring, and many feel they are the most strongly motivated to directly intervene for us, since we are their legacy.

What does all of that matter? Well ask yourself: why do we honor the ancestors and Otherworldly beings? I'd argue for many of the same reasons we honor the Gods: because they are worth honoring and they are able to help and bless us, and ultimately if we create the right relationship with them they will be good to us and our lives will benefit. The more immediate spirits in our lives, the ones in our homes and home-places, the ones in our family, are the ones who have the greatest motivation to intercede – for good or ill – in our lives because they are intimately a part of every day we live, whether we see them or not, whether we honor them or not.

And so in Fairy Witchcraft we honor all these Powers – Gods, ancestors, spirits – because such reciprocity is what creates the relationships that nurture positive things (luck, blessings, health) in our lives. We give to them and they give to us, from the greatest God to the lowest spirit of place. That is what it is to live in right relationship with the seen and unseen worlds.

I have heard it said that the spirits of the Otherworld are bound to specific places and many people use this idea to argue against honoring culture specific spirits like the aos sí outside Ireland. Now I grant you that land spirits generally are tied in this way to a location; however, I do not believe that applies to the Good People. In stories they are clearly said to change their homes (their sí) at certain times of year and are wont to travel, which is why building on fairy roads is such a bad idea. Yeats speaks of a woman whose mother had a fairy woman as a friend and the woman would tell her of things occurring in America;

this can be interpreted as the fairy woman having oracular abilities, or perhaps she was able to travel there herself and directly see the events. I'd argue each possibility is equally likely. Many folk stories in Ireland mention the Fairy Host going abroad to France or Spain. Spirits, like people, move and travel and explore new places. They also in my experience tend to follow those who believe in and offer to them. There are spirits of place and spirits of stationary things like trees or rocks that do not move around, but there are other spirits that are not anchored to a specific thing that go where they will. And it is possible that how we perceive them plays a role as well – one person's alf may be another's elf, may be a third person's daoine sí.

When we move from place to place we bring our Gods and many of our spirits with us, and we also have a chance to meet new ones. We carry them with our traditions and practices and beliefs into new territories and new opportunities. When the Norse arrived in Iceland they found alfar there, and to this day there is a rich tradition around the Hidden Folk in Iceland – but were they really there before the Norse or did they arrive with them, following those who honored and offered to them? I do not know for certain, but I do know that in my own life in America I have encountered many different kinds of spirits, and I feel this variety reflects the multiculturalism of the place I live.

When I teach on topics relating to the Good Neighbors most of the people who attend end up talking about wanting to connect to the spirits of the land or Fey Folk, and this is almost always followed by a wistful regret that the person doesn't live in a rural area or can't get to a specific sacred site. While I encourage this urge to connect to the spirits, I don't understand the idea that we need some wild place or sacred place to do so – in fact the spirits of those places are the least likely to appreciate our intrusion. The reality is that all places have spirits and it is just as easy to connect to them in a city as in a forest. I believe very strongly actually that it is even more important for us to connect to the spirits that share our homes than it is to connect with spirits of places we are only visiting, because the ones we live with can directly affect us every day.

In my own opinion there are two main types of fairy spirits: spirits of place, also called land spirits, and Otherworldly spirits, also called the Fair Folk, Good People, or fairies. The biggest difference between the two is that land spirits are tied to a location and do not travel, while the Fair Folk can and do wander. Land spirits also tend to be less focused and aware and somewhat harder to communicate with because their consciousness, in my experience, operates on such a vast scale. The Good Neighbors are more like dealing with humans, except you have to think of them as people from an utterly foreign culture.

All places have spirits, and in many cases there are layers of spirits. Land spirits may manifest as vague feelings or impressions associated with an area, but more often they appear with a clear physical form. The island of Iceland is said to have four spirits that appear as a bull, bird, giant, and dragon; one might argue that the red dragon of Wales is another such embodied spirit. On the smaller local scale, your property and your home might have a spirit that could appear as an animal or person. Spirits of place may be the manifestation of a place's spirit or they may be a spirit that is strongly tied to a certain place, but either way they have the ability to influence a person or family's luck, health, and mood.

Gods and Fairies

In Christian myth it is said that the fairies exist as beings that are between the nature of angels and demons; many people dismiss this as later propaganda, but I believe it represents a reflection of genuine older belief. In pagan times the fairies were seen as being of the same nature as the Gods, but on a lower level, existing somewhere between the Gods and humans. Within modern Fairy

Faiths, the fairies – as well as the old Gods – have been greatly diminished and reduced to beings that are often seen as less than human, but this is not true to the older view.

In Grimm's *Teutonic Mythology* we are told:

> *On the nature of Elves I resort for advice to the ON. [old Norse] authorities, before all others...the Elder Edda several times couples æsir and âlfar together, as though they were a compendium of all higher beings, and that the AS. [Anglo-Saxon] ês and ylfe stand together in exactly the same way. This apparently concedes more of a divinity to elves than to men.*
> (Grimm, 1882)

From this we can understand that in both Norse and Germanic as well as Anglo-Saxon belief the Alfar, who were roughly equivalent to the Irish sí, were seen as a semi-divine race of beings that were often placed alongside the Gods.

Robert Kirk's book *The Secret Commonwealth*, based on his 17th century experiences with fairies, says: '*These Siths, or fairies...are said to be of a middle Nature betwixt Man and Angel, as were Dæmons*[19] *thought to be of old.*' (Kirk, 2007). This also shows the idea of the fairies as beings that exist above humans, but below Gods in the universal hierarchy.

Evans Wentz, writing 200 years later, says: '*In the Book of Leinster the poem of Eochaid records that the Tuatha De Danann, the conquerors of the Fir-Bolgs, were hosts of siabra; and siabra is an Old Irish word meaning fairies, sprites, or ghosts.*' (Evans Wentz, 1911) This connects the Irish Tuatha de Danann, often seen as the old pagan Gods, with the fairies. Wentz goes on to say:

> *In the two chief Irish MSS., [manuscripts] the Book of the Dun Cow and the Book of Leinster, the Tuatha De Danann are described as 'gods and not-gods'; and Sir John Rhys considers this an ancient formula comparable with the Sanskrit deva and adeva, but not with*

> *'poets (dée) and husbandmen (an dée)' as the author of Cóir Anmann learnedly guessed.*
> (Evans Wentz, 1911)

Some modern authors do indeed see the reference to 'Gods and not-Gods' as referring to the division between the people of skill and the common laborers. However, I agree with Rhys that it more likely refers to the separation of the Gods and the fairies, in the same way that we see the Aesir and alfar referred to in the Norse/Germanic material. There are many additional references in Irish myth to the sí, particularly the riders of the sí, acting with or at the request or direction of the Gods. It can be difficult to discern if these references are meant to indicate that the riders of the sí are the Tuatha Dé Danann or if they represent a separate force under the command of the Tuatha Dé, but I tend to favor seeing them as the 'not-Gods' who are allied with the Gods. If this is accepted along with the references to the fairies existing between men and Gods, then it becomes clear that the fairies exist as beings part of, but separate from, the Gods, and would likely have arrived in Ireland before the Gods and have been in the mounds before the Gods were driven into them.

Are the fairies the 'not-Gods' of Irish myth? It is impossible to know with certainty, but it is a possibility, and one I embrace. Whether they are or not, it can be said that they have long been viewed as powerful beings that are less than Gods, but more than humans, and should be given our respect. Using the framework of the old Fairy Faith provides an excellent way to do this.

Within the loose category of the term 'fairy' there are a huge array of different beings and it is far beyond the scope of this book to discuss them all. However, it's important for us to look at several specific types. To start we are going to gain a better understanding of the most powerful of the Fair Folk, the aos sí and the alfar, and then look at some of the ones you should work to know and have a relationship with, the land spirits and house spirits. After that we will discuss the more dangerous ones that you may run across, the Wild Hunt and the Slua sí, and also look at several types of fairy animals that you may encounter.

It's also always best to keep in mind that although we are seeking these beings out as allies and even friends, they must be treated with respect and caution. As Terry Pratchett said:

Elves are wonderful. They provoke wonder.
Elves are marvelous. They cause marvels.
Elves are fantastic. They create fantasies.
Elves are glamorous. They project glamour.
Elves are enchanting. They weave enchantment.
Elves are terrific. They beget terror.
The thing about words is that meanings can twist just like a snake, and if you want to find snakes look for them behind words that have changed their meaning.
No one ever said elves are nice.

Aos Sí – The Irish Fairy Folk

It can be hard to make any definitive statements about the Irish fairies, the aos sí, because the folklore is so diverse[20]. It is, however, important to have at least a basic understanding of who they were and are and how to safely interact with them and honor them. This section takes a very general view and it should be understood that there will be exceptions to what is said here, but that this represents the most common or widespread beliefs.

The terms daoine sí and aos sí both mean 'people of the fairy hills' and come from the belief that these beings dwell within the hollow hills, called sí, which are entrances to the Otherworld. Although the emphasis is on the fairy hills, the daoine sí were also associated with mystical islands, usually located in the west, which were sometimes seen in the distance, but could never be reached (McNeill, 1956). Looking at Irish fairy lore we see that the aos sí are found living in the mounds and islands and are associated with islands, bogs, lakes, trees, and the air (O hOgain, 2006). This clearly reflects the complex layers of belief around the Otherworld and its inhabitants, often called the Other People or Other Crowd.

The daoine sí are often referred to with euphemisms like Good Neighbors, Gentry, Mother's Blessing, and Fair Folk; sometimes they are called fairies, which may be a shortened form of Fair Folk (Wedin, 1998). In the older belief it was thought to be bad luck to call the daoine sí by that name (or any name using 'sí', previously spelled sídhe), but interestingly this prohibition seems to be shifting to the term fairies, which of course was originally used as a way to avoid offending them. In modern practice many people have a strong prohibition against referring to them by any form of sí or using the word fairy, sticking instead to euphemisms (O hOgain, 2006). However, in contexts like this book or classes on the subject it is difficult not to use terms the majority of people are familiar with, so sometimes cautious compromises must be made. In some cases they are also referred to as wee folk or little people, likely something that began as a way to minimize their power or influence, but has come to reflect a belief that their physical stature has literally shrunk.

The lands within the Otherworld are described as beautiful beyond belief, rich in resources of all kinds, and peaceful. Often mortals taken into Fairy were content to stay there, sometimes forever, sometimes for many years until a sudden homesickness seized them and drove them to return to our world. Such visits rarely end well because time flows differently in the Otherworld than it does here, meaning that the person might return only to find that hundreds of years had gone by since they left. As soon as they touch mortal earth all the years they missed catch up to them and they die.

Although they are strongly associated with these Otherworldly locations, the daoine sí are in no way limited to these places, nor are they tied to the areas around them. In many stories they travel in our world, moving their homes from one fairy hill to another, attending mortal fairs, and traveling on fairy roads. Usually they go unnoticed among mortals, using the magic of glamour to blend in; sometimes they may be seen by a person who has the second sight or who has dealt with them before and for some reason retains the ability to see them. For example, in many stories where a midwife is borrowed to attend a fairy birth she is given a salve to rub on the newborn's eyes and intentionally or accidently rubs some on one of her own, which allows her to see through fairy glamour. In such cases she often encounters the fairy father later, perhaps in a public place like a market, and when he realizes she can see him he puts out her eye. There are also tales of the Fairy Queens traveling and of the Fairy Rade[21] riding out. Fairy Rades were dangerous to any humans who might cross their path, but could also be helpful in offering the opportunity to free captives, such as in the case of Tam Lin who is rescued by his lover Janet from a Fairy Rade.

There are many roads and paths, called Fairy Roads, that exist between the different fairy hills and which most people cannot see. The Good Neighbors travel on these roads, especially at night, and building on or near one always leads to bad luck and often death (O hOgain, 2006). An equally bad idea was any activity that disturbed the homes of the daoine sí, whether that was digging into the fairy hills or cutting down their trees; both actions were likely to result in ill-luck or death (O hOgain, 2006). This belief exists to this day and has resulted in protests to divert roads around fairy trees and outrage over the destruction of fairy hills. There was a case in Ireland not too long ago of telephone poles placed too close to a fairy hill, which kept falling down; this inexplicable inability of the company to keep the poles up so close to the hill lead many people to say it was the result of the offended daoine sí.

Physical appearances of the daoine sí are fairly consistent, they are generally described as very similar to humans, usually finely dressed, pale, and fair (O hOgain, 2006). Yeats describes a fairy woman in an anecdotal tale as being of human height and appearance, with brown hair and dressed in human fashions (Yeats, 1966). In stories, they are often said to wear green or grey primarily and may have blond or brown hair; they can appear alone or in groups and be male or female. Groups of fairy men sometimes appeared seeking a human to play hurling with them, apparently a requirement for them to play the game, while fairy women might appear with messages or warnings (Yeats, 1966). The Good Neighbors are usually invisible to mortal eyes thanks to their magic, which hides them, unless they wish to be seen or the person has the second sight. However, their presence and especially their passage can be perceived in other ways. People may hear the sounds of horses, hounds, and riders, or of laughter and talking. The passage of the Fairy Host also creates a sudden gust of wind, called sí gaoithe or séideán sí (MacKillop, 1998). The Fairy Host will be discussed in depth in a separate entry. The ability to pass by unseen relies on the use of a type of magic called glamour, one of the fairy folk's most famous powers, which can deceive mortal senses into thinking one thing is something else. This magic is seen in many different fairy stories where a handful of leaves might seem to be a pile of gold coins, for example, or a deserted cave appear as a rich mansion.

Both the Tuatha Dé Danann and the aos sí have been known to intermarry with and have children with humans. There are a multitude of different versions of stories of a bride stolen by the fairies on her wedding day and taken to marry a man of the sí instead. Often this stolen bride is thought to have died by the people in her community, but may later be seen by a midwife who has been borrowed by the fairies to help the girl deliver her Otherworldly husband's child. The belief is that the birthrate among the fairies is low and that they use human women and babies to increase their own numbers, being fond of taking brides as well as unusually beautiful or pleasant children and infants.

The aos sí also take musicians and midwives, but these are usually only borrowed for a time and later returned to the mortal world. Some, like Thomas the Rhymer, are taken for a specific amount of time, while others – often those who eat or drink anything in Fairy – can never leave. In some tales a person might join the fairies for a single night of dancing in a fairy ring or enter a fairy hill for what they think is only one night only to emerge and find that anywhere from seven to an hundred years have passed. The aos sí were also famous for stealing cattle and horses that they wanted, usually by making the animal appear to sicken and die, but sometimes by taking them outright (O hOgain, 2006).

The Fairies are often divided into two courts, what we today might call the good fairies and the bad fairies. In Scotland they were referred to as the Seelie, or blessed, Court, and the Unseelie, or unblessed, Court. The words Seelie and Unseelie come from the Scots dialect a language spoken in the lower parts of Scotland, which is a blend of Scottish Gaelic, English, and German. We often see the phrase 'Seelie wights' with Seelie being equated to good or benevolent. The word wight was borrowed into Scots from German and is a general term for any being, but is used to denote supernatural beings as well. McNeill refers to these as the Seely and Unseely, or good wichts (wights) and wicked wichts (McNeill, 1956). In Ireland the two courts sometimes battle during the night leaving behind traces of fairy blood, a white liquid, which people see in the morning (O hOgain, 2006). The Gentry are ruled by a monarchy, but there are also lower class fairies as well as the nobility, and these working class fairies may interact with humans (O hOgain, 2006). The Fair Folk ride on fine horses and are seen in the company of hounds; generally these animals are either black, white, or grey. In some stories it is said the deer of the forest are the cattle of the fairies (McNeill, 1956).

In folklore the daoine sí are seen as being especially active on the quarter days, Samhain, Imbolc, Bealtaine, and Lughnasa. It was believed that on these days the fairies moved house, processing forth from one hill to another along set fairy roads (McNeill, 1956). Samhain and Bealtaine are the strongest times of fairy influence and so are times when great care should be taken to avoid running afoul of them (O hOgain, 2006). At Bealtaine it was believed that the Fair Folk might travel abroad, appearing as a stranger at the door asking for milk or a coal from the fire; to give either would mean giving the household's luck away for the year to come (Wilde, 1887). At Samhain the daoine sí are known to move from one hill to another, from their summer to winter homes, and it is quite dangerous to meet them on a fairy road that night (Estyn Evans, 1957). The Fair Folk are also especially active at twilight and midnight, and the Slua sí, the airborne malicious fairy host, is most active at night.

The Fey and the dead have long been overlapping and intertwined groups, and it can be difficult to entirely separate them even in discussions. The ranks of the daoine sí are often said to include the dead, particularly those who have recently died, and a common theme in folklore is for someone in a market or at a fair to accidently run into a neighbor or former friend thought to have died, but actually now among the Fair Folk. Usually it is explained in the context of a person – a new bride or other attractive young person – who was taken to join the Other Crowd and had a changeling left behind, which died and was buried. Even the sí that the Fair Folk live in are places of the dead, often ancient burial mounds, such as Brugh na Boyne (Newgrange). In many fairy stories a person is believed to have died, but appears, often in a dream, to a loved one and explains that they have been taken into Fairyland and can be rescued in a certain way, perhaps by the living person going to a crossroads at midnight when the Fairy Rade will pass by and grabbing their loved one from the horse he or she is riding (O hOgain, 2006; *The Ballad of Tam Lin*). Many people say that the Slua sí, the fairy host of the air, are spirits of the mortal dead (McNeill, 1956).

The daoine sí can bless or harm people, and a main motivation for keeping on their good side is to receive the blessings and avoid the ill luck. Fairies are reputed to give gifts, but these gifts too can be either a blessing or curse, as they might result in prosperity or luck, or they could be illusions that would turn to leaves or grass at dawn. The sí gaoithe (fairy wind), which was a sign of the presence of the fairy host, could bring illness or cause injury (MacKillop, 1998). Elfshot is another well-known fairy malady, a sudden pain, cramp, or stitch caused by an invisible fairy arrow shot into the body by angered daoine sí. In many cases it was also believed that elfshot was a power given to witches, which they learned from the fairies – indeed many Irish and Scottish witches were thought to have learned both malediction and healing from the Fair Folk with whom they dealt (Hall, 2005). In contrast though, those who were considered friends of the daoine sí could be privy to special knowledge and taught things like healing and magic, or a musician might be given great skill (O hOgain, 2006). The daoine sí might appear as a stranger at the door seeking to borrow something or needing milk or a coal from the fire, alone in a field or wood, or might be encountered on the road; those brave enough to seek them out might choose to sleep on a fairy mound, knowing that the result would either be blessing or madness.

There are a variety of protective charms against the Fair Folk far too numerous to get into here and many of which we've previously discussed, but I'll offer some specific examples. To keep a new mother and infant safe they would be given milk from a cow who had eaten the herb mothan (McNeill, 1956). To get the host, particularly the slua, to release anyone they may have taken one should throw the dust from the road, an iron knife, or your left shoe and say, 'This is yours; that is mine!' (McNeill, 1956). Should a person be suffering from the ill-willing attention of one of the fairy people a Fairy Doctor must be found, that is a person with special knowledge of the fairies, who can diagnose the exact issue, be it elfshot or fairy blast, and come up with the appropriate charm, chant, or herb to cure the person (Wilde, 1887). Tying a red ribbon on cattle or horses was thought to keep fairies away, as was tying a rowan twig on to a cow's tail, or lightly striking the animals with rowan or hazel switches (O hOgain, 1995; O hOgain, 2006). Rowan and red thread is another well-known protection, as is anything made of iron, a material that the Fair Folk cannot bear.

Honoring and offering to the daoine sí are vital aspects of Fairy Witchcraft. We seek not only to live in friendship with the aos sí, but also to form alliances with them. The Fair Folk have long been offered to and this is a practice that we must continue in our thoroughly modern world, rather than turning our backs on the Otherworld, which has so long existed side by side with ours. Honoring the daoine sí not only prevents ill-luck, but can grant good luck and blessing and more importantly helps create a reciprocal relationship between us and the Fair Folk based on respect and friendship. We must also know the signs of fairy trouble as well and how to protect ourselves and others against them. Humans have a long and complex relationship with the daoine sí – as long and complex as the history of the Fair Folk themselves – and they are just as present today as they have ever been.

A Norse View: the Alfar, Huldufolk, and Elves

One of the challenges in understanding the Norse and Germanic material is that many different Otherworldly beings are translated into English as 'elves', just as many different Irish beings are called fairies. The Norse word alfar appears in German as alp or elb, and English as elf, while in modern Icelandic they are known as both alfar and Huldufolk (hidden folk), although Huldufolk is also used as a generic term, like elf, that can describe alfar, trolls and land spirits. Landwights are also sometimes conflated with the alfar, because the two have many commonalities, but also key differences that indicate they actually are separate types of beings (Gundarsson, 2007). The modern view of elves as tiny laborers is vastly at odds with the traditional view of the alfar as tall, beautiful, and powerful beings. If you are familiar with Tolkein's elves then you have some idea of the older view of the alfar.

The alfar were created when the Gods created the world and in Norse myth one of the nine worlds belongs to them: Ljossalfheim (Light Elf Home). Properly there are at least three groups referred to as alfar in Norse myth: the Ljossalfar (light elves), svartalfar (literally black elves; often conflated with duergar – dwarves), and drokkalfar (literally dark elves; mound dead), although it is difficult to know with certainty if these were originally seen as different beings altogether, which were all later simply called alfar for convenience, or if they were always seen as related beings. Jacob Grimm tried, in his *Teutonic Mythology*, to make a literal division of the groups by color, so that the ljossalfar were white, the svartalfar black and the drokkalfar grey, but this is almost certainly his own invention (Grimm, 1883). I think it is more likely, personally, that alfar was sometimes used as a term to describe supernatural beings who were neither Gods nor giants and so could be used in a more general sense, as well as specifically with the ljossalfar probably being the original beings under that name. In the lore, however, we do see beings referred to as alfar at one point and elsewhere as other types of beings, including Gods or giants, so it can be difficult to have any real clarity on this (exactly like the Irish material). There is some clear distinction between the ljossalfar, the more traditionally understood Otherworldly elves, and the drokkalfar, who are understood to be the mound-dead, but there is also significant crossover as well, which may indicate an understood connection between the two groups (Gundarsson, 2007).

The alfar are known to interbreed with the other beings, particularly humans, and some mythic heroes and kings (as well as the king's half sister in the *Saga of King Hrolf Kraki*) were said to be half-elven. Icelandic patronyms sometimes show this possible ancestral connection (Gundarsson, 2007). This may reflect the common belief that the birthrate among the elves is low or that females are rare; a common theme in mythology is the stealing of brides and babies or of midwives to help at births. In the older Norse material, alfar always appear to be male, although in later Icelandic folklore we see females as well, and in the Swedish material we mainly see alf women (Gundarsson, 2007).

Alfar are associated with their own world, ljossalfheim, of course, but are also believed to live in or access our world through natural sites including mountains, cliffs, and boulders. They are known to be associated with certain places, and particularly certain individual trees, and it is believed that to disturb the places belonging to the Hidden Folk is very bad luck (Gundarsson, 2007). As recently as October 2013 protesters in Iceland were trying to block a highway project on the grounds that the construction passed through an area belonging to the alfar, who would be angered (Scherker, 2013). It is believed by many that disturbing the alfar with construction will result in bad luck and machines breaking down and often a special person who is known to be able to see and communicate with the elves will be brought in to negotiate (Gruber, 2007). Those who are brave enough to enter an alf-hill or visit the realm of the alfar may find that time moves very differently there, and sometimes the alfar will not release those who have gone among them.

In folklore, the alfar are seen as being especially active during the twelve days of Yule and at Midsummer. Gundrasson suggests – and I have long agreed – that the summer activities of the alfar, while still potentially perilous to humans, are less dangerous in nature and intent than the Yule activities (Gundarsson, 2007). The alfar ride out in full procession at Midsummer and Yule, an activity that may convey blessing on the areas they pass through, but in Iceland the Yule ride of the alfar, the alfarieth, is equated to the Wild Hunt and is extremely dangerous to see or contact (Gundarsson, 2007).

Interacting with the alfar is always a tricky business, as they can give blessings or lay curses on a person. In many traditional tales those who encounter elves and please them – often with good manners and generosity – may receive gifts, but those who offend them are killed or driven mad. When offered a gift from the alfar one should not refuse, and these gifts might include food, drink, or worthless things like leaves that will later turn to gold (Gundarsson, 2007). The alfar can also heal illnesses and injuries, if properly petitioned, and can be called on with a specific ceremony to protect a baby (Gundarsson, 2007).

The alfar are angered by several types of human activity including the aforementioned disturbance of their places. They are also driven out of an area by the placing of an alfreka or by people urinating on the ground (Pennick, 1993; Gundarsson, 2007). When angered, they can cause bad luck, sickness, madness, or death. Elves were also thought to be able to inflict illness on humans through the use of alf-shot or an elf-blast; the first being a small, invisible arrow that created diseases including bone cancer and arthritis, the second being a method where the elves would breathe or blow sickness into a person. There are several surviving charms aimed at curing alf-shot (Gundarsson, 2007). There is also a reference in older material to 'alf-seidhr', which is possibly a type of magic worked by the alfar against humans to cause madness and death (Gundarsson, 2007).

In Norse lore iron and steel are used as a protection against dangerous alfar and other spirits, although it is not effective against giants (Gundarsson, 2007). Any item made of this metal may be used, but traditionally bladed weapons and nails were the most commonly seen, and iron or steel nails might be hammered into a post or doorway to protect a home. Sulfur, rowan, and juniper are also traditional Norse protections, as well as a blend of woody nightshade, orchid and tree sap, which was said to protect against the 'unwanted attentions' of the huldufolk (Gundarsson, 2007). It is also said that church bells ringing will drive off the alfar, as will Christian prayers, although this may perhaps represent more of a reaction by the alfar to a religion that offends them than a sign of any power that faith actually has over them.

In a modern context it would be wise for Fairy Witches, especially those in Germanic lands or areas settled by Germanic peoples, to remember to honor the alfar, with rituals and offerings. The alfar are closer to us and our world and affect us more often than the Gods generally do, and they should be respected. It is also a good idea to understand how the alfar can affect us, for good and ill, and ways to best deal with them.

House Spirits

All places have spirits, from immense tracts of land to tiny streams. On the smaller local scale, your property and your home also have a spirit that could appear as an animal or person. In our home our house spirit appears as a dark-haired girl of about 12, dressed in white; my husband and I have both seen her in this form and my children have seen her as a flash of white out of the corner of their eyes. In Norse tradition house spirits may be called Tomte or Nisse and appear as short old men.

Most homes will have more than one house spirit, and if the house has an attached yard there will likely be spirits associated with those areas as well. How many spirits are there depends on many different things, but in my experience there will always be at least one main one that feels strongly possessive about either the home itself or the family. If the spirit is attached to the family then it will follow the family should the people move. Spirits of place may be the manifestation of a place's spirit or they may be a spirit that is strongly tied to a certain place, but either way they have the ability to influence a person or family's luck, health, and mood.

One of the first and most basic steps in practicing Fairy Witchcraft is to build a relationship with your house spirit. Connecting to the spirit of the place you live in is actually very easy and begins with cultivating awareness. Know that the spirit is there and let yourself be aware of its presence. Be respectful of it in word and action. For home spirits traditionally this would involve keeping your home and, if you have one, yard in good order, being kind and generous in your life, and acknowledging their presence. Consider setting an area aside, no matter how small, dedicated to your house spirit where you can leave offerings. In most traditions for home spirits this would be done near the hearth; in my house it's in the kitchen. I know some people who set up a small box that belongs to the house spirit, while others create elaborate shrines. Follow your own intuition in creating an area that your house spirit will like, but remember the most important detail is that it should be a small place set aside only for this spirit.

Offerings can be made weekly, monthly or yearly and might include fresh water, milk or cream, and baked goods. In Norse practice house spirits are especially honored at Midwinter with offerings of porridge with a large pat of butter prominently displayed on top. Generally you want to avoid giving any articles of clothing as in folklore this will cause the spirit to leave, either by offending it or pleasing it too much. The offerings serve as an acknowledgement and sign of gratitude for the spirit's presence and beneficial activity, but it's the everyday awareness and respect of the spirit that matter most. Choose a schedule for making offerings and stick to it. Consistency is important.

In Fairy Witchcraft it is also important to connect to home spirits and communicate with them directly. Those who have second sight or experience as a psychic medium can use these skills while those who don't can reach out through the use of divination tools or spiritual journey work. How the spirit of place communicates will vary greatly depending on the spirit, but the same general rules of contact apply to them that would apply to any spirit or fairy: be considerate and be respectful. Sometimes direct communication can be a good idea because it will allow you to establish a rapport with your house spirit and you can tailor your offerings and actions to what the spirit would like. At its most basic you can communicate with them by speaking out loud to them and by letting yourself be open to responses. Sometimes you may perceive answers as shifts in emotions or mood in a room or area, other times you may get more direct responses, including audible knocking or objects moving.

As with any relationship it takes time and effort to build a strong connection with your house spirit, but it is worthwhile. House spirits in many ways are the heart of the house itself and can affect the home's atmosphere as well as influencing the inhabitants' moods and physical health. I recommend starting with house spirits before moving on to other spirits of place because house spirits tend to be friendly and have a vested interest in a reciprocal relationship with us. Most home spirits are more open to human connection and more willing to be friendly than some of the spirits of the wild places, although all the same general rules apply. Start at home and slowly move outward from there.

Land Spirits

This is an important one for me to discuss because I find a most people conflate land spirits with Otherworldly beings; most popular authors I know of blithely refer to the aos sí as nature spirits or land spirits, for example, which I think misses the nuanced difference between the two. Of course it is murky waters at best, as all these things are, because there is a lot of crossover in folklore between the two categories, where landveattir are part of the huldufolk and spirits of the land are usually seen as fairies. However, while land spirits fall into the broader category of Hidden Folk, they do not represent all of the beings of the Otherworld and there are many key differences between true land spirits and other kinds of Fair Folk.

The Norse view of land spirits, called land wights or landvaettir, is reasonably straightforward. They are the spirits of a place, which encourage growth and prosperity there when they are properly inclined. The best description of landvaettir from myth might come from the Heimskringla, where we are told that Iceland is full of land spirits and has four guardian spirits. These spirits are landvaettir who appear in the forms of a dragon, eagle, bull, and giant.

It was believed that the landvaettir were important to the success of a household, and to offend them or lose their presence meant disaster. In *Egil's Saga* we see Egil setting up a Nidstang to drive off the landvaettir in order to curse his enemies, for example. Similarly the dragon head prows on longships were taken down before entering friendly harbors, to avoid frightening the land wights, and were likely used in raids for the purpose of driving off the native land wights to make the raid more successful (Gundarsson, 2007). To avoid offending the land spirits around a home, offerings were made onto the earth, something that was prohibited during the later Christian period. It was a pagan practice to take food and drink to sites associated with land spirits, to enjoy a meal there, and leave some of the food at the site (Gundarsson, 2007).

It is important to ask permission of the land spirits before doing any work on the land, because the health and success of the landscape is based on the happiness of the land wights. Land wights do not like loud noises or bloodshed, and Gundarsson supposes that they also would dislike pollution and litter (Gundarsson, 2007). Asking permission first allows the spirits to prepare for the change if you intend to alter your area. It is also important to properly maintain the land, which means not littering or unnecessarily destroying natural features.

The Irish view of spirits of the land is complicated. There is a very blurry line between a spirit that embodies a place and a spirit that inhabits it, which can make it difficult to distinguish between the two. Adding to the complication are spirits of sovereignty, which are often described as spirits of the land; I think though that sovereignty spirits are not properly land spirits, but are a higher level of being that do not embody the spirit of a place so much as represent the power to rightly rule that place and the spirits – corporeal and non – within it. Land spirits are best understood as the spirit of a specific place, the embodiment of that location's energy or soul, if you will. Unlike some other kinds of spirits, land spirits are strongly tied to a single location or natural object, such as a tree or well, and in folklore are rarely able to leave that place or object. The other types of daoine sí are well known to move their homes and travel, even far abroad. As with the Norse, Irish land spirits may appear in human form or as birds or animals (O Suilleabhain, 1967).

The role of land spirits in Irish is difficult to study because, unlike the Norse, they are not often viewed as a separate category of being, although there is a tradition of malefic spirits of place. These dangerous spirits are viewed as being bound to a location and have names like Sprid na Bearnan (spirit of the gap), Sprid na Charraig an Eidhin (spirit of Carriganine), and Sprid an Tobac (spirit of the tobacco), each with their own story (O Suilleabhain, 1967). Because these spirits are largely malevolent it was believed they must be protected against using things like iron (a chain or black handled knife specifically), holy water, or a rooster crowing (O Suilleabhain, 1967). It is possible though that these represent a later Christian attitude towards these spirits, rather than an older pagan one, as priests were often called to banish the spirits of these places.

In both the Irish and Norse views, land spirits are associated with specific features of the land. In the Norse this is usually a large boulder, although it can also be a tree (Gundarsson, 2007). Both cultures also see land spirits as able to take different forms, including human and animal. A Welsh example comparable to the Icelandic guardian land spirits might be the red dragon of Wales described in the *Historia Brittonum*.

In my own experience there is a distinctly different feel between spirits of place and other spirits. Spirits of place have a more immediate, primal feel to them and often take a simpler approach to relating to things outside themselves. They may communicate directly with people who are able to hear or see them, often taking the form of a person or animal for this purpose, something that is supported in folklore. They may also appear in dreams or visions to people in order to communicate with them (Gundarsson, 2007).

Although daoine sí and huldufolk can travel – and do – and may be found in unexpected places, land spirits are sedentary. The spirit of a tree, or boulder, or well, has physical limitations within this world, in my experience, because it is anchored or rooted by the physical item it belongs to. Similarly while the Other Crowd can influence people directly – stealing things, harming, blessing, or gifting – land spirits are more subtle. They influence us through our emotional states and through the wider flourishing or failure of a place. In my experience, while land spirits will accept, and even want, tangible offerings many of them seem to feed on energy from living things: happiness, creativity, love, and in some cases fear or other dark emotions. In response they nurture the energy they need.

I believe that not all land spirits want to be acknowledged or honored. Some just want to be left alone, and some have some very old anger towards people that will not easily be overcome. Land spirits, in my experience, view humans much the way many of us view squirrels or birds, that is as a generic group of animals; there isn't an immediate understanding by a land wight that you are a unique individual separate from the other general humans who may have previously done it harm. To establish a relationship with an angry land spirit is a tricky business, and involves some risk and a great deal of effort.

It is worthwhile to consider connecting to and honoring the spirits of the land you live on. Not only is this an important aspect of animism, in my opinion, but it is also essential to living what I would call a good life. Being in proper relationship to the spirits of the land you live on, the foundational spirits that influence the atmosphere of the space we occupy, may take time, but results in a strong bond with that place and a powerful reciprocal relationship with those spirits.

The Wild Hunt

The Wild Hunt is a collection of spirits – some say ghosts or fairies – that travel through the air in storms led by a Huntsman. Who the Huntsman is varies as widely as the geographic areas the hunt is found in and the names it is known by. There have been entire books written about the Wild Hunt – and I highly recommend Claud Lecouteaux's *Phantom Armies of the Night: The Wild Hunt and the Ghostly Processions of the Undead* – so this section will by necessity be very limited in its scope, but I'd like to offer an overview. I have encountered the Wild Hunt myself a time or two and it is likely that another follower of a fairy-based witchcraft tradition will also meet them or see it at some point and it's best to go into that with an understanding of who and what it might be.

So, to begin, the Wild Hunt is found in Germany, France, Denmark, Normandy, Sweden, Norway, England, Scotland, Ireland, Wales, and the United States (Jones, 2003). The Wild Hunt is interesting though in that although found across a wide geographic area and among different cultures, it always takes on a unique local character, often with a specific local spirit or God taking on the role of Huntsman. In the Germanic areas the Wild

Hunt is often led by Odin (Wodan), Frau Hulde, or both together, the Welsh Hunt is led by Gwynn ap Nudd, and the English by Herne, while in France it is led by Harlequin, and in other areas a variety of fictional or historic figures including sir Frances Drake (Jones, 2003). The Wild Hunt in Germany is also sometimes led by Frau Perchta or the White Lady, Frau Gauden, who led groups of dead children or witches through the sky and was seen as good a omen of abundant crops in the coming year (Berk, & Spytma, 2002). Some modern sources try to relate the Hunt led by Harlequin to the Norse Goddess Hel, but it is more likely that the name derives from the 12th century term 'Herlethingus', a word used to describe wandering spectral troops during the time of King Henry II (Berk, & Spytma, 2002). In Orkney the Wild Hunt is led by Odin, but may also be the trows riding out on pale horses to steal cows (Towrie, 2013). In Scotland the Hunt is the Unseelie Court, perhaps relating to the Irish idea of the Slua sí, the fairy host who travel through the air attacking the unwary. Often when the Huntsman – or Huntswoman – is not a God or Otherworldly spirit it is said to be a person who so loved hunting in life that they rejected any other afterlife but to continue hunting and were rewarded or cursed to perpetually hunt for all eternity (Grimm, 1883).

The Wild Hunt is known by many names. In Orkney it is called the Raging Host (Towrie, 2013). Associated with Odin, the Hunt was called Odin's Hunt/Odensjakt, Odin's Army, Wilde Jagd, the Wild Ride, Asgardeia, Oskerei, Horrific Ride, Thunderous Ride, and also the Ride of the Dead, and the Family of Harlequin (in France) (Towrie, 2013; Berk, & Spytma, 2002). Other names include the Furious Host or Wild Host and in America, the Ghost Riders.

The Wild Hunt travels in the air, and appears as a group of dark riders, led by a Huntsmen who may be headless, with a pack of fearsome hounds, accompanied by a horde of spirits who sometimes appear as the newly dead or battle dead (Jones, 2003).

When the Hunt is led by Gwynn ap Nudd the hounds are white with red ears, and are called the Cwn Annwn or Gabriel Hounds (Berk, & Spytma, 2002). The Hunt always includes horses and hounds, both usually black, but sometimes white or grey, and always fierce; in some accounts the animals breathe fire and they are often missing limbs or with extra limbs and may display the same gruesome wounds as the battle dead accompanying the Hunt (Berk, & Spytma, 2002). The presence of the Hunt is signaled by the unearthly sound of hooves, hunting horns, and baying hounds appearing usually in the night sky and sometimes in storms (Towrie, 2013).

Mary Jones gives us a classic description of the Hunt from 1127 CE:

> *...it was seen and heard by many men: many hunters riding. The hunters were black, and great and loathy, and their hounds all black, and wide-eyed and loathy, and they rode on black horses and black he-goats. This was seen in the very deer park in the town of Peterborough, and in all the woods from the same town to Stamford; and the monks heard the horn blowing that they blew that night. Truthful men who kept watch at night said that it seemed to them that there might be about twenty or thirty horn blowers. This was seen and heard...all through Lenten tide until Easter.*
> (Jones, 2003)

This description gives the time the Wild Hunt appears as during 'Lent', which might be assumed to be roughly March and April. In Switzerland the Hunt was said to appear during summer nights, and those who do not quickly get out of the way of the passing Hunt would be trampled by it (Grimm, 1883). More often in folklore the Hunt was said to ride in late fall and winter, particularly during the twelve nights of Yule. Grimm tells us that in Germany it was believed the Hunt rode during the time from Christmas to Twelfth Night or whenever the storm winds blew

(Grimm, 1883). Yule was seen as a time of high supernatural influence when the dead were more present (Towrie, 2013). In my own experience with the Ghost Riders of America they appear around Samhain and ride until the first week of January, but in times of great unrest or disturbance they may appear as well.

In many cases the Hunt is connected to Fairy in some way, but it is equally strongly connected to the spirits of the dead. Towrie conjectures that the Orkney trows, themselves connected to the Wild Hunt, may have originally been considered spirits of the dead (Towrie, 2013). The dead are often seen in the retinue of the Hunt and that includes both those who may be recognized as recently dead as well as the ancient battle dead, some displaying hideous wounds. Some folklore also says that the Wild Hunt rides out seeking the dead, chasing certain types of ghosts or spirits.

The Hunt appeared for different reasons depending on where it was – in some cases hunting a mythic animal or creature, in others pursuing lost souls or even seeking to punish wrong-doers (Towrie, 2013). As a Fairy Rade, the Hunt is usually hunting human beings, either with the purpose of kidnapping them or tormenting them; in some cases the person might go mad (Berk, & Spytma, 2002). In some cases the Hunt might offer to take a living person to ride with them, but the risk of doing so was great; the person might never return or might become a permanent part of the host[22]. Seeing the Hunt could be an ill-omen and the Hunt itself could kill or drive a person mad, but conversely in some areas it was believed meeting the Hunt bravely and politely could earn a person great reward. There are several folk tales, like the story of Wod, the Wild Huntsman, where the main character meets the Hunt and comes away with gifts of meat and gold as a reward for his cleverness. Showing proper respect would also earn a person a reward, but conversely rudeness would result in the person being thrown a severed human limb, if he was lucky, or his own dead child, if he wasn't; in some cases the Hunt would turn on the person mocking them and tear the person to pieces (Berk, & Spytma, 2002; Grimm, 1883).

Protection from the Wild Hunt is best achieved through avoiding them by not traveling at night, especially during Yule or other dangerous times. Shelter can also be sought at the first sound of hunting horn or hounds in the air. However, should those fail or not be possible and should you meet the Hunt, and do not feel like taking your chances with them, there is this charm from 14th century Germany:

Woden's host and all his men
Who are bearing wheels and willow twigs
Broken on the wheel and hanged.
You must go away from here.
(Gundarsson, trans. Höfler; Berk, & Spytma, 2002)

The Fairy Host

Whenever the subject of the fairies comes up it is best to remember that they are not the twee little things of pop culture, and I really can't emphasize that enough. Even among the diverse groups of fairies, though some deserve more caution and respect than others. One group that was particularly feared is the Slua sí, the fairy host. In Scotland the Slua are considered the most daunting of the fairies (Briggs, 1976). This fairy army would travel on the wind, especially the whirlwind, which was called the séideán sídhe, fairy blast, or sitheadh gaoithe, meaning thrust of wind, and often called by the similar sounding name of sí gaoithe, fairy wind (O hOgain, 1995; MacKillop, 1998). Although most often described as invisible to mortal eyes and traveling in the form of a wind, in Scotland the Slua is also said to appear in the form of clouds (Carmichael, 1900). The Slua traveled most often at night, but was especially active around midnight (Evans

Wentz, 1911). Anyone who had reason to be out at night, and more so if they were out alone, needed to be careful to avoid the fairy host. This does not mean that the Slua appears only at night though, and in fact the fairy host may appear anywhere at any time.

In Ireland it was said that the Slua sí would often force a human to go along with them while they engaged in their malicious endeavors (O Suilleabhain, 1967). In tales these endeavors often included kidnapping brides, a common theme in many different types of fairy stories. A hapless traveler out alone at night or wandering where they shouldn't be might be taken up by the Slua and find themselves with no choice but to go along where the fairies took them. People taken this way might be said to be 'in the fairies' (O Suilleabhain, 1967). In folklore people taken by the Slua sí may go as far afield as France or Spain and be left there to find their own way home, or else may be returned to the place where they were taken mostly unharmed. There are also tales of those, out traveling at night, who would see another person who had been or was being taken by the Slua. To get the host to release anyone they may have taken one should throw the dust from the road, an iron knife, or your left shoe and say, *'This is yours; that is mine!'* (McNeill, 1956).Those known to have been taken and released were gone to for advice relating to the fairies and seen as being quite knowledgeable about them (O Suilleabhain, 1967).

In Scotland some people believe that the Slua sí, the fairy host of the air, are spirits of the mortal dead[23], specifically those who died with unforgiven sins (McNeill, 1956; Briggs, 1976). Alexander Carmichael described them as the ghosts of men who died full of sin and Evans Wentz related stories of the Slua as both the mortal dead and as fallen angels (Carmichael, 1900; Evans Wentz, 1911). In Irish folktales related by authors like Yeats and Hyde, however, the fairy host seems distinct from the human dead and appears to act like fairies in other tales, engaging in behavior such as stealing human brides. It's possible that no simple line can be drawn between the two groups, but rather that crossover existed that is reflected in the different folk beliefs.

The fairy host would appear in a sudden wind and the sound of voices, armor clinking, or people shouting (O Suilleabhain, 1967). Hyde describes it in the story Guleesh Na Guss Dhu this way: *'He heard a great noise coming like the sound of many people running together, and talking, and laughing, and making sport, and the sound went by him like a whirl of wind...'* (Hyde, 1890, p 76). Some say it appears as a dust devil that moves over roads and hedges as the Good Neighbors travel (JCHAS, 2010). When the whirlwind appeared people would avert their eyes, turn their backs, and pray, calling on saints or their guardian angels or else saying, *'Good luck to them, the ladies and gentlemen.'* (O hOgain, 1995; JCHAS, 2010, p. 319). This was done to avert any harm caused by the close proximity of the host and to hopefully avoid drawing their attention. The sí gaoithe (fairy wind), which was a sign of the presence of the fairy host, could bring illness or cause injury as it passed by, contributing to its fearsome reputation (MacKillop, 1998). The Slua had a reputation for being mercurial and prone to malicious behavior and unlike more sedentary types of Fair Folk they are not easily appeased but most often must be warded off, usually with iron, driven away, or out-witted.

I've encountered the Slua sí twice and that is enough for me. Their reputation is what it is for a reason.

Fairy Animals

Cu Sí

There are many different types of fairy animals, both the more intelligent beings like the pooka who can take animal form and animals that are part of fairy. One of the more interesting ones is the fairy hound, or cu sí (pronounced koo shee). The cu sí are known by many names including cu sith (Scottish), cwn annwn (Welsh), and when riding with the Wild Hunt may be called the Gabriel Ratchets, dandy dogs, or Hell Hounds. They are also sometimes conflated with the ghostly hounds known as the black dog, black shuck, Hell Hounds, Padfoot, Bogey, Moddey Doo or the Grim. Katherine Briggs divides these supernatural dogs into three categories: supernatural beings, human ghosts in dog form, and ghosts of dogs (Briggs, 1978). For our purposes we will discusses all appearances of Otherworldly dogs, but it is important to understand up front that the subject is complex and that what appears to be a dog may or may not actually be a dog. That is really just par for the course with anything of Fairy actually.

The cu sí may appear as huge shaggy black or dark green dogs, or as swift white hounds with red eyes and ears, sometimes missing a limb. They are known by their enormous size, often described as being as large as a calf with huge round eyes (Parkinson, 2013). These spectral dogs may be male or female and may appear alone, in pairs, or in packs (Campbell, 2008). A cu sí may also appear as a black dog with a white ring around its neck, usually seen on a fairy hill (Evans Wentz, 1911).

The cu sí, when associated with the Wild Hunt, usually frighten people, as the Hunt itself is an omen of war, death, and madness, although it can also bring blessings. The black dogs are seen as omens of death, although it is a bit murky as to whether, like the Irish banshee, the dog shows up to warn of an impending death or whether the dog causes the death (Parkinson, 2013). However, not all black dogs are bad omens; in at least some cases the appearance of the black dog was protective as in one story from Swancliffe where a man had a black dog appear and accompany him through a dark wood, twice, only to find out later that the dog had saved him from being robbed and killed by highwaymen (Parkinson, 2013). They may also appear as guardians of treasure, something they are known for in Scotland (Parkinson, 2013). In Ireland cu sí are often associated with specific fairy locations where they are known to be seen over the course of multiple generations and are known to sit and watch people, but they are only considered dangerous if they are disturbed, otherwise they will remain peaceful (Lenihan & Green, 2004). In at least one Irish example a small white fairy dog appeared as an omen of the coming of the daoine sí to a home, to warn the inhabitants to prepare (Evans Wentz, 1911).

Fairy dogs may appear with the daoine sí during Fairy Rades, or they may appear wandering on their own, guarding fairy hills, or going ahead of the Gentry to warn of their presence. Black dogs seem to be territorial, favoring churchyards, roadways, and crossroads, especially where gallows have been (Parkinson, 2013). In stories they are often associated with a particular area that is considered haunted (Campbell, 2008). Cu sí may appear standing motionless on fairy hills or even among mortal dogs on occasion (Evans Wentz, 1911).

Many people assume the cu sí and black dogs are ill-omens, and indeed they may be, but not always. While the appearance of such a hound – especially if it is baying or howling – is usually an omen of death, the fairy hounds may also appear for other reasons. Sometimes they can be protective, either of a location in which case simply leaving them and the area alone will allow you to walk away unharmed, or of a person. They may also appear for unknown reasons, without directly harming or affecting anyone.

I have seen fairy hounds twice in my life.

The first time, many years ago, a friend and I were trying to do some magical work to cleanse and ritually protect a mutual friend's business in a city. As the sun sank and twilight took over we sat on the front steps by the door and burned herbs in a small cauldron. We had been chatting as we worked and full dark fell, but we both suddenly became silent as the realization sunk in that all the sounds around us had stopped. No traffic noises, no other voices, nothing. Curious we both leaned forward looking down the now empty street for any cars and instead saw two huge black dogs trotting towards us down the sidewalk. No one was with them, but they walked calmly and with a purpose. Nervously my friend joked that maybe they would cross to our side of the street; as soon as he had spoken, sure enough, both dogs turned and walked calmly across the empty road towards our side. In what is best described as comic flailing we fled back into the store and hastily closed the door. As soon as it was safely shut we both looked out the big front window of the shop to watch the dogs pass, but to our surprise the street was empty again. No dogs anywhere. Venturing back out we saw the dogs walking down the sidewalk away from us, although it was impossible for them to have passed where we were without us seeing them. They disappeared when the road curved and moments later the sound and traffic returned.

The second time I saw a fairy hound happened when I was working as an emergency medical technician for a local ambulance company. My partner and I were on a layover at 5am on a winter morning in a city by the shore of Long Island Sound and we had parked in a lot next to a large field fenced off for construction. I had decided to get out and stretch my legs while we waited for our next scheduled transfer and my partner was sitting in the ambulance reading a book. I wandered over to the chain link fence that surrounded that field and was standing there looking at the dark sky when I noticed something white moving on the far side of the open space. As I watched in the darkness the white shape moved steadily towards me; it seemed to be moving quickly across the field and eventually I realized it was a dog, although the way it was moving seemed strange. Searching the field I could not see any sign of a person with the animal. The white dog, some sort of hound by its shape, was so white that it almost glowed in the pre-dawn darkness and I stood there watching it come straight towards me, trying to puzzle out why it was alone in a fenced in field and why the way it moved seemed so disturbing even though it was moving quickly and apparently easily. When it had crossed about two-thirds of the space between us I finally realized that it had only one front leg – not that it was missing one, but that its front leg was placed in the center of its chest. A wave of fear went over me and I responded instinctually, running, and jumping back into the ambulance. My partner looked up, startled, and asked me what was wrong, and I told him there was a dog. Looking out he asked me what dog. Sure enough when I looked there was no dog to be seen anywhere, despite the fact that there was nowhere for it to go in the empty field and no time for it to have gone anywhere.

Fairy Horses

Fairy horses are well known in Ireland and Scotland, where there are two main kinds of fairy horses seen in stories: the Kelpie and the Water Horse. The Water Horse is also called Aughisky and Each Uisce (Irish Gaelic for Water Horse). In Orkney, they are called Nuggles, in Wales Ceffyl Dwr. In Shetland, they are Coofiltees, and on the Isle of Man they are called Cabbyl Ushtey or the Glashtin. Water Horses and Kelpies are seen in all parts of the Celtic world under these different names and also in parts of the Norse world. In Scandinavian folklore they are called Bäckahästen or 'Brook horses'; in Norway they are Nokken and in Iceland they are called Nykur. It is likely that the Water Horses and Kelpies, like other European fairies, have followed the people who believed in them to new countries so that they can be found all over the world now.

These water fairies usually appear as black horses or ponies, but sometimes may be white or even green with a black mane. They appear to be unusually beautiful horses and act very tame and friendly; however, a Water Horse or Kelpie can be recognized by the seaweed or other water plants that are sometimes seen tangled in its hair and the water that drips constantly from its mane and tail. Water Horses may take the shape of people, usually women, but sometimes a good looking man, but even in this form they can still be recognized for their dripping hair and seaweed or other water plants.

These fairy horses are known for trying to trick people into climbing on their backs for a ride. Kelpies are said to do this in order to take the person on a wild ride before dumping the person on the ground, in a ditch, or in the water, although some say that Kelpies will trick people in order to take them to a body of water and drown them. The Water Horse is more sinister, tricking the person into riding, and then running into the nearest body of water where it turns on the person and tears them apart, eating everything but the liver. Water Horses are also known to eat sheep and cows.

Some people say that the fairy horses that live in lakes and ponds are less dangerous than those that live in running water, such as rivers or the ocean. Other people say that the less dangerous Kelpies live in streams and rivers, while the more dangerous Water Horses live in lakes and the ocean. In general it is never a good idea to try to ride a strange horse, just in case it is actually a Water Horse or Kelpie of some type.

Another fairy that is similar to the Water Horses and Kelpies, but is not the same, is the pooka. In ireland they are called pooka, phouka, puca, or puka. They are also called pwca in Wales and bucca in Cornwall. These fairies are shape-shifters that can appear as many different things, including men, dogs, goats or bulls, but they are most often seen as horses. Pookas are dark colored in whatever form they take. As a horse, the pooka will trick a person into riding them and then run off before dumping the person on the ground. Pookas are seen by some people as mischievous, but by others as dangerous. It is said that all the unpicked blackberries and raspberries belong to the pooka after Samhain, and that people should never eat them after this date because the Pooka urinates on them.

The Roan

The Seal Folk, called roan, roane or rón in Ireland and selkies or silkies in Scotland, are a fairy found in the sea that, if you live near water with seals in it, you may encounter. Roan are liminal by nature, existing between land and sea, between human and seal form.

Roan can be either male or female, and appear in either seal or human form, as they are true shapeshifters. As seals they are indistinguishable from ordinary seals; as humans they are usually average height, with dark brown or black hair, and dark, sad eyes. They can be very difficult to stop in human form, but they will always show a deep longing for the sea. The key to their shapeshifting is the power of their seal skin, which they take off to become human and put back on to return to seal form.

In folklore roan will sometimes appear in seal form and aid fisherman during storms, although it was also said that they could raise storms to avenge their kindred (Briggs, 1976). They have been known to help drowning sailors by supporting them and helping them safely to shore, in much the same way as dolphins are known to do. Many believe that the roan are the gentlest of the fairies (Briggs, 1976). In other tales they will herd fish towards the sailors' nets to help them get a big catch, particularly if the fisher's family is tied to the roan.

Most stories about them, though, center on a roan marrying a human. Male roan are known to take human lovers although they do not remain long on land (Briggs, 1976). In many of these stories the roan will return many times to the woman over the years and she may have many children by him, but they will all be born with webbed hands and feet as a sign of their Otherworldly heritage (Briggs, 1976). The stories involving human men and Seal Women, however, are much different. They always involve a man who stumbles upon a group of roan on the beach, and watches them change shape from a hiding place. Once in human form they leave their seal skins to go dance along the shore and the human sneaks down and steals one of the skins. When the roan return to the ocean the one whose skin was stolen is trapped in her human form, and the man emerges and claims her as his bride. They will live peacefully together, with the Seal Woman as a faithful wife, so long as she never reclaims her seal skin. In most lore the couple will live happily for years, raising a family until one of the children discovers the hidden seal skin and tells the mother. Once she regains her skin she returns to the ocean, and no bonds – not even love of her children – can keep her on land. After leaving the woman is said to follow her husband's fishing boat in seal form and help him in any way she can, although she can never return to him as his wife. The children of these unions are thought to be gifted fisherman, with a passionate love of the sea, although they are often prone to melancholy. Even many generations removed, families that have roan blood will sometimes produce children who show the fairy blood, which have an uncanny love of the sea.

Cat Sí

In Celtic folklore there are stories about cat si (fairy cats) also called cat sith in Scottish Gaidhlig. These are closely tied in folklore to witches and it behooves a Fairy Witch to be aware of them and their stories. Cat si are believed to be large, Otherworldly black cats with a single white spot on the chest. The descriptions somewhat resembles the Kellas cats, large wild cats of Scotland, which has led some to theorize that sightings of them may have been the origin of the cat si stories (Matthews, 2005).

These cats are generally seen as malevolent and some people believe they are actually shape-changed witches. In particular a witch was believed to be able to take cat form nine times, but legend says on the 9th time the witch would have to remain a cat forever (Old Farmer's Almanac, 2012). There is a very good children's book by Jane Manning called *Cat Nights* based on this story, about a young witch who has adventures each night as a cat. For eight nights in a row she goes out in cat form, and is then faced with the choice of transforming again and staying a cat forever or remaining a witch. As with the aos sí and alfar there are also stories of cat sí taking human form and marrying into human families. The MacGillivray family claims to have a cat sí among its ancestors, and it is said that the clan motto 'touch not this cat' comes from this ancestry (MacGillivray, 2000).

Fairy cats are often seen as dangerous spirits and they have a strong association with the dead. In Scotland the bodies of the newly dead are carefully watched and special protections are used to ensure that a cat sí doesn't sneak in and steal the soul before it has separated from the body (MacGillivray, 2000). Most of these protections depend on doing things to distract the cat sí and keep it away from the body, such as sprinkling catnip about the other rooms, or playing games that would draw the cat sí's attention (MacGillivray, 2000).

Certain special days have been associated with the cat sí. One source mentions August 17th in connection to the cat sí as transformed witches, and says that it was on this night that a witch might make the ninth transformation into permanent cat form (Old Farmer's Almanac, 2012). Another cites the folk belief that on Samhain a saucer of milk should be left out as an offering to the cat sí to gain their blessing, while failing to do so could earn a curse on the household (MacGillivray, 2000).

Miscellaneous Animals

Fairy Deer

Another type of fairy animal that you might see, especially in dreams and journeywork, are fairy deer. These deer often appear to be pure white and may be stags or hinds. Fairy deer can act as guides in the Otherworld or may be sent to lead a person to a specific place.

Fairy Cattle

Fairy cattle, whether they are cows or bulls, are generally seen as positive and even good luck for mortals to encounter (Briggs, 1976). In Welsh stories fairy cows are often associated with lake maidens, but in the Irish they may belong to the daoine sí.

Swans

I have always been told that swans are often not what they seem, and may be fairies or witches shape-changed. In much folk belief, harming a swan in any way was strongly prohibited lest the animal actually be a fairy in disguise (Carmichael, 1900).

Butterflies

Particularly in German belief the elben (elves) were known to take the form of butterflies. They are associated with all three life stages: caterpillar, chrysalis, and butterfly (Grimm, 1982).

I will add that in my own experience I have also known them to take the form of moths.

Ancestors

Honoring ancestors is an important part of any Fairy Witch's practices. The spirits of our ancestors are always with us, watching over us, and they have a vested interest in our success that most other spirits don't. As we've already established a few times over, it is a thin and blurry line at best between the dead and the Fey so it shouldn't come as any big surprise that respecting your ancestors and including them in what you do is important. So let's take a look at a couple specific kinds of ancestral spirits and ways we might choose to honor them.

Honoring Ancestors

Honoring ancestors is an important aspect of Fairy Witchcraft because our ancestors are closer to us and more willing to help us, although it tends to be a more passive practice than working with other spirits. What I mean by that is that, for me personally, while I am active in my honoring of and connecting to the Gods and Fair Folk I see my relationship with my ancestors as already established. I don't have to work to create it, only to maintain it, and that requires less effort because they are family, just like my living family automatically has a stronger connection to me than people I don't know. Keep in mind that ancestors do not have to be related by blood necessarily, but can also be people who were very close friends or who loved you like family. If you are adopted and do not know your birth family don't worry; blood relationship is not required and adoption had long been seen as something that makes you part of a new family line, meaning that your adopted kin are just as much your family as your blood kin. It is up to you to decide who does and doesn't qualify as family for you. Also remember that dying does not change a person's personality. Someone who was a certain way in life will be that same way in death so dealing with them after death tends, in my experience, to be much the same as dealing with them in life. Someone who was quick to interfere and eager to help will still be so, while someone who tended to prefer to be left alone and didn't like to be involved in other people's problems still won't be quick to interfere.

I tend to treat my ancestors with less formality and more of a casual respect. Not because they can't still influence my life, but because they are family and there is a certain inherent intimacy in familial relationships that changes the tenor. They have an altar of their own in my house, which includes pictures and tokens from loved ones who have passed. Besides personal pictures and tokens I also keep a stylized resin skull, which represents all of my ancestors whose names I don't know but who I also want to acknowledge and honor. In Fairy Witchcraft the head and skull are the seat of the soul and represent a person's soul. If you lack the space for a full altar or shrine, or prefer not to have one there are other options. You might choose to keep a small area of your main altar set aside for the ancestors, or, if you prefer a more subtle approach, you could arrange pictures of deceased loved ones together somewhere in your home where you would be able to see them regularly.

Offerings for ancestors can include food and drink that the person liked in life, if you are aware of their preferences. General offerings may include tea, coffee, and bread. Traditionally white candles are also lit to honor the dead (Danaher, 1972). In my family we not only light white candles, but also incense as offerings for the dead. The ancestors are honored especially at Samhain and at Yule, and the time between the two holidays belongs to them, and is when the dead are most active in the world.

Communicating with the dead is important and can be done in several ways, although direct communication requires a great deal of practice and training. It was an old belief among the Celts that if a message was written and burned it would go to the Otherworld and the ancestors (Freeman, 2002). Because of this belief you may choose in ritual, especially those dedicated to the dead or memorializing ancestors, to write down and burn messages you want them to receive. You can also speak out loud to them, although I have found it helpful to do something to get their attention first; the dead are not omniscient or omnipresent after all. I have had luck with repeating an ancestor's name three times to draw their attention to me. The dead can speak to us in dreams or through divination tools, although it can be difficult to interpret the messages they send. Some people have natural abilities to see and speak to those who have passed from this world and they may be able to communicate more directly, but in many cases it's important to remember that the message is still being relayed through an intermediary and will not be precise.

For those who have never honored ancestors before the initial practice might seem strange, but there is a comfort in knowing that our beloved dead never truly leave us. Some part of that person always remains with us, as long as they are remembered, and our kin have the most reason to want to stay with us and help us. If you are new to ancestor worship don't be afraid to go slowly and ease your way into it, perhaps starting just with one or two pictures of people you were very close to in life and building from there over time.

Honoring Difficult Ancestors

Fairy Witchcraft is, in many ways, about balance: balance between this world and the Otherworld, balance between darkness and light, between the dark half and the light half. We occupy a liminal place and because of this we try to take a wider view, to see beyond the easy answers of good and bad. One way this manifests for us is in how we relate to difficult ancestors.

People like to worship the ancestors that they liked and are quick to repudiate those they didn't, but this isn't always the best approach. I'm not talking about ancestors who genuinely deserve to be disowned, which a serious matter but does occasionally happen, I mean the ones we just don't like, the ones who weren't nice people, who were difficult, or who struggled with personal demons. Of course it's easy to honor our ancestors who we perceive to be good people, and it's hard to find the worth in those whose flaws are written large in our memory. I think we forget though that even the ancestors we like were not perfect and those we are so quick to reject often have value if we look for it.

I have two paternal grandfathers; one of blood and one of love. My step-grandfather was my grandmother's third husband and, I believe, the love of her life, a man my father considered his dad, but that's another story. My biological grandfather was my grandmother's second husband, the son of a German immigrant and an Irish immigrant. He was a mean drunk who, according to my father, threw fists, words, and dinnerware with equal viciousness. He spent most of his money on his beer and his own food, making my grandmother fix him steak and potatoes for dinner while she and their seven children sat and ate whatever the church food pantry had to spare for them. Having said that I am sure there are at least some people out there who are reading this and thinking that they would never honor such an ancestor, and some who may even be thinking they would never speak of him and let his memory be forgotten.

I may not honor him actively, but I do include his picture on my ancestor altar and I include him in the general offerings and attention that my ancestors, collectively, get for three reasons. Firstly, my father maintained a cordial relationship with his biological father until my grandfather's death and I do not believe it is up to me to decide to cut off an ancestor I never knew based on his flaws when my father never did so during his life. Secondly, my grandfather was not wholly bad. He had a strong sense of loyalty and family, even if he didn't treat them well when he was drinking. When he met my grandmother she was a 19 years old with two small children from her first husband, a man who had decided to abandon his family to seek greener pastures. My grandfather loved her, married her, and adopted her children; in his life he never treated them any different than the five children he and my grandmother had together. From what everyone in the family says, as far as he was concerned, my eldest uncle and aunt *were* his children. He also had an indomitable will. At one point in his life he owned a small grocery store; when closing up one night, as he turned to lock the door, a man who meant to rob him stabbed him in the back with a meat cleaver, opening a wound from shoulder to hip. My grandfather turned and fought back, forcing the man to run away; he was able to get help for himself, which probably saved his life (I often wonder if this incident was a major factor in his drinking problem). I have a lot of respect for anyone who can fight through that type of injury in the moment and who has that strength of will.

My third reason is less personal to my grandfather and more

general, but it's the reason I chose my paternal grandfather as an example. No ancestor is perfect and I think we do ourselves a disservice to think we can cherry pick the 'good ones' based on our own limited information about people's lives. The reality is we never know more than a fraction of a person's story, especially those who died before we were born or when we were very young. Certainly if we know for a fact that an ancestor did something deserving of being cut off, and we have no doubt that there were no extenuating circumstances or other mitigating factors than we may choose to cut them off from our memory. Families are complicated things and what exactly would qualify as across that line will be different for all of us – my grandmother cut off her biological mother after her mother abandoned the family leaving my nine-year-old grandmother to care for her four younger siblings; until the day she died she would not even tell anyone her mother's name or anything about her. She made a choice to totally cut her mother out of her memory, and consequently the memory of subsequent generations, and to me that is a very serious thing to do. My grandmother did it based on direct experience with the person; on the other hand my father took the other road and kept the relationship. I choose to respect the choices of those who actually knew the people when they were alive. I don't believe that I should cut off an ancestor, in death, who was not cut off in life, or conversely to reconnect to one who was.

When I look at the strengths and weaknesses of my family, living and dead, I see things in all of them that can be remembered with pride and things that are, at best, warnings for future generations. Even the ancestors that I love best have flaws, and when I think of myself and how I will be remembered, I hope that my children and their descendants don't just pass on the good stories but also the balancing points. Ancestors may be dead, but they are still family, with all the attendant imperfections.

The Disir – Protective Ancestresses

Once the Idisi set forth, to this place and that;
Some fastened fetters; some hindered the horde,
Some loosed the bonds from the brave—
Leap forth from the fetters! Escape from the foes!
– Merseburger Zaubersprüche

In Norse and Germanic paganism we see the concept of beings called Idises (German) or Disir (Norse). These words can best be understood, perhaps, as female ancestors who guard the family line. The word used in this sense is plural, Idises or Disir; the singular (Idis or Dis) can mean the same or be used for a living female relative, Goddess, or demi-Goddess (Our Troth, 2006). The Idises are explicitly connected to ghosts and the dead – *''konor hugðak dauðar koma î nôtt,' dead women, i.e., dîsir, come at night,'* (Grimm, 1882). They are also associated with the Goddess Freya who is called Vanadis and with Valkyries who are called Herjan's Disir (Herjan being another name of Odin). From this we can see the fine line that exists with these spirits between ancestors, deities, and related spirits like the Valkyries. This sort of liminal spirit is one that we often deal with and honor in Fairy Witchcraft, while trying to understand them within the cultural context that they are mentioned in, we also connect to them in our own individual ways. Everyone has Idises, whether you are aware of them or not, because they are protective spirits attached to your family line.

We can see some aspects of what the Idises do in the Merseburg Incantation above, where they are described as going forth and binding or hindering the enemy while encouraging their own side. The Norse Disir are described in the same way as both helping and hindering (Grimm, 1882). They are also associated with giving aid during childbirth, collecting the dead, and the fertility of crops as well as the harvest, especially around

Winternights – what we would call Samhain (Our Troth). Our Troth volume 1 suggests that the Disir and the idea of the tribal mothers is ancient and ties into the worship of the Matronae, which we have previously touched on. The Idises are associated with the maternal ancestral dead and protect their family line; they appear sometimes as omens or to deliver warnings (Grimm, 1882). In at least one story the Idises foresee danger to a man and protect him by delaying his departure (Our Troth, 2006).

Historically we know that the Norse honored these spirits and sacrificed to them at Disirblots (Grimm, 1882). Some people celebrate a special Disirblot in the spring or fall, although honoring them around Samhain would also be appropriate. Additionally the Idises are honored on Mothernight, the first night of Yule. And of course the Idises can be honored or prayed to at any time; I like to make a small offering at least once a week.

In Fairy Witchcraft we call these protective ancestral spirits 'the Ladies' or 'the Ancestral Ladies' since lady is the meaning of the words dis and idis. Honoring these spirits is very important because of their protective nature and the way they watch over the family. A Heathen friend once told me that the Disir have a vested interest in the wellbeing of their descendants and strong motivation to help us, and I have found this to be true. They tend to respond well and quickly to being acknowledged and honored and can help us in many ways including with healing, protection, fertility, childbirth, and offensively by binding or hindering those who may hurt us.

It is a good idea to have a small shrine to the Ladies. Some people choose to place this shrine in the kitchen, while others prefer the living room; mine adjoins my main ancestor altar on a fireplace mantle. Many choose to use images of deceased female family members, but I prefer to keep all my ancestor images together so I use female statues in a range of styles from many different time periods to represent these spirits. In front of the statues I have a candle and a small offering dish. Sometimes I offer milk and sometimes I offer food shared from our kitchen, especially baked goods. My youngest daughter, who calls them 'the Lady ancestors', likes to have me light the candle and some incense when she sits at the altar to talk to them. In all honesty I have to admit we are closer to our male ancestral dead – or perhaps I should say we feel they are closest to us – but we always honor the Ladies as well. You may choose to include them in with your other ancestors or acknowledge them separately.

Modern Experience

At one point my family had an extended family member move into our home, and the house spirits did not like this person being there. The day she moved in the door inexplicably jammed and could not be opened. It actually had to be forced open, which broke it in the process. Once her things were moved in she was plagued with mysterious difficulties limited only to her room: her phone line would cut out and often have severe interference, despite repeated assurances by the phone company that it was fine; her computer died; her internet access failed over and over; her room, normally the warmest in the house became frigidly cold; she was kept up at night by knocking sounds in the walls.

In short the house spirits were not happy and they were making their feelings known.

The ideal solution was for this person to move out, but in the interim I was put in the position of trying to make peace. I, of course, was caught in the middle between the unhappy spirits who wanted this person to leave and the person who I'd offered hospitality to and who was now unhappy about all these problems. Sometimes there are no perfect solutions either and the best that could be managed was a lot of offerings and a long conversation about why the person would need to be tolerated at least temporarily. Peace was restored, but until the day the person finally moved out it was a tentative peace at best.

Chapter 5

Tools and Ritual Space

You—you will make no terms with the spirits of fire and earth and air and water. You have made the Darkness your enemy. We—we exchange civilities with the world beyond.
– Yeats, 1893

The exorcism by knife appears to be a Welsh notion; though there is an old superstition of wide prevalence in Europe that to give to or receive from a friend a knife or a pair of scissors cuts friendship. I have even encountered this superstition in America; once an editorial friend at Indianapolis gave me a very handsome pocket-knife, which he refused to part with except at the price of one cent, lawful coin of the realm, asserting that we should become enemies without this precaution.

In Wales, according to Jones, the Gwyllion often came into the houses of the people at Aberystruth, especially in stormy weather, and the inmates made them welcome—not through any love they bore them, but through fear of the hurts the Gwyllion. might inflict if offended—by providing clean water for them, and taking especial care that no knife, or other cutting tool, should be in the corner near the fire, where the fairies would go to sit. 'For want of which care many were hurt by them.' While it was desirable to exorcise them when in the open air, it was not deemed prudent to display an inhospitable spirit towards any member of the fairy world. The cases of successful exorcism by knife are many, and nothing in the realm of faerie is better authenticated.
– Wirt Sikes, 1880

The tools of Fairy Witchcraft are straightforward and fairly simple. Our tradition is, at heart, a pragmatic one and while each tool does have symbolic significance they are also meant to be used as working tools. The guidelines for your tools are very general, as each one should be an expression of your own practice and something you can really connect to. The only hard and fast rule is that they must not be made of iron or steel as these materials will drive away fairies, which is antithetical to the purpose of Fairy Witchcraft, otherwise you can choose any material you like and make your tools as simple or fancy as you please. Also, while the required tools for this type of witchcraft are fairly minimal, you can of course add in whatever else you want to use.

Tools

The Cauldron

The cauldron is the central tool of Fairy Witchcraft and is used to burn offerings and herbs and to focus magical workings. It is symbolic of the Dagda's cauldron, a great treasure of the Tuatha De Danann, which was brought from the Otherworld when the Gods first came to mortal earth and it represents abundance and plenty. My cauldron is made of bronze and is unadorned, sitting on three legs. I suggest finding one large enough to easily work with, at least the size of a three-quart cooking pot. You will use your cauldron for many things and you want to have one that you like and are comfortable working with. This may take some time and meanwhile you can make do with something smaller. I also have a cauldron I made myself out of clay that works just as well, although it is not large enough for some types of workings.

The Ritual Knife

This can be made of bronze, silver, or other non-ferrous metals, or alternative materials such as wood, bone, antler, or stone. The knife is used to direct energy and in certain types of healing magic. It is symbolic of the sword of Nuada, another of the four treasures of the Irish Gods; the sword was a mighty weapon from which no enemy escaped once it was unsheathed. The ritual knife in Fairy Witchcraft is used in any magic that involves commanding.

The Wand

The wand is also used to direct energy and is the main tool for magic. Each type of wood has its own quality and purpose so you want to study the different materials and choose the one you prefer. I have one main wand that I use most of the time, but I also have an assortment of other wands that I also use for different purposes based on their unique qualities:

Oak: Strength, power
Birch: New beginnings, birth, breaking hexes
Rowan: Magic, enchantment, cleansing
Hazel: Wisdom, knowledge
Yew: Shapeshifting, ancestors
Apple: Love, healing
Maple: Friendship, peace, compromise
Blackthorn: Cursing, protection

The wand symbolizes the spear of Lugh, another treasure of the Tuatha De Danann. The spear was a weapon of defense, which it was said no battle could be sustained against.

The Broom

The broom should, ideally, be made of ash with birch twigs and willow binding, but any fairy-friendly material is acceptable (keep in mind the plant broom is a protection against fairies and should not be used). This tool is used to purify and cleanse areas and in certain kinds of spells. Birch has strong cleansing properties and is a protection against the more dangerous and malicious types of spirits, so I would suggest that even if you choose alternative material you affix a small amount of birch to the broom as well.

The Quiach

The quaich is a bowl with two handles that is used to make food and liquid offerings, because it symbolizes friendship. It can be made of wood or metal.

The Fairy Stone

The fairy stone is a found stone that is kept on the altar as a symbol of the connection between the witch and the land. Ideally the stone should be found as a gift from the Fair Folk. There is no right or wrong in what this stone will be like and it may be used for other purposes as well, such as healing or blessing magic. The stone represents the fourth treasure of the Irish Gods, the Lia Fal, which was symbolic of sovereignty.

Mortar and Pestle

Connecting to the spirits of local trees and plants is important in Fairy Witchcraft and a Fairy Witch is encouraged to make her or his own incenses and, with proper training, teas and medicines. One mortar and pestle should be kept only for making incense and a separate one for anything that will be consumed. Personally, I have a small ceramic one for making incense and a small brass one for other purposes, as that way there is no worry about remember which is used for what.

Additional Tools

Besides the main tools listed above there are a few others that you might consider using. These are not necessary, per se, the way the others are, but they can be helpful and important. Whether you decide to include any of these is entirely up to you.

The Staff or Walking Stick

Preferably made of blackthorn, this tool is used somewhat like a large wand and in many ways is simply a bigger version of a wand. Whereas a wand is generally going to be kept on the altar at all times, a walking stick can be kept with the witch and has the advantage of being a tool that can go with them into the wilds or into the city if needed without attracting too much attention.

The Sword

The sword is a larger version of the ritual knife. It is used for the same purposes, but on a grander scale, and as with the ritual knife you would not want it to be made of iron or steel.

An Iron Blade

Although this is not often used in Fairy Witchcraft, there are certain situations, such as exorcisms of specific types of spirits, where an iron blade may be needed. In those cases by tradition you would want an iron knife with a black handle, and I recommend having one knife for this purpose that isn't used for anything else.

Making Your Own Tools

One decision that you will face as you begin your practice – even if you are a more experienced practitioner – is whether to buy or make your own tools. On the one hand making your own is an amazing experience and creates a feeling of connection to the things you use like nothing else. On the other hand buying tools allows you to support pagan artists and companies and can provide better quality. There are pros and cons either way and obviously your personal circumstances and abilities will dictate some of what you can and can't make or buy. That said I wanted to talk about some of the items I use that I have made with my own hands and why I think you should make at least one thing for your own ritual use.

First, a little back story. When I was in high school I planned to go on to be a fine arts major in college so I took every art class my school offered, including ceramics. I adored ceramics and figured out early on that I could use the class projects to make my own ritual items, an especially appealing idea since I had very little money (I was 13 and 14 at the time I was taking the classes). I made my own cauldron, decorated with leaf designs from five trees I considered significant. I made my own altar plate, with three oak leaves on it, and my own chalice, censer, and candle holder.

All of these are items I still use today, although I certainly could have replaced them with nicer store bought versions in the past 20 years. But I keep them and use them because there is something powerful in knowing I made them with my own hands. They are the physical representation of my skill and my dedication to my spirituality. And when I look at them I remember not only the decades of use, but also the time and effort that went into their creation.

My main motivation in making my own tools has been necessity, but I think there is also value in having something I've made myself. And if I can do it I think each of you can do it as well. I believe there is something physical that you can use in what you do, that you can make for yourself and that the process of making that item is as valuable as the item itself.

For anyone interested in giving this a try without a huge financial investment consider trying salt dough. It's easily made with just salt, flour and water and can be hardened and painted after shaping. Obviously this can't be used to make a cauldron or censer, but you could make a serviceable altar plate with it, or deity statues, or a quiach for food offerings. It's also a great way to make poppets for image magic and can be incorporated into spellwork in other ways as well.

Basic Salt Dough Recipe

1½ cups flour
1 cup salt
1 cup warm water

Mix flour and salt until they are well blended then slowly add in the water. Mix the dough until it has a nice smooth consistency. You can shape it fairly easily, although if you make anything too thick it won't dry properly. I like to use tinfoil to build off, by wadding the tinfoil up to create a base shape to mold the dough around, and I try not to go more than a half inch thick on the dough. Once you have shaped your piece you can leave it out to dry or bake it for a few hours in the oven at 200 degrees. After it's completely dry you can paint it however you like and then varnish it to preserve it. I like to use acrylic paints and a spray-on varnish, both of which should be available either at a local craft store or online.

Altars

By the technical definition an altar is a place to make offerings, and to expand on the dictionary idea a bit for witches, an altar is also a place for magical working. An altar may be a permanent structure or it may be temporary; it may be simple or complex. Although some traditions can be very strict in what is required in setting up an altar, Fairy Witchcraft takes a more fluid approach – your altar should reflect your own personality and should work for your practice, rather than follow a rigid structure. As long as it serves the ultimate purpose of giving you a place to honor the Gods and spirits and make your magic, then it really doesn't matter where you place your cauldron or your knife. Simply put, an altar is a place where we can go to connect to the Gods and spirits and as long as it is serving this purpose effectively how it looks is – pardon the pun – window dressing.

Exactly what is on a modern altar and how the altar is used can vary widely, but there are some general things to keep in mind. As a rule a flat surface works best; if you want to use a stone outdoors you'll need to find one that has a mostly smooth top surface and that is fairly level or you run the risk of things falling off and sliding, which is never good when candles are involved. Also keep in mind when fashioning an outdoor altar that you don't want to cause too much damage or disruption to the area, as the point is to work with the area not to be at odds with it. Most altars that I have seen will include sacred images, candles, and a place or bowl for offerings, but some may also include a variety of objects and tools. My own altars tend to get very elaborate as I try to include a variety of things that are important to me, but I have seen some that are as simple as a candle and incense burner. In Fairycraft I would recommend placing all your tools on the altar during rituals and spellwork, but even that is open to personal preference.

I am lucky enough to have several permanent altars in my home, and I will describe several of them here to give everyone an idea of different ways altars can be approached. For some people, setting up an altar may be easy, but I know when I first started out I was nervous about doing things the right way and it took me a while to learn to trust my own intuition. Having a template to follow is reassuring, so maybe some people will find inspiration in these ideas.

My main altar is fairly large and includes all my working tools as well as representations of the liminal Gods. At the back of the altar is a large tree sculpture from which I hang various items, from charms to hag stones, that I call my blessing tree. This represents the Living and Dying Tree, which is something like the World Tree of Fairy Witchcraft – it is the central point upon which all things revolve. At one point I tried to use statues to represent the liminal Gods, but that never felt right so eventually I opened up to trusting my intuition and instead of modern, aesthetically pleasing statues I started using more organic primal objects to symbolize the Gods. The Lady of the Greenwood is represented during the light half of the year by a painted rabbit skull, and the Lord of the Wildwood by a pheasant's wing. During the dark half of the year the Queen of the Wind is represented by a crow wing and the Hunter by a painted deer skull. These are of course only my own choices for representations, and individual witches can and should decide for themselves what feels most appropriate, rather than taking my suggestions as written in stone. In front of the tree sits my cauldron, a large brass, three-legged one that I use for my spellwork and for blessing items; in front of my cauldron is my fairy stone. To the left I have my wands, offering bowl, and both mortar and pestles. To the right is my incense burner, ritual knife

I have one altar that is dedicated entirely for honoring several healing Goddesses; this altar is where I go when doing any healing magic or when praying for healing. Although my main focus is the spirits of this world and the Otherworld I do also honor some Irish and Germanic Gods, including Brighid and Airmed. This altar features statues representing those deities as well as tokens for them and a small brass cauldron. The cauldron is used in healing spells; I write down the names of people who need healing on small slips of paper and place them in the cauldron. When the person feels better or their health has improved the paper is taken out and burned.

I have altars dedicated to my ancestors and to the daoine sí. My ancestor altar has pictures of all my beloved dead and a few objects that are things owned by them, as well as candles and a deck of oracle cards. My altar for the Other Crowd is often changing, but at the moment it has a small collection of statues that remind me of the aos sí – and it took time to find good ones without wings – as well as a few other images representing other Fey beings I am familiar with. There are sacred objects, an offering cup, an incense burner and candle, and a deck of cards. These altars serve the same purpose as the other altars, but are very specifically focused. I find that they are excellent for connecting to non-divine Powers and go to them no less often than the others.

Sacred Space

> *Every religion must have its holy places, affording a means of communication between man, gods, spirits, and forces of nature.*
> – Hilda Ellis Davidson

In our post-modern paganism there is a tendency to view all space, all nature, as sacred and yet it has been said – and rightly so – that to make all space sacred is to lose any sense of genuine sacredness. Without the profane there can be no appreciation of the sacred, just as without the darkness the light has no value. In Fairy Witchcraft our view of sacred space is layered, both by an understanding of the traditional views of it and also by an appreciation and respect for naturally occurring sacred spaces.

At its most basic, sacred space is a special area or space that is set aside for worship or a natural place that provides a special connection to Powers beyond ourselves. Sacred space may be created or exist temporarily or permanently (Viking Answer Lady, n.d.). Additionally the formation of sacred space may be based in an acknowledgement of a place's inherent sacredness, such as we see in the Celtic practice of worshiping in groves of trees or by sacred wells, or may be an entirely human construct where a specific area is declared sacred or made sacred through ritual actions. Both the Norse and the Celts seem to have originally sought out natural sacred spaces for worship and to leave offerings, and the places seen as sacred in this way were the same for both cultures: clearings in groves of trees, hilltops, and near bodies of water (Ellis Davidson, 1988). The Norse continued to favor the use of open sacred spaces for worship until the Christian period, although there are examples of man-made temple structures as well, although these are usually smaller and associated with family use (Viking Answer Lady, n.d.). Historically we see the intentional creation of places of worship, which had their own sacredness in both cultures. In Norse cultures we see the creation of fridr-gardr, or peace areas, which were used for worship and also for law courts (Viking Answer Lady, n.d.). In the Celtic areas we find rectangular and square earthworks, called veirechschanzen, which are believed to have been temple sites from around the first century BCE, and contain examples of offering pits (Ross, 1970).

Both Celtic and Norse cultures acknowledged natural sacred spaces, places that by their very nature had a sacred quality; this included special groves of trees, hilltops, lakes where offerings were given to the waters, swamps, and certain meadows or fields (Ross, 1970; Viking Answer Lady, n.d.). These places were sacred because of an inherent quality recognized by worshipers, such as the presence of specific trees or healing waters, or else were seen as sacred due to omens that occurred to indicate this sacredness or because of specific uses, such as leaving offerings at the sites, which sanctified them. These natural sacred sites might belong to specific Gods or spirits or might be general places of worship (Viking Answer Lady, n.d.). In Fairy Witchcraft we also seek out places that we consider sacred because of the presence of the Fair Folk, such as the fairy mounds or ancient sites associated with them – or new places we may find where we feel their presence. In my area there is a state park that many local pagans feel has a very strong Fey presence and many of us consider this a sacred place.

Constructed sacred spaces might be simple or elaborate. These places were called hofs in the Norse and could be anything from a simple one-room wooden building or a large multi-roomed temple (Viking Answer Lady, n.d.). The Irish word for a sacred space was nemed or fidnemed, terms that were likely used for both the natural sacred places as well as the human-built temples (Ross, 1970). Both cultures seemed to have used the man-made structures to honor their Gods with offerings and for community celebrations. The Celtic examples include deep pits that contain the remains of ritual offerings and sacrifices. Although neither culture initially seemed to use physical representations of Gods, later temple sites may have included such images, and the Celtic temples are believed to have included a central pole or pillar, which may have symbolized a sacred tree.

In the end I believe that modern sacred space is really no different from ancient sacred space; it is what we create and what we find and acknowledge in nature. What makes space sacred is sacred use and, in the natural world, the organic focusing of sacred energy by the landscape and particular features. Anyone can create a sacred space through ritual use, and repeated use can make a temporary sacred space more permanent; this can also be done intentionally through focus and intent. The greatest challenge for us today may be learning to recognize the natural sacred places on our own and properly honoring them. So many of us live divorced from the natural world that it is easy to see why we might begin to feel that all the natural world is sacred, yet if we make the effort to get out and connect with our environment we will begin to see that while we can nurture connection with the sacred anywhere, there are special places that are, in and of themselves, sacred. These places deserve to be found and recognized, and honoring them through ritual use, even something as simple as meditation, not only teaches us to appreciate the sacred, but also honors the spirit of that place in way that is mutually beneficial. Whether we are creating a sacred space or appreciating one we have recognized, we will doubtless find that an appreciation of sacred space deepens our own spirituality.

The Directions, the Elements and the Year

We've already discussed the importance of moving with or against the sun. When it comes to ritual space we should always remember that we want to enter sacred space by circling it, preferably three times, sunwise. We also associate certain directions, qualities, and elements with these movements.

In *The Silver Bough, Volume 1* F. Marian McNeill discusses the airts, or the different directions in Scottish tradition. This concept of the directions relating to seasons is also a part of Fairy Witchcraft, where we associate each season with a cardinal point. Each direction is related to a season, with spring in the east, summer in the south, fall in the west, and winter in the north (McNeill, 1956). She mentions that this progression was seen as being connected to the path of the sun through the sky, but that she believes this clockwise movement may also connect to the constellation of Ursa Major. This constellation, which is also called the Farmer's Clock, points in each of the directions in the corresponding season.

In Fairy Witchcraft we acknowledge five elements: air, fire, water, earth, and spirit. Each element is associated with a direction, season, color, and specific qualities. The qualities we assign to each element are based on the Irish story Suidigud Tellaich Temra, which suggests specific characteristics for each one. All things are intrinsically linked to all other things, and each has importance and power.

Correspondences

East: Air, white, spring, land spirits, abundance, prosperity, support

South: Fire, red, summer, humans, music/poetry, speech, inspiration

West: Water, blue, autumn, ancestors, knowledge, wisdom, history

North: Earth, black, winter, aos si, battle, conflict, pride

Center: Spirit, green, the entire year, Gods, sovereignty, power

Circle Casting[24]

Unlike many other modern witchcraft approaches, Fairy Witchcraft doesn't often use circles. They aren't used for basic offerings, or most spellwork, and only rarely in rituals because when we cast a circle we are opening a gateway into Fairy. The only time a circle would be used in specific kinds of guided mediations or journey work, or in rituals where it is necessary to have that extra connection. Be aware though that shifting your ritual space in this way can have some interesting effects; it is very common for time to be distorted and appear to either slow down or speed up, sometimes drastically.

The five elements are invoked to anchor the circle space and give it stability while it is acting as a bridge. They are invoked first, and then the circle itself is cast and the gateway opened. When the ritual is ended the process is reversed to close this opening down. It is very important to understand before doing this that this is not a neopagan circle whose purpose would be to protect the caster from outside influences or contain raised energy. As a Fairy Witch, you need to be able to handle the energy you raise and to ward yourself from any spirits that might be drawn to what you are doing. A Fairy circle is an opening connecting to the Otherworld, and should not be done lightly.

If you are working indoors, before casting the circle take the broom and walk three times sunwise around the space. Sweep with strong motions outwards while chanting or singing a simple blessing, such as:

Bless this space
Bless this place
Three times round
This blessing's bound.

If you are outdoors and do not have a broom you may either choose to create a temporary one using an available branch from a tree, or you can simply walk three times around the space chanting the same thing.

To cast the circle start in the east. Raise your hands and envision a strong wind blowing. Say:

Element of Air, Power of the East,
I call you to attend this circle
Ground my circle between the worlds
Join me now!

Turn to the south, raise your hands, envision a roaring fire, and say:

Element of Fire, Power of the South,
I call you to attend this circle
Ground my circle between the worlds
Join me now!

Turn to the west, raise your hands, envision a driving rain, and say:

Element of Water, Power of the West,
I call you to attend this circle
Ground my circle between the worlds
Join me now!

Turn to the north, raise your hands, envision fresh turned earth, and say:

Element of Earth, Power of the North,
I call you to attend this circle
Ground my circle between the worlds
Join me now!

Finally stand in front of your altar, raise your hands, and open your heart. Say:

Element of Spirit, Power of the Center,
I call you to attend this circle
Ground my circle between the worlds
Join me now!

After calling the elements, pick up your ritual knife. Starting in the east, walk the perimeter of your ritual area, visualizing the blade cutting a line of energy that expands into a sphere surrounding you. When you have completed the circuit, return to your altar. Set the knife down. Clearly and strongly say:

I stand now between the worlds
Where time is timeless
I stand now between the worlds
Where mortal earth and Fairy join
I stand now between the worlds
Where wish and will unite

Once the circle is cast you want to invite the fairy folk, but this has to be done with extreme caution. It's important to extend the invitation because this is one of the ways that alliances and friendships with the fairies are built, but you must be careful not to invite in fairies that want to do you harm or are dangerous. Say:

I welcome all goodly inclined friendly spirits.

Now perform the body of your rite. This can including calling in the ancestors and the Gods as well as different acts of magic or prayers and offerings. When finished, stand before your altar and say:

To all goodly inclined spirits who joined me here, may there be peace and friendship between us.

Then say:

The doorway to Fairy is closed
The flow of time returns
The doorway to Fairy is closed
I stand again on mortal earth
The doorway to Fairy is closed
As I will it, so it is.

Walk the boundary of your space again with ritual knife, this time seeing the energy returning into the blade. When done stand before your altar again and put your ritual knife down. Lower your head slightly and say:

Element of Spirit, Power of the Center,
I release you from this circle
In peace and power.

Offer some of the energy from the ritual to the elemental spirit. Turn to the east, lower your head slightly and say:

Element of Air, Power of the East,
I release you from this circle
In peace and power.

Offer some of the energy from the ritual to the elemental spirit. Turn to the south, lower your head slightly and say:

Element of Fire, Power of the South,
I release you from this circle
In peace and power.

Offer some of the energy from the ritual to the elemental spirit. Turn to the west, lower your head slightly and say:

Element of Water, Power of the West,
I release you from this circle
In peace and power.

Offer some of the energy from the ritual to the elemental spirit. Turn to the north, lower your head slightly and say:

Element of Earth, Power of the North,
I release you from this circle
In peace and power.

After taking down the circle it is essential to be sure you ground your energy. Eat and drink something, lay out flat on the earth or on the floor if you are inside, or put a small amount of salt on your tongue.

Modern Experience

Sometimes my spiritual practice and my role as a mother come into conflict. One such incident happened a few years ago and presented a unique challenge for me.

My youngest daughter was five years old at the time. She is very intuitive; my grandfather would have said she has what the Irish call the second sight, the ability to know the future and to see spirits. Although my house is also home to a variety of spirits it had never been an issue, until she started to say that she was afraid to sleep in her bedroom because of a scary ghost. Now I knew nothing in the house was dangerous to her or meant any harm, but obviously something was frightening her just by being in there. I tried giving her a stuffed toy made by a friend of mine called a 'Monster Getter', telling her it would catch any bad spirits. I was hoping that if she was just going through a normal childhood phase that would be enough, but that didn't work. I was stumped because I didn't want to banish the helpful or friendly spirits that were around, but my only previous experience with banishing spirits was designed for the entire home and got rid of all spirits present. I also wanted her to feel she had control over her own space and was safe. She should be empowered and in control of the situation, not just dependent on me to come in and take care of it.

In the end I decided on a mixed approach using several different methods to make her room its own separate space with its own ghost-proof protections. I know children are very concrete thinkers so I wanted to have something physical, something she could see and touch, in her room as a talisman. I thought this would also help her whenever she started to feel frightened by giving her a reminder that her room was safe, and I felt that such an item could be tailored to only affect her room, not the entire house. I also wanted to incorporate something she could participate in so that she felt part of the process.

I used two rune staves for banishing and keeping out spirits. I thought this would be perfect because my children are used to seeing runes and runic staves around so while they don't know what the symbols are, per se, they believe in their power. I wrote the staves on a piece of heavy parchment along with the English words 'No Ghosts Allowed' to reinforce the message in a way that the children could understand. I mixed up and burnt an herbal blend for cleansing with juniper and rosemary and then my daughter and I stood in her room and she repeated, 'This is my room and no scary ghosts or mean spirits are allowed here. No ghosts allowed!' Afterwards we hung up the sign on the wall next to the door, facing into the room. She was satisfied with the procedure and felt confident that her room was fixed, as she put it. I was happy that she felt better about sleeping in her room.

And she hasn't complained about any ghosts in her room since.

Chapter 6

Holidays and Prayers

On November Eve they are at their gloomiest, for according to the old Gaelic reckoning, this is the first night of winter. This night they dance with the ghosts, and the pooka is abroad, and witches make their spells... After November Eve the blackberries are no longer wholesome, for the pooka has spoiled them.
– W.B. Yeats, *Irish Fairy and Folk Tales*

...but presently he mentioned that the following night the fairy king and queen would hold a grand court and feast in Glen Rushen, in the southern part of the island, near Ballasalla, in honour of Re-Hollys-Vooar-Yn-Onyr, the royal festival of the harvest moon, and that every elfin in Ellan Vannin would have to attend. He described to her wondering and delighted ear how the dancing would be kept up till the moon ceased to shine, and sank behind the head of South Barrule, and the ruddy rays of the coming sun began to show signs of rising from the eastern sea.
– Edward Callow, *The Phynodderre and Other Legends of the Isle of Man*, 1882

Fairy Witchcraft, like many other neopagan faiths, celebrates eight holidays throughout the year, roughly one every six weeks. Of these there are four greater holy days – Samhain, Imbolc, Bealtaine, and Lúnasa – and four lesser holy days – Midwinter, Spring Equinox, Midsummer, and Fall Equinox. The greater holidays are also called the quarter days, and it is on these four occasions that the Fair Folk are especially active, being out and about, and some say it is on these days that they move their homes, traveling from one fairy hill to another via the ancient fairy roads. The lesser holidays are the cross-quarter days, the solar festivals of the solstices and equinoxes.

Samhain: October 31st
Winter Solstice: Varies between December 20th and 23rd
Imbolc: January 31st
Spring Equinox: Varies between March 20th and 23rd
Bealtaine: April 30th
Summer Solstice: Varies between June 20th and 23rd
Lúnasa: July 31st
Fall Equinox: Varies between September 20th and 23rd

Samhain

Samhain occurs for us on October 31st. It is more accurate though to say that Samhain begins at sunset on October 31st and ends at sunset on November 1st, as all the holidays for us begin at sunset and go into the next day.

Samhain marks the end of the light half of the year and the beginning of the dark half, and also the end of the old year and the beginning of the new. It is at Samhain that the rule of the liminal Gods transitions, and the Queen of the Wind and Hunter step up as Queen and King of the next six months. This turning of the year from light to dark is a time when the spirits of the dead are more likely to return to visit us, and we make a practice of leaving out fresh water, food, and lighting a white candle for them. Samhain is also the time when the people are most likely to encounter fairy beings, as they are at their most active and present in our world (Evans, 1957; McNeill, 1962). The Gentry that are abroad at Samhain are a dangerous sort though and care must be taken if they are encountered at night; both the Wild Hunt and Slua sí are out at this time, among others. Should you happen to be confronted by the host it is best to thrown the dust of the road at them, as the belief is that they must then release anyone they have taken (Danaher, 1972).

In Fairy Witchcraft we prefer to celebrate Samhain as a three-day holiday when possible, dedicating the first day to the Fey folk, the second to the liminal Gods, and the third to the dead. Offerings are made of milk, bread, apples, porridge, and perhaps a shared meal. Prayers for a good New Year can be said, and divination should be done for the year to come.

The first day of the holiday is dedicated to the daoine sí and wandering ghosts. Since we also celebrate secular Halloween with trick or treating, my children give the sí a tithe of candy from their take at the end of the night. Porridge is offered as well, left out near the woods and I tell the kids fairy-stories. After the children go to sleep, I will do my own ritual honoring these Powers and re-affirming my friendship with them.

One thing I personally do every Samhain morning (November 1st) is walk through my house fumigating with a blend of juniper, rosemary, and vervain to bless my home. As I do this I will say a prayer based on one from the *Carmina Gadelica*:

Gods, bless to me this new day,
Never seen by me before;
As I bless You on this morning,
Embracing the time I am given.
Bless my two eyes,
May my eyes bless all I see;
I will bless my neighbor,
May my neighbor bless me.
Gods, give me a clean start,
Let me remain under your protection;
Bless my children and my husband,
And bless my life and my possessions.

The second day is dedicated to the Gods. We honor the Queen of the Wind and the Hunter as they come to prominence. I also tell my children stories about the Gods or spirits and things that happened on Samhain, of which there are many to choose from in Irish myth. As part of my ritual I extinguish all the candles on my altar and relight them to symbolically re-enact the Samhain fire lighting at Tlachtga, and represent the end of the old year and birth of the new. We have a small ritual feast as well, of pork and apples with seasonal vegetables, some of which are offered to the Gods, spirits, and ancestors.

The third and final day is for the ancestors. I light candles on my ancestor altar and tell my children stories about the family members who have passed from this life. We set an extra place at dinner and leave out a plate of food for the dead. I also often talk to my children about the turning of the seasons and the approach of winter now. We take our Halloween pumpkins and offer them to the woods to feed the deer and other wildlife.

The Winter Solstice

We celebrate the Winter Solstice on the shortest day and longest night of the year, which usually happens between December 20th and December 23rd. Most of the traditions and practices for the Winter Solstice in Fairy Witchcraft are drawn from older folk practices, both Celtic and Norse. Many of the Irish practices come to us from later traditions tied to Christian celebrations because the older pagan traditions have been lost in the shadows of time. Although there is no solid evidence connecting Christmas in Ireland to older pagan practices, there are some hints of traditions that may pre-date Christian influence. As Estyn Evans tells us: *'Although Christmas is the outstanding Christian festival of the year its traditional 'Twelve Days' of holiday are steeped in pagan lore and in folk practices relating to the winter solstice...'* (Estyn Evans, 1957, p 279). It is possible that the older solstice customs shifted to Christmas (O Suilleabhain, 1967).

Preparations begin before the holiday, with a thorough cleaning of the home and the gathering of appropriate decorations. In my family we generally do this either the last weekend in November or the first weekend in December. These decorations traditionally include boughs of evergreens including holly, ivy, bay, and laurel (Danaher, 1972). We use these as small decorations around the house and also have a tree that we decorate every year. For us the tree represents the hope of life in the midst of the cold and dark of winter.

Gift giving was, and remains, an extensive practice, virtually a social obligation. Historically in Ireland shopkeepers gave gifts to customers, the well-off gave to the less fortunate, and friends and family gifted each other; these gifts could include firewood, food, special seasonal treats, and clothes (Danaher, 1972). In this way gift giving both reinforced social bonds and also acted as charity to support the lower levels of society. This concept is maintained in Fairy Witchcraft – where we emphasize generosity anyway – by the practice of giving gifts to those we interact with. In our family this includes everyone from my children's school bus driver to the men who collect our garbage every week, and the gifts usually emphasize food, often being either gift cards for food or seasonal treats. We also make food offerings to the various spirits.

This time of year, like Samhain, is a time to remember and honor the dead (O Suilleabhain, 1967). One older practice was to leave out three plates on the table and a bowl of water left on the windowsill to be blessed by the spirits of deceased family members during the night; this water is then thought to have healing properties (Danaher, 1972). There is also an old practice of lighting a candle at this time for a family member who has died in the past year, and decorating the graves of family members with holly or yew (Danaher, 1972). In Fairy Witchcraft we may do all of these as part of our solstice celebrations.

One similar traditional practice is the lighting of a large white candle in the kitchen window the night before the holiday, which may be decorated with holly (O Suilleabhain, 1967; Danaher, 1972). The candle would be allowed to burn either all night or until midnight, and if it was put out or went out early it was thought to be a terrible omen, sometimes seen as foretelling a coming death in the family (Danaher, 1972). In Fairy Witchcraft we incorporate this by lighting a single white candle, decorated with holly, on our altars during our solstice ritual. We often do this to help guide the wandering souls as well, since we believe that the Wild Hunt is especially active at this time, as are other dangerous Fey. It is also at this time that an offering of porridge is made to the house spirit in gratitude.

In Scotland we see a blend of Celtic and Norse beliefs. During the period of Yule all household work, like spinning and weaving, was strictly prohibited as it was believed that to do such work, even drawing water, during the twelve days of Yule would risk the girls of the house being taken by a Kelpie. The hearth was cleaned and decorated to please the Gods and garlanded with rowan to keep out mischievous spirits. On the eve of Yule the family would go out to collect the Yule log, which would be brought in with great ceremony, an offering of ale poured over it, and then placed in the fire to burn through the night. In some parts of the Highlands the Yule log is associated with the Cailleach, the spirit of winter and in those places the Yule log chosen would be the stump of an old tree. Special breads and cakes were baked on Yule eve, and ale and sowans were made with omens taken from how they cooked. First thing on Yule morning, weather omens were taken to predict the year to come; green Yule meant snow in spring, warm Yule a cold spring, and a light Yule a good harvest.

Beef, roasted or boiled, was the most popular meal for the holiday (Danaher, 1972). Sweets, apples, and baked goods were also traditional foods. Generally speaking a large meal would be prepared including as much variety as the household could manage. We continue this practice as well by having a large family meal with beef as the main dish, and apple pie as one of the desserts. In my family we also bake a cake, which is shared among the family and partially offered to the Good Neighbors.

There are several omens that might be taken on the day. To hear a cricket was a good omen, as was hearing a rooster crow at night (Danaher, 1972). Snow, frost, and cold weather were seen as good omens, signs of a pleasant spring to come (Danaher, 1972). The special candles lit were also used for divination, as previously mentioned.

Imbolc

Traditionally Imbolc is celebrated when the lamb's first come into milk – an old name for the holiday, Oimelg, literally means 'ewe's milk' – and we celebrate it from sunset on January 31st to sunset of February 1st. It is a time to welcome the growing light of the returning sun and the hope of the returning warmth in the darkness. In Irish custom it is strongly associated with the Goddess Brigid.

There are many older Irish folk traditions connected to Imbolc. Weaving new Brighid's crosses – symbols of protection, health, and blessing – was an important Imbolc tradition in many places. One ritual that was enacted in Connaught, Sligo, Leitrim, Mayo, Roscommon, and Ulster before the Brighid's crosses were woven for the new year on the eve of the festival was for the eldest daughter to take the part of Brighid and wait outside carrying the material for the project (Danaher, 1972). She would then knock three times, proclaiming herself to be Brighid requesting entrance; she would be warmly welcomed in and the family would sit down to dinner with an elaborate blessing prayer (Danaher, 1972). The meal often prominently featured dairy products, and, if the family was wealthy, might also include fresh mutton (Danaher, 1972). After eating the meal the family would sit and weave the new crosses, with the largest sprinkled with water and hung up on the wall until the next Imbolc (Danaher, 1972). Another tradition was to create an effigy or doll, called a brideog (little Brighid), representing Brighid.

The Brideog might be made of straw from the last sheaf of the harvest, leftover rushes from weaving the crosses, a re-purposed child's doll, or the dash from the butter churn. In those homes that used an effigy as a Brideog a small bed would be prepared, made of rushes or of birch twigs, on the eve of Imbolc (Estyn Evans, 1957). The doll would be taken outside and then invited in to bless the home.

In Fairy Witchcraft we celebrate this holiday with a dairy based meal, perhaps also featuring lamb or mutton. Part of the meal is offered to the Good Neighbors and some also to the Queen of the Wind and Hunter. We look for signs of spring, of early plants like (in my area) the crocus pushing up from the snow and we observe the weather for omens, such as:

As far as the wind shall enter the door
On the Feast Day of Bride, [Imbolc]
The snow shall enter the door
On the Feast Day of Patrick. [Spring Equinox]
(*Carmina Gadelica*)

For us this is also primarily a holiday focused on cleansing. In ritual we symbolically wash or anoint our heads, hands, and feet to prepare for the work of the year to come. This is the ideal time for any dedications or to begin any long-term projects. We honor the Queen of the Wind and Hunter as both the heart of winter and the hope of spring.

Spring Equinox

There is very little historic evidence in Fairy Faith traditions relating to the spring equinox, although it does fall suspiciously close to a certain patron saint of Ireland's feast day. The spring equinox varies each year, but is usually between March 20th and March 23rd. I do tend to borrow a bit from that other holiday, and on the equinox I celebrate my closest ancestors, as opposed to my ancestors in a more general sense. I listen to traditional music and tell my children stories of their close relative who have passed on. And I cook a big meal of corned beef and cabbage with carrots and potatoes, because it's part of Irish-American culture and I don't think my closest ancestors would forgive me if I didn't.

In Fairy Witchcraft we believe that the Fairy Folk move their homes at the equinoxes, although in traditional Fairy Faith belief it is at the four Fire Festivals that they are said to be the most actively out and about. This confusion comes from the fact that in Ireland the Fire Festivals are called the quarter days, but those same holidays are called the cross-quarter days in some parts of the British Isles; at some point the belief about the fairies moving about on the quarter days (Fire Festivals) was confused with their moving on the non-Irish quarter days (solstices and equinoxes).

At this time when day and night are balanced and the warmth is noticeably beginning to overtake the cold, we focus on setting goals for the growing season and choosing what we will nurture and put our energy into. Those with actual physical crops might look at starting seeds indoors around now, but for those of us without literal plants to grow we look at what other things in our lives need to be planted. Offerings are made as usual to the Good Neighbors at this time, and also to the liminal Gods for a safe spring, as the dangerous season of thawing and storms begins.

Bealtaine

Bealtaine is celebrated from sunset of April 30th until sunset of May 1st. The focus of Bealtaine is on welcoming back summer and celebrating the return of warm weather and its life-affirming qualities. Beltane stood opposite Samhain on the calendar and in many ways represented opposite themes; where Samhain was a time of harvest and of the dead, Beltane was a time of blessing and planting (McNeill, 1959). At this time some believe that the Wild Hunt leaves until the next winter, leaving behind a single hound called the Windhund who brings good weather, fertility and luck (Hodge, n.d.) This hound is offered a slice of bread with butter and honey on the morning of May 1st to ensure its blessing on the home (Hodge, n.d). The night of April 30th is particularly associated with witches, who were said to gather to celebrate and in a modern context is considered a time of magic and enchantment.

There are many traditions associated with this holiday, in both the Celtic Fairy Faith and German paganism that are incorporated into Fairy Witchcraft. The German traditions include offerings to the spirit hound left by the Wild Hunt, burning old worn-out tools, blessing bonfires which may be jumped over, the creation of May bushes – that is a small bush or decorated branch covered in yellow ribbons, flowers, and eggshells – and the gathering of flowers brought in to bless the house (Grimm, 1888; Hodge, n.d.). May bushes are also found in Irish practice as are bonfires, which would be jumped over to increase a person's fertility and show their bravery (Evans, 1957). In some areas instead of jumping them two fires were made and the herds driven between them for cleansing and luck.

The fairies were thought to be especially active and powerful on Beltane, and in some sources for the first three days of May. It was said in Ireland that it was on Beltane eve that the faeries moved from one hill to another and were most likely to steal children or cause mischief (Danaher, 1972). Caution was needed to guard against faeries stealing the household's luck, dairy products, or herbs, and the best protection against this was strewing primroses across the threshold (Wilde, 1991). This belief also meant that strangers were looked on with great suspicion, lest they actually be fairies in disguise, and there were strong prohibitions against giving away or lending milk or fire on Beltane. Offerings of food might be made to appease the faeries, or else a bit of iron or rowan would be carried as protection (Danaher, 1972).

In German practice, this holiday, called Walpurgisnacht, is a main holiday for witches. Grimm specifically mentions, in his section on witches: *'The Witches' Excursion takes place on the first night in May... They ride up Blocksberg on the first of May, and in 12 days must dance the snow away; then Spring begins.'* (Grimm, 1888). This may indicate a belief that the welcoming of summer was a process of banishing winter, and only after rituals being done for the right amount of time – 12 days – would winter actually retreat and summer begin. In the German-American practice of Urglaawe the holiday includes the 12 nights of Wonnetdanz when frost giants fight against the thawing of the land and are repelled each night (Schreiwer, 2013). In Fairy Witchcraft we see Bealtaine as the time when the dark half of the year turns to the light half, winter turning to summer, and the liminal Gods again change rulership. The Queen of the Wind and Hunter return to the Otherworld while the Lady of the Greenwood and Lord of the Wildwood step forward to take over here.

In Fairy Witchcraft, Bealtaine is particularly a fertility holiday, when we rejoice in the new growth all around us. Physical unions are celebrated and any children who are conceived at this time (who will be born around the next Imbolc) are thought to have a special connection to Fairy.

Midsummer

We celebrate Midsummer on the longest day and shortest night of the year, usually between June 20th and June 23rd. Midsummer has long been associated with the Fair Folk; in Ireland the Goddess Áine – who is often seen as a Fairy Queen – is especially celebrated on this night and in Swedish belief the Wild Hunt rides out. Although the Wild Hunt is fearsome, overall the Fair Folk who are about at this time of year tend to be the most kindly inclined towards humans and while they may still be prone to mischief – Shakespeare's A Midsummer Night's Dream isn't an unfair depiction by any means – it is still one of the best times to interact with them.

The Lady of the Greenwood and Lord of the Wildwood are honored and offerings of sweets, candies, milk, honey, and flowers may be made. In my family we also bake and offer a cake, with pieces given to the Gods, Fair Folk, and ancestors and shared among the family. The overall feel of this holiday is very light-hearted and joyous with an emphasis on dancing and singing.

Lunasa

In Fairy Witchcraft we celebrate Lunasa starting at sunset on July 31st until sunset of August 1st. This holiday represents the first harvest, the time when we begin to see the return of whatever we planted and chose to nurture earlier in the year. It is also a period of abundant resources, which feature strongly in the offerings we make.

There are several themes surrounding this celebration that include the mundane, the spiritual, and the blending of both. Lúnasa celebrates, at its core, the beginning of the harvest and the new abundance of food being gathered; because of this it is strongly associated with porridge and bread, which symbolized the fresh foods of the new harvest, often with fresh seasonal fruit being incorporated (Danaher, 1972). The period just prior to the beginning of the harvest was the leanest of the year, making the celebration of fresh fruit, vegetables, and grains all the more special to the people (MacNeill, 1962). Although in our modern world we are not usually dependent on the cycles of the agricultural year the way our ancestors were, in our tradition we nonetheless strive to appreciate these cycles. In my area around Lunasa every year is when the first leaves begin to turn and despite the blistering heat of summer the signs of autumn start to appear.

In Ireland, one of the traditional folk practices was for the community to gather to celebrate at a site chosen for both its beauty and remote location (Danaher, 1972). There are references to blessing cattle on the eve of Lughnasa and of making blessing charms for the cattle and milking equipment that the blessing would remain for the year to come (McNeill, 1959). For us we implement this practice by blessing our ritual tools and charging them with energy for the year to come.

Divination was practiced, with a particular focus on the weather during the harvest and this seems to have been based on observations of the weather so far during the year and on atmospheric conditions on Lughnasa, with color and appearance of certain landmarks indicating either fair or foul weather to come (Danaher, 1972). In my practice it is at Lunasa that we do divination for the weather of the winter to come, making note of whether the omens indicate a mild or severe winter to come. Methods used for this will vary from observing natural signs to drawing lots or cards.

Lughnasa was also the time in Ireland, Scotland, and the Orkneys for handfastings and weddings, or the dissolution of unions formed in the previous year (McNeill, 1959). This is an ideal time for weddings in our tradition, whether they are legal marriages or less formal year-and-a-day handfastings. Trial marriages of this type were used to see if the new couple was compatible; should they choose to separate after a year there was no shame in it and any child that was produced from the union would be ranked with the father's legal heirs (McNeill, 1959).

Finally Lughnasa was also well known for harvest fairs and an assortment of athletic competitions and horse races; it is important to note that the ancient fairs, or oenacha, were not occasions of commerce, but of social gathering and celebration (MacNeill, 1962). Many different types of games were held, as well as competitions of agility and strength, fire leaping, and swimming races of both men and horses (Danaher, 1972). A general party atmosphere prevailed with dancing and music, storytelling, feasting, and bonfires (Evert-Hopman, 2008). We may choose to continue this tradition ourselves by seeking out local harvest fairs and similar harvest celebrations held by the wider community.

The Fall Equinox

The equinox falls between the 20th and 23th of September on most years, and is the time when day and night are equal. The things we set as goals in the spring are ready to be harvested now and this is very much a holiday of reflection and introspection.

The closest holiday with folk practices to the autumn equinox in Ireland is Michealmas, occurring about a week after the equinox. On the eve of Michaelmas carrots are harvested; finding a forked carrot is a sign of good fortune. The women of the house, especially the oldest daughter, bake a special cake out of a blend of flours made from all the types of grain harvested that year, as a symbol of the prosperity of the land. The cake is baked on a fire of sacred woods and prepared with special chants and songs. The night before Michaelmas horses are stolen, at least temporarily since they will be returned later, and the men either stay on guard to protect their horses or are out acquiring their neighbor's horses. On the day of Michaelmas itself a lamb or goose is prepared as well as the cake and food is shared with the poor. The people visit the graves of their ancestors, riding horseback around the graveyard, and then return home to engage in a series of games and contests. Horse racing is popular, and is done without saddle and sometimes without bridle. After this comes a dance and the exchange of small gifts between friends. In general, the day is associated with the apple harvest, cider making, and the opening of the hunting season.

Much of our Fairy Witchcraft practice is based in the older Irish Michaelmas traditions. Before the ritual special cakes are made to eat and to offer, a graveyard can be visited. After walking sunwise around it, I would suggest politely entering and cleaning around the graves. As with Lúnasa, races can be run and games can be played. The ritual itself, focused on the Lady of the Greenwood and Lord of the Wildwood, should focus on gratitude for the harvest, blessing of the fertility of the land, and protection of the community. A feast of lamb or goose should follow the ritual, with portions of the food shared among the Gods and spirits; ideally this should be as part of a party or at least festive atmosphere. In a group gifts can be given or for a solitary person a random act of kindness or gift to a stranger might be considered. Because a main focus of Michaelmas is charity I believe it is appropriate on the equinox for pagans to donate money, food, or other supplies to an organization that helps the poor, ideally within the person's own community, such as a food locker.

Prayers

Fragment 216 (modified)

As it was,
As it is,
As it shall be
Evermore,
O Ancient ones
People of peace!
With the ebb,
With the flow,
O Ancient ones
People of peace!
With the ebb,
With the flow.
(Based on material from the *Carmina Gadelica, Volume 2)*

Prayer to Honor House Fairies

I offer this to the spirits of my home,
Spirits of place, I honor you
Spirits of peace, be welcome
May there be friendship between us

Prayer to the Daoine Sí

Ancient Ones of the Otherworld
Wise People of skill and power
I offer this to you as a sign of goodwill
Honey and cream, sweetness and life,
May there be peace and friendship
always between myself and the daoine sí

Prayer for Patience

Gods above, Gods below,
Give me patience
As I come and go
As I strive and work
As I rest and play
From morning to night
All through my day

Prayer for Patience at Work

God of smiths,
Patient during adversity,
Masterful craftsman,
Help me to find my strength
To endure my own trials.
Help me to master
My own work over time.
God of skill,
Help me learn patience.

Prayer to the Ancestors for Patience (A Parent's Prayer)

Ancient mothers and fathers
Primal parents of many children
Who have patiently nurtured
Untold generations of the past
Be with me now as I seek

To nurture a new generation
Help me find the patience
To endure a parent's trials

Hiking Prayer

Spirits of the land
I will walk gently here
Spirits of the stones
I will step lightly here
Spirits of the plants
I will tread softly here
Spirits of the trees
I will be peaceful here
Spirit of the animals
I will speak softly here
Spirit of the earth
I will respect you here

Travel Protection Prayer

I am protected from sky to ground,
From sunrise to sunrise
Above, below, and all around,
As I travel out and return
Safe from all harm and ill will
Safe from all mischance and ill luck
From the moment I set out until
The moment I happily return
By sea, earth, and sky
It is so

Children's Prayers

Meal Prayer

We give thanks
For this food
To the Gods
To the Good People
And ancestors too

Sleep Prayers

A general version for all the pagan parents of little kids out there:

Now I lay me down to rest
I pray that my home and kin be blessed;
ancestors guard me through the night
Gods watch over me by starlight
Guardian spirits are always near
and keep me safe, no need to fear
Loving spirits will dance and sing
Happy dreams they always bring
And when I wake to a new day
The shining sun will light my way

And more Irish version:

Now I lay me down to rest
I pray that my home and kin be blessed
ancestors guard me through the night
Gods watch over me by starlight
Guardian spirits are always near
and keep me safe, no need to fear
Goodly spirits will dance and sing
Happy dreams they always bring
And when I wake to a new day
Aine's bright sun will light my way

Modern Experience

The first time I ever experienced the passage of the Wild Hunt it was just after Yule. I had been experiencing assorted Otherworldly things my entire life, but while I knew that the Hunt existed I had never done more than read about it. Consequently, I didn't really fear the Hunt, although I knew it was frightening.

This particular year wasn't anything out of the ordinary. Yule had been a day or so before, and that night my family happened to run out of milk during dinner and told my husband I would go get some. Not a very exciting errand, but with small children and a baby it was a chance to get out of the house alone for a bit, even if only to run to the grocery store. The air was cold and crisp, the night completely black. I jogged to my car quickly, wanting out of the cold.

As my hand touched the door the wind suddenly picked up and I could hear, very faintly a sound like dogs barking. I hesitated, looking up and squinting into the biting breeze, but there was nothing but darkness to be seen. Nonetheless I could hear dogs barking more clearly, and something else, something to this day I can't entirely put into words, like something big rushing in the trees where nothing was. The hair stood up on my arms and the back of my neck and a feeling of absolute awe went through me. I jumped into my car with the distant sound of hunting horn carrying on the wind, and huddled behind the wheel. A moment later the feeling passed and the wind died back down.

I've experienced the Wild Hunt since then as well, and sometimes it is frightening and sometimes it fills a person with an overwhelming desire to join it. Sometimes both at once.

Chapter 7

Rituals and Practices

I've always believed in experiencing everything in life. When you walk out with blinders on, you cut yourself off from the angels and the fairies.
– Alyssa Milano

There was a man named Bill O'Dooley who lived by Killarney lake and one day it happened that it was a Quarter Day and his rent was due. But Bill was a poor man and the season had not been a good one for him. He knew that his landlord would send someone out to collect the rent and when he couldn't produce it he and his wife and all his little children would be turned out. He wandered over and sat on a rock near the lake wringing his hands and moaning over his situation.

Without warning a strange, stout man appeared, stepping out of the brush nearby. 'What ails you, you poor man that has you wailing so?'

Bill was startled and answered without thinking, 'It's rent day, good sir, and I haven't any way to pay as I've no luck lately that isn't bad. My family will be homeless and I am dreading it.'

The stranger shook his head in sympathy. 'A sad tale, but can't you plead your case to your landlord's agent? Surely he won't have the heart to turn your family out.'

'Heart?' Bill said, shaking his head. 'Neither my landlord nor his agent have a heart, only a stone where a heart should be.'

'Take this then to pay your rent,' the stranger said handing Bill a pouch with enough gold to pay his rent in full. 'Although I swear to you neither your agent nor landlord will get any good from this.'

Bill stared at the bag in utter disbelief, and when he finally gathered his wits enough to look up and thank the stranger he found the odd man had disappeared.

Later that day Bill paid his rent to the agent, but remembering the stranger's last words he insisted that the other man count each coin and give him a written receipt. The next morning as the agent gathered all the rent to bring to the landlord he found that all the coins Bill had paid had turned to gingerbread. Furious and baffled he threw the perfectly formed bread coins to the floor, but there was nothing he could do since Bill had a receipt to prove he'd paid.

And from that day on Bill had nothing but good luck and success.

– Retelling of traditional Irish story

Ritual

Unlike other traditions, ritual in Fairy Witchcraft emphasizes an organic structure and aims for either ecstatic experience or strengthened connections. Because of this there is a loose ritual structure, but ritual itself is often unique and personal. The central focus is inviting in the (friendly) fairies, ancestors, and Gods, or any one group alone, offering to them, and usually using divination to see how the offerings are received. Offerings may include everything from food, liquids, jewelry to song, dance, and raised energy. You may include other things in ritual as well including magical workings and, in the case of the moons, giving thanks or ritually setting goals, and for the solar holidays, prayers or offerings unique to that holiday. Specific prayers can be used, drawn from whatever culture you prefer – I like modifying prayers from the *Carmina Gadelica* or writing my own. How you personally choose to do ritual beyond that is up to you, although it's recommended to invite in only goodly inclined spirits, and instead of thanking them at the end, to ask that there be peace or friendship between you.

The basic ritual outline is:

- Burn something cleansing
- Light candles
- Invite Powers
- Pray
- Magic/meditation/body of ritual
- Offerings
- Divination
- Closing

Unlike most neopagan traditions, Fairy Witchcraft does not usually cast circles; sacred space is created through intention and repeated ritual use of one area or occurs naturally. When circles are used in rituals, the fundamental purpose is very different from the idea of creating a boundary or containing energy; rather the circle in Fairycraft is used to temporarily shift a space to the Otherworld.

Some people may find that simple and short is what works best for them in ritual – perhaps a quick prayer and offering, then a moment to look for an omen – while others may prefer a more elaborate and involved ceremony. An elaborate ritual would start with the area being ritually cleansed with the broom and then the altar would be set up for the ceremony. The spirits would be invited in with prayer, chant, or song, and the body of the ritual can include anything from spiritual journeywork or magic to seasonal rites. Offerings should be made and then divination done – of whatever sort you are most adept with – before the spirits are parted with. It is not uncommon during fairy rituals for time to shift in odd ways so you should not attempt a more involved ritual if you have limited time to work with. Short or long the ritual begins when the spirits are invited in and ends when they are acknowledged and parted with. A basic ritual might be as simple as a weekly offering of milk to the house fairy.

More ecstatic ritual will include singing, drumming, or dancing, all of which can raise energy, which may be offered to the spirits being invited. Burning candles or incense can also be offerings, as can jewelry, art, poetry, alcohol, milk, cream, and food; I do personally recommend not using meat as a general offering as this can attract the wrong sort of Otherworldly being, but for specific situations it's alright.

Another difference with fairy ritual is the fluid nature of the experience. Many people find that the energy that comes in ritual brings feelings of peace or comfort that may make the person want to stay in ritual. You might enter a ritual with one intention and find yourself drawn to another, or you may intuitively decide to change your focus part way through. Fairy is a liminal place and tapping into its energy, even in the most basic ritual, can have unforeseen effects. The witch must learn to trust his or her instincts in guiding a ritual and allow the experience to flow as it needs to.

Offerings and 'Elves'

In November of 2014 I taught several classes about the Daoine Maith (Good People) at the Changing Times, Changing Worlds conference in New England and one of the most common questions I was asked was about offerings. I thought it might be helpful here to talk a bit about the most common traditional offerings and the way they have been historically understood. Regular offerings to the Good Neighbors should be an essential part of any Fairy Witch's practice.

Why do we offer to the Gods and daoine sidhe? When the sons of Mil defeated the Tuatha De Danann the land was divided between the two, with the Milesians taking what was above the earth and the Tuatha De taking what was beneath it. But soon the Gaels found that their cows would not give milk and their crops would not grow, because the Tuatha De destroyed all the produce. The sons of Mil reached an agreement with the Dagda that they would offer a portion of their harvest in exchange for the friendship of the Tuatha De. After that time, offerings of milk and grain were made to the Gods and later to the daoine sidhe as well, to ensure a good harvest and abundant milk. Today we offer to receive blessing and luck in our lives.

Probably the most common offering is milk. We see multiple references to this in many sources, both to the milk being offered regularly and to it being given as type of appeasement when disruptive behavior is occurring. Evans Wentz in the seminal *Fairy Faith in Celtic* countries tells us: *'Milk was set at night for piskies [pixies], who had been knocking on walls and generally making nuisances of themselves.'* (Evans Wentz, 1911). It should be noted that if you begin to make regular offerings and then stop it will bring you bad luck; an anecdote is related in *Fairy Faith in Celtic Countries* of a woman who always poured out an offering to the fairies when milking her cow. However, after becoming Christian she stopped the practice; one of her cows was then taken by the fairies, prompting her to resume making the offerings (Evans Wentz, 1911). Yeats mentions that offerings of milk were left out on windowsills for the Good People to ensure good fortune (Yeats, 1888).

Offerings to the Other Crowd may also include butter and bread, left either by a door or at the roots of a fairy tree, and small amounts of anything a person is drinking could be poured out onto the ground as an offering (Estyn Evans, 1957). The custom of pouring out a bit of your drink is something I was familiar with from my grandfather and is easily done. Milk that was spilled on the ground belonged to them and milk might sometimes be thrown in the air for the fairies or butter buried near a bog as an offering to them (Evans Wentz, 1911; O hOgain, 1995). On the quarter days, a heavy porridge was offered by pouring it into a hole in the earth and bread was offered, which could be left out or tossed over the shoulder (McNeill, 1956; Sjoedstedt, 2000). It was also once the custom to bleed live cattle on Beltane and offer the blood to the fairies (Estyn Evans, 1957). The most common modern offerings are milk, cream, bread or other baked goods, honey, and portions of meals, as well as alcohol.

Finnish and Germanic cultures also offered to these spirits, usually called elves. In Finland it was believed that elves could be helpful in many domestic areas and appreciated offerings of food, alcohol, coins, silver, or gold (Nenonen, 2014). Guerber tells us that:

> *In Scandinavia and Germany sacrifices were offered to the elves to make them propitious. These sacrifices consisted of some small animal, or of a bowl of honey and milk, and were known as Alf-blot.*
> (Guerber, 1908).

As Jacob Grimm tells us:

> *The hill of the elves, like the altar of a god, is to be reddened with the blood of a slaughtered bull, and of the animal's flesh a feast prepared for the elves... [a]n actual âlfabôt.*
> (Grimm, 1883).

The alfablot, or ritual offering to the elves, was a practice throughout the Norse lands that occurred roughly at the end of the harvest season and was celebrated by the entire family unit (Gundarsson, 2007). Offerings to the elves traditionally included milk, ale, silver, and crafted metal (Gundarsson, 2007).

And, for those who are curious, the Good Neighbors do not actually consume the physical item but rather its essence. Evans Wentz refers to this as the astral portion, as he says: '*Apparently the piskies only drank the 'astral' part of the milk.*' (Evans Wentz, 1911). Robert Kirk calls it the 'pith' or 'quintessence' (Kirk, 1893). In practical terms what this means is that the physical item remains, but the fairies take its substance, so that afterwards what's left can be discarded or left for animals.

Regular Offerings

It is important to make regular offerings to the Fair Folk, the liminal Gods and the ancestors. The Gods can be offered to any time, as can the ancestors; in Irish tradition Friday is the day when the fairies are most active and so this day is a good one to make offerings to them. It is believed that on this day they have the most influence over everything (Wilde, 1887).

For modern practitioners of Fairy Witchcraft there are many resources, including several very good books written at the turn of the 20th century by people trying to preserve the old folk ways in writing. One of my favorites of these is Lady Wilde's *Ancient Legends, Mystic Charms,* and *Superstitions of Ireland,* written in 1887. Although far from being a scholarly work, this slim book offers a treasure trove of folk beliefs and practices, which can easily be applied to modern spirituality. In this section, I want to look at several quotes from a section of that book and show how those particular portions still apply today and shape the practice of Fairy Witchcraft.

> *The Sí passionately love beauty and luxury, and hold in contempt all the mean virtues of thrift, and economy. Above all things they hate the close, stingy hand that gathers the last grain, and drains the last drop in the milk-pail, and plucks the trees bare of fruit, leaving nothing for the spirits who wander by in the moonlight. They like food and wine to be left for them at night, yet they are very temperate; no one ever saw an intoxicated fairy.*
> (Wilde, 1887)

Looking at this section we immediately see one of the key principles of modern Fairy Witchcraft, the idea of generosity of spirit. Fairies hate those who take everything for themselves and who leave nothing at all for the spirits. They are not greedy themselves, but have an expectation that a certain portion is due to them as their share, especially the last portion, as Lady Wilde says, the last drop, the last grain, the last fruit. An offering of food and drink should be left out for them at night, and because they love beauty and luxury, it should be of good quality. I have found it best to have a special set of dishes for this purpose – in this case I have a very nice china tea cup and saucer, which serve to hold both food and drink. As the above passage illustrates it is never wise to try to scrape by with the cheapest option when it comes to fairies, although they seem to expect only the best of what we can afford.

> *But people should not sit up too late; for time fairies like to gather round the smouldering embers after the family are in bed, and drain the wine-cup, and drink the milk which a good house-wife always leaves for them, in case the fairies should come in and want their supper.*
> (Wilde, 1887).

In the old days the fairies would gather around the family's hearth fire to socialize and enjoy the offerings left for them, often wine or milk. In a modern context not many of us have a hearth fire, and certainly few of us still keep the fire burning at all hours, so it is necessary to decide what part of your house represents its 'hearth'. Some people choose the kitchen as a modern alternative to the old hearth fire, while others might decide the living room reflects the idea of a family gathering place. If you have a fire place that can also be a good area to leave offerings for the fairies.

> *A vessel of pure water should also be left for them to bathe in, if they like.*
> (Wilde, 1887).

My grandfather, who came from Cork, used to say that fresh water had to be left out for the fairies to wash their babies in;

Wilde echoes this sentiment in her writing as well although she doesn't say what the water is for. Whatever they actually do with the water, it does seem to be appreciated, so it is a good idea to at least occasionally leave out some clean water for the fairies. Although be cautious in dumping it out afterwards, as it is an offense to the fairies to simply toss water on the ground without first warning any invisible spirits that might be nearby that the water is coming. A simple 'Beware' or 'Water coming' should suffice.

> *And in all things the fairies are fond of being made much of, and flattered and attended to.*
> (Wilde, 1887)

My own experience echoes this; fairies like being given attention and hate being ignored. This can be a double-edged sword as once you begin to honor them they may not appreciate a change of heart on your part. It is best before embarking on the path of Fairy Witchcraft, or any honoring of the fairies, to be certain you are willing to continue with it.

> *...and the fairy blessing will come back in return to the giver for what-ever act of kindness he has done to the spirits of the hill and the cave. Some unexpected good fortune or stroke of luck will come upon his house or his children; for the fairy race is not ungrateful, and is powerful over man both for good amid evil.*
> (Wilde, 1887)

Fairies are well known to reward those who help or honor them and this reward most often takes the form of good luck. In our cynical age it is easy to dismiss any turn of good fortune as mere coincidence, but for those who honor the fairies this luck may be very odd or unusual indeed, or wholly unexpected. Keep an open mind and watch for synchronicity and omens that might indicate fairy involvement. Fairies reward those who are naturally generous and who give without expectation, as Lady Wilde says:

> *Therefore be kind to the wayfarer, for he may be a fairy prince in disguise, who has come to test the depth of your charity, and of the generous nature that can give liberally out of pure love and kindliness to those who are in need, and not in hope of a reward.*
> (Wilde, 1887)

So it is best to simply make a habit of generosity, and let the results come as they may. She who gives generously for the sake of giving is often rewarded; she who gives seeking reward does not find one and may indeed be punished for greed.

> *If treated well, the fairies will reveal the hidden pot of gold, and reveal the mysteries of herbs, and give knowledge to the fairy women of the mystic spells that can cure disease, and save life, and make the lover loved.*
> (Wilde, 1887)

In some cases beyond luck the fairies may reward a person with special knowledge, particularly of healing and magic. Some people say that Biddy Early was rewarded in this way, as was the Brehan Seer. Good luck is more likely, but certainly special knowledge is always also possible, if one is open to it.

> *But some small courtesies they require. Never drain your wine-glass at a feast, nor the poteen flask, nor the milk-pail; and never rake out all the fire at night, it looks mean, and the fairies like a little of everything going, and to have the hearth comfortable and warm when they come in to hold a council after all the mortal people have gone to bed.*
> (Wilde, 1887)

Make the fairies welcome in your home by making your home inviting to them. Leave out a bit of food and drink and a warm environment that seems friendly. Be open and friendly and share freely of what you have – these are the ways to welcome Fairy into your life.

Rituals for Moon-Days

We honor two phases of the moon with ritual and acknowledge another with a small action and prayer. This is because the liminal or transitional phases of the moon are important times for us to connect to the energy of Fairy that we are honoring in both our religion and our witchcraft practice.

The moon figures strongly in magic as well; during the waxing moon the energy is right for all things relating to growth and increase and so we might focus our efforts on anything we wish to nurture or draw more of. It was during this phase that branches from trees like hazel and willow would be harvested, romantic unions made, and healing charms prepared (McNeil, 1956). There is a folk belief told to me by my friend Allison Joanne that I also try to follow, that cutting your hair on the full moon will make it grow faster. On the full moons we hold ritual to connect to the Otherworld and to honor the liminal Gods of the light half of the year, the Lady of the Green Wood and Lord of the Wild Wood.

The waning moon is a time of decrease and banishing. On the dark moon all other plants are harvested, and the earth is turned for planting, and anything that needs to be cut back is trimmed now (McNeil, 1956). At the dark moon our ritual honors the deities of the dark half of the year, the Queen of the Wind and Hunter.

Additionally we always acknowledge the new moon that is the first sliver of moon visible in the sky after the dark moon. It is an old tradition in many parts of the Ireland and Scotland to acknowledge the first sighting of the new moon in some way. Some people nod their heads or bow to the moon and it's considered lucky to touch silver as well, usually the coins in your pocket or rings you are wearing. When I see the new moon, that first thin sliver of silver crescent in the sky, I kiss my hand to the moon and turn the silver on my hands, saying:

Hail to you, new moon tonight,
You are always the light of the poor,
However well you find me tonight
May you find me seven times better next month,
New moon of blessings.[25]

Rituals for the full and dark moon are fairly simple, as most rituals in Fairy Witchcraft are. I prefer to do any serious meditation work or journeywork on the dark moon if possible, and will often do so during my ritual. The full moon is a time for magic and for renewing any alliances or fulfilling any pledges I've made, perhaps to make a specific offering at that point. I renew my dedication to the path on the full moon closest to Imbolc each year.

I begin by burning some rosemary for purification. For both types of ritual I will light a couple candles and ask whatever Powers I would like to join me to be welcome. I may pray at this point or recite some appropriate poetry. Any magic or meditation is done at this point then offerings are made. If I am going to do any divination it will happen after the offerings. Then I ask that there be peace and friendship between myself and the Good Neighbors, and thank the Gods and ancestors.

Rituals for Holy-Days

Celebrating holidays in Fairy Witchcraft, like celebrating the moons, is not a big, complex process. It's mostly about simple ways to acknowledge the turning of the seasons as we move from one to the next, and honoring the different energies that flow at each time. In the modern world, for so many people, this flow is lost. We don't notice the subtle changes in the earth from one holy day to the next – but they are there. Even just taking the time to really, truly look around and observe the world and what it is doing at each point is vitally important.

Samhain

Burn juniper, light candles Invite in your ancestors, all goodly inclined spirits, and the Queen of the Wind and Hunter.

On your altar light a white candle for your ancestors. Say something like:

Ancestors of blood, flesh, and bone,
Family gone but not forgotten,
Friends that I had known
In life and remember now
Witches who are kindred souls
Spiritual brothers and sisters,
Kindred hearts with kindred goals
We honor you on this Samhain night.

Light a candle for the Fair Folk and say:

Spirits of the Otherworld,
Spirits of the Land,
May there be
Only friendship
Between us now
And forever.

Light a third candle for the liminal Gods (or two separate ones if you prefer) and say:

Queen of the Wind, Hunter of the Winter Wood,
I welcome your return to the mortal world

As summer passes into shadow and
The old year goes to its rest once again
May you bring with you renewal and rebirth.

Offerings of apples and bread are made. Do divination for the year to come. Perform closing words or actions.

Winter Solstice

Move clockwise around your ritual space hitting the ground with your birch branches to symbolically drive away negative spirits.

Burn juniper, rosemary, or a cleansing incense; light candles; invite Powers.

An appropriate prayer might be:

I have news for you:
The stag bells,
Winter snows,
Summer has gone;
Wind high and cold,
The sun low,
Short its course
The sea running high;
Deep red the bracken
Its shape lost,
The wild goose has
Raised its accustomed cry;
Cold has seized
The birds' wings
Season of ice
This is my news[26]

For the main body of the ritual I often honor my house spirits with an offering of porridge with a large pat of butter on top, but songs to welcome back the sun, or other similar activities would also be good.

Offerings should be of cookies and milk, or other appropriate foods. Do divination. Perform closing words or actions.

Imbolc

Burn something cleansing; light candles; invite Powers.

An appropriate prayer might be:

The new growth emerges from the earth
The spark of life dances in winter
Queen of the Wind, let us see
The blessing in the darkness,
Hunter, let us see
The strength in our hearts
To endure the cold.

Wash your head, hands and feet with blessed water to cleanse yourself for the coming year.

Do a dedication/renewal if appropriate. Offerings of any dairy product are good. Divination should be done. Closing words or actions.

Spring Equinox

Burn something cleansing; light candles; invite Powers.

Say something like:

As day and night are equal
As dark and light are balanced
May I find the way
Walking between two worlds.

Choose three colors of yarn or thread that represent energy or goals you want to nurture in the coming six months. Weave a bracelet from three colors of thread to either wear or keep on your altar. Offerings of milk and eggs are appropriate. Divination. Closing words or actions.

Bealtaine

Burn something cleansing; light candles; invite Powers.

Say:

On this day of blessing we welcome back summer
We welcome back the Lady of the Greenwood
We welcome back the Lord of the Wildwood
With joy and with laughter, with love and with pleasure
We honor the Light you bring, May you bless us
Bless our homes and bless our families
Bless our lives and bless our prosperity,
Bless our land and bless all within it.

Light a small fire in your cauldron using either herbs or wood. Pass an object you wish to bless as a talisman through the fire. When the fire is entirely extinguished, keep the ashes to use in blessing charms. Offerings of milk, bread or, if you are feeling adventurous, whiskey may be made. Divination should be done, Closing words or actions.

Summer Solstice

Burn blessing incense or rose petals; light candles; invite Powers.

A good prayer might be:

Midsummer has arrived again
A night of mischief merry
When the woods are filled
With spirits earthly and airy
When much magic is afoot
And the Fair Folk do abound
Riding out on fine horses

Traveling from elfin mound.
May we join in the celebration
On this the shortest night
And may no harm come to us
As we dance beneath starlight.

Midsummer is an ideal time to seek out new allies and make new friends in the Otherworld. This can be done through journeywork, meditation, or extending offerings to new Powers. This is also a good time to remember to honor your land spirits.

Offerings of cake or bread with honey work well. Do divination.

Closing words and actions.

Lúnasa

Burn something cleansing; light candles; invite Powers.

A good modern Lunasa prayer:

Bless my harvest
Bless my home
Bless my work
Bless all I own
Gods above
Gods below
Gods of power
That I know
Bless my reaping
What I've sown
Bless the harvest
That I've grown

Magic or meditation can form the body of ritual. Offerings of any baked goods are appropriate.

Divination can be done. Closing words or actions.

Fall Equinox

Burn something cleansing; light candles; invite Powers.

An appropriate prayer might be:

As dark and light are balanced
My harvest is in full swing
I gather together what I've grown
As I watch birds on the wing
Flying south as winter comes
In summer's final nights
I honor the effort I've put out
And honor all goodly wights.

If you made a bracelet charm at the spring equinox you might consider burning it now to symbolically harvest your intentions. Otherwise, you could write your achievements on a piece of paper and burn it.

Offerings should be done. Divination. Closing words or actions.

Rites of Passage

Like any other religious practice Fairy Witchcraft has a selection of rituals and prayers for different rites of passage. These are by no means required of anyone to practice, but can add depth to a person's spiritual life.

Birth

When a woman is in labor she should make sure her hair is loose and that any knots or ties in her clothing are undone, the old belief being that such knots will make the birth more difficult. She or anyone who is with her assisting might say this prayer:

As leaves fall from a tree,
So may the child slip easily from her womb,
By the strength of the firm earth,

By the power of the flowing sea,
And of the shining Sky that covers all;
Firm earth and flowing sea,
And shining sky that covers all.

Baby Blessing

This is what might be called 'Morgan's All-Purpose Baby Blessing' in that it's the one I use as a witch or as a Druid. It was previously published in my book *Where the Hawthorn Grows*, but this version is specifically tailored for use in this tradition.

The child should be dressed in something beautiful and meaningful for the family. If indoors, a small altar can be created with a bowl of sacred earth and a bowl of blessed water, as well as something representing a tree. If outdoors, the altar should be prepared in front of a tree and contain the bowls. The officiant should walk three times sunwise around the altar holding the infant and chanting:

Once for the Lady of the Greenwood,
mother of the people of peace,
We go around the path of the sun, beloved one
Once for the Lord of the Wildwood,
Guardian of all living things,
We go around the path of the sun, beloved one
Once for those who have gone before,
We go around the path of the sun, beloved one
To aid you from the Fairy-kin
To guard you from the Host
To aid you from the Fairy-hound
To shield you from the specter
To keep you under the mantle of the Fairy Gods
To shield you, to surround you,
To save you from powers that threaten
To fill you with blessed inspiration

Three times round we go
To wash you in inspiration.

The child should then be passed over the bowl of earth to the father, back across to the officiant, and then across a third time back to the mother. The officiant should then pick up the bowl of water and dipping their fingers in should drip water onto the child's forehead for each line of the following:

A little wave for your form,
A little wave for your voice,
A little wave for your sweet speech.
A little wave for your means,
A little wave for your generosity,
A little wave for your appetite.
A little wave for your wealth,
A little wave for your life,
A little wave for your health.
Nine little waves for you
By land, sea, and sky
In the names of the Gods of my people
the spirits of the Otherworld,
and the ancestors whose blood lives within you.

The remaining water should be poured out at the roots of a tree, offerings should be made of honey to the Powers invoked to bless the child, and the gathered family and well-wishers should feast and celebrate.

Dedication[27]

If you are certain that Fairy Witchcraft is the path for you then you can perform a ritual to dedicate yourself to following it and to the liminal Gods. There is no need for a ritual to dedicate to honoring the fairies, as that is less about words than it is about actions; however, the charm pouch you will make for this dedication ritual does also symbolize your honoring of those spirits. It should be noted that even if you do work with other people or a group this ritual is always done alone and on your own. Fairycraft has no initiation within a group setting, only private dedication between yourself and the Gods. For this reason you cannot say that you are initiated into this path, only that you are dedicated to it.

Make a small pouch out of green silk or cloth that you can wear around your neck. In the pouch place some earth from your home, nine herbs for luck, blessing, protection, health, power, wisdom, magic and at least one of the nine should be a fairy plant. Add tokens from three animals whose qualities you want to draw to yourself. Add three drops of your own blood on a small piece of cloth and a lock of hair. Tie the pouch closed and place it on your altar.

Cast a circle to open a portal to the Otherworld and call in your ancestors, the goodly-inclined fairies, and all of the liminal Gods. Light a white candle and say:

Gods of the Otherworld,
Everlasting joy
Is in my soul
With good intent.
And for every gift of peace
You bestow on me.
My thoughts, my words,
My deeds, my desires
I dedicate to You.
I make offerings to You,
As I ask for Your protection,
And Your guidance,
Shield me tonight,
And walk with me each day.

Make an offering of oats, honey, and milk to each of the Powers you have invoked. Then pick up the pouch and say:

I am a Witch
I respect the fairy folk
I honor my ancestors,
I worship the Old Gods
From this day forth
I walk the path
Of Fairy Witchcraft
Joyous and solemn
Foolish and wise
Wild and gentle
I am a Witch.

Put the pouch on. Close the circle. It is done. You should wear the pouch every day, but especially whenever you are doing any magic.

Marriage

A true Fairy marriage requires only that the oath of fidelity be made. However, in our modern world marriage is a bit more complicated than that. If you're looking for a legal wedding Fairy Witchcraft style then you can really do as suits you, but you might choose to add in this prayer and have the groom prepare a small pouch containing a coin, an acorn, flax seed, a bit of cloth, and some earth from a place that is special to the couple as a gift for the bride. The bag is a charm to bless the new couple with abundance, prosperity, and security as they begin their new life.

I learned this wedding prayer in Irish from a Druid friend of mine named Niall, but I'll give it here in the English. I have used this in weddings I officiated at in the past as a blessing for the couple:

May the strength of oak protect you,
May the gift of grain sustain you,
May the stillness of earth ground you,
May the rhythm of the rain soothe you,
May the voice of the wind teach you,
May you dance the spiral of life together,
Your bonds forged in the sacred fires of your hearts.

Death

Death is always difficult for the living to come to terms with, although it is said that to die to this world is to be born into the Otherworld. In Fairy Witchcraft we see death here as re-birth there and rather than a cause for mourning we try to celebrate the person's life. Cremation and the keeping of ashes on ancestral altars are common, but there is no strict requirement. At the time of death or soon after this prayer, based on material from the *Carmina Gadelica*, can be said:

Since we know the soul is immortal–
At the time of yielding the life,
At the time of pouring the sweat,
At the time of offering the life,
At the time of shedding the blood,
At the time of balancing the beam,
At the time of severing the breath,
At the time of loosing the soul,
Peace upon the soul's journey;
As it returns to the land from whence it came,
Peace upon the soul's journey,
As it returns from whence it came.
And may the Hunter, gentle and kindly,
Lord of the winter woods and guide across worlds,
Take possession of the beloved soul,
And shield it home,

Oh! Where it may rest and be reborn again.

Many witches choose to be buried or cremated with at least some of their ritual tools; others may be passed on. How you handle a funeral or memorial service is really up to you, but it would be in keeping with the beliefs of the religion to emphasize joy and happy memories as much as possible. Death is only the beginning of a new life, from our point of view.

Generally it is best to wait about six months after death before the new ancestor is added to the ancestor altar or called on, but you may find that in the months immediately following death the person's spirit seems especially active. Messages can be relayed to the dead by writing them down and burning them; what is burned in our world is manifested in the Otherworld and it was an old Celtic custom to write down letters to the dead on wood and burn them in funeral pyres in order to get them to the ancestors (Freeman, 2000).

Modern Experience

My father and I were extremely close, especially after I moved out of my parents' house. I talked to him every day on the phone and saw him quite regularly; we had a very similar sense of humor and liked many of the same things. He died when I was 25 years old, a few days before his 57th birthday.

My father was a very spiritual man, but also very Catholic. He was part Cherokee, and would often talk about the more mystical things his mother and grandfather had passed on to him as well as the Irish culture passed down from my grandfather which included respecting the Good Folk, but he had also been in seminary to be a Jesuit priest. Probably the best anecdote I can give to sum up my dad's approach to religion was that after my daughter was born (shortly before he died) he insisted I have her baptized, even though I was pagan and the church wouldn't do it, as he said: 'If it means us going in there ourselves and baptizing her out of the holy water font by the entrance when no one's looking.' He felt it was that important and so he was going to see it done, and the details be darned.

His special animal was the owl, and I had never seen a live one except in a zoo until after he died. When he was alive they would come to him, either live ones or images of them, as omens of good things about to happen. After he died I started seeing them too, and I have always felt that each time (there have been four so far) it was my father trying to convey a message to me.

About four months after he died I started having experiences where I would wake up with the overwhelming sensation of someone standing over me. It was always jarring and frightening. As soon as I would sit up in bed, startled, the figure would disappear and I would immediately realize it had been my dad. Finally, after the fifth or six morning, this happened; I had a talk with him and explained that I appreciated his concern and liked knowing that he was still watching over me, but that he was freaking me out each morning. After that it stopped, although he sometimes relays messages now in dreams – not to me but through other people.

And he'll always get his coffee just the way he likes it, black and thick enough to stand a spoon up in it, every time I make an offering to my ancestors.

The dead never really seem to leave us until they are ready to, and our ancestors often stay to keep an eye on us.

Chapter 8

Stones, Plants and Animals

Have a mouth of ivy and a heart of holly.
– Lady Wilde, Irish Proverb

The story goes that a group of boys was heading up the mountain for a holiday bonfire, carrying peat to add to it, when they started to argue about the Good People. One boy was adamant that the siogai existed, but the other boys teased him and called it all nonsense. They asked him if he'd ever seen the fairies himself and he admitted he hadn't – but insisted that his grandmother had and he believed her stories. As they walked they argued and the other boys teased the one who believed unmercifully, until they all grew tired of walking and decided to stop and rest for a little bit.

They sat down in the grass and as they sat a strange red-haired boy appeared and joined them. No one knew who he was, but he asked them if they were going to the bonfire and when they said they were he stood up and joined them going up the mountain. He led the way, moving so quickly that they all had to run to keep up and by the time they reached the summit where the people where gathered they were gasping and exhausted, although the red-haired boy was not even out of breath.

The bonfire was built and the boys enjoyed the dancing and revelry, watching the red haired stranger leap through the flames and move among the villagers as if no one noticed him at all. After a time the boys grew bored and decided among themselves to go to Gortnashee, so they snuck off, none noticing what had become of the strange boy. As they went the air grew dark, so that they could barely see where to place their feet, and just as they were debating turning around they saw lights flickering in the distance, which they thought might be torches – although the boy who believed in the Good People worried they were fairy lights. A sudden strong wind suddenly came up, pulling their hair and stealing their hats, and before they knew what was happening the doubting boys had been turned, to a one, into horses and the Fair Folk were leaping on their backs delighted. Only the boy who had insisted they were real the entire time remained a boy, and he was seated on a fine white horse in the middle of the procession.

The poor boys – now in the forms of horses – were ridden to Gortnashee and then all across Ireland by the Fair Folk, spurred to run at a furious pace and given no rest until the dawn broke in the morning sky. Only then did the boys wake up – back in the form of boys – and found themselves lying underneath the fairy thorn at Gortnashee, all aching and exhausted from the night's exertions. All except the boy who had always believed in fairies, who with shining eyes related a beautiful dream he'd had of passing the night riding with the Good People.

All the boys gave up their doubt after this and never again said a word but that fairies were real, and everything they spoke was kind and respectful about them. And in time a friendship grew between the boys and the fairies.

– Retelling of a traditional tale, based on Oíche na Féile Eion from the book *Faery Nights*

The Use of Stones and Crystals for Healing[28]

In modern neopaganism and the new age movement using crystals and stones for healing is an almost ubiquitous practice. In Fairy Witchcraft, however, we look less at the modern practices around the use of stones and more at the older folk beliefs and practices in the Irish and closely related Celtic cultures. These are very pragmatic in nature and don't rely on spending huge amounts of money to buy rare precious stones, but rather on using what is locally available to the witch. Or, put another way, it isn't about what you can buy, but about what you can find in rivers and streams and in the ground around you.

When we look at folk practices from Ireland and Scotland we can find evidence of the use of stones and crystals for several purposes. We do look at the older archaeological evidence to understand the history of stones and crystals being used. It is these more recent practices that we look to for our own understanding of how to use stones and crystals in our magic.

Archeologists excavating Iron Age graves in England have found balls of rock crystal (clear quartz, I think) wrapped in bands of silver, or less often gold or bronze (Fraser Black, 1894). It is unknown what these were used for, whether they held a magical significance or were purely decorative; however, similar balls of crystal were used in later periods in the belief that they could ensure victory in battle or bring healing. In Glenlyon there was such a wrapped crystal that was called either 'Clach Bhaui' (powerful stone) or 'Clach Buaidh' (victory stone); similarly another such stone is called the 'Clach-na-Bratach' (stone of the standard) (Fraser Black, 1894). The Clach-na-Bratach belongs to Clan Donnachaidh. It was found by the clan chief in 1315 on the way to battle and was believed to be a good omen; as such it was consulted before every following battle and carried into the fray until 1715 when an internal flaw was seen (Fraser Black, 1894). After that it was retired from battle, but people believed that this stone also had healing powers especially for cattle. Another named stone in Scotland is the Clach Dearg (red stone), which is reputed to have the ability to charge water with healing power, following a certain ritual process (Fraser Black, 1894). Some say the Clach Dearg was originally part of the wand of an arch Druid, while others believe it was imported from the east (McNeill, 1956). In Keppoch the MacKenzies are said to possess a healing stone associated with the holy well of Brighid, which would be dipped into the water from the well for a healing charm (McNeill, 1956). The majority of these stones range in size from one inch across to an inch and a half, and most are mounted with silver bands.

When used for healing purposes we see both the above described crystals and also references to similarly sized but more oval or egg-shaped crystals being used. Curing stones might be used in one of two ways, either dipped in water, which was then drunk or otherwise used on the afflicted person or animal, or rubbed directly on the injured or ill body part. When used in water the stone was often wrapped with silver bands, usually four, with a loop for hanging or wearing; the crystal would be dipped into water, while the person chanted:

Let me dip thee in the water
Thou yellow, beautiful gem of power!
In water of purest wave,
Which Bridget didn't permit to be contaminated.
In the name of the Apostles twelve,
In the name of Mary, Virgin of virtues,
And in the name of the High Trinity
And all the shining angels,
A blessing on the gem,
A blessing in the water, and
A healing of bodily ailments to each suffering creature.
(Fraser Black, 1894)

For my own purposes I prefer to use a slightly different version:

Let me dip you in the water
You beautiful gem of power!
In water of purest wave,
Which Brighid kept pure.
A blessing on the gem,
A blessing in the water, and
A healing of bodily ailments
to each suffering creature.

Besides these crystals there is also a history of the use of other types of stones for healing. Both saints Columba and Fillan were said to possess 'curing stones', all white, which could heal when dipped in water that was then consumed. Saint Molio also possessed such a healing stone, but that one was green and was rubbed on the afflicted area to effect a cure; interestingly this stone is also said to grant victory in battle and is alleged to have belonged to Clan McDonald. Many churches had healing stones on their altars, and some could be found next to holy wells. These might resemble the body part they were best used to heal, such as the eye or heart (McNeill, 1956).

In Scotland there are also accounts of several named curing stones: Clach Leigh (medicine stone) was a green tinged stone, Clach Ruaidhe (red stone) was used for healing cows by rubbing it on the udder, and the Clach Spotaiche (spotted stone) was a piece of black basalt that was used in healing horses (Fraser Black, 1894). Whenever these or similar healing stones were used by rubbing a charm might be said at the same time, such as this one from Strathspey:

This day well, next better,
After that nothing but a scar
(Fraser Black, 1894)

A similar use can be seen in Irish lore, but instead of a known curing stone, all the person needs is to find three green stones in a running stream, after midnight but before dawn, and in silence. These stones are rubbed on the afflicted body part, from the top down towards the feet, while the person chants:

Wear away, wear away,
There you shall not stay,
Cruel pain – away, away
(Wilde, 1896)

Less commonly curing stones might be used for other purposes. A type of curing stone was one used for curing infertility. One example from Scotland is an egg-shaped quartz that was passed from one 'wise woman' to another upon death, and was used by placing the stone in running water (preferably south-flowing) in which the woman would then wash her feet (Fraser Black, 1894). Stones of rock crystal would also be drilled to create a hole and then worn to protect against the evil eye (McNeill, 1956). The famed stone of the Brahan Seer was a white stone with a hole in it, said to be a gift of the fairies, through which he could divine the future (McNeill, 1956).

These stones are described as being worn and carried in the pocket, but may also receive special care. One curing stone was said to be kept in a locked chest, wrapped in linen and then wool (Fraser Black, 1894). Another was said to be wrapped in cloth, kept in a silk bag, and wrapped in a napkin (Fraser Black, 1894). In many cases they were passed down in families as an heirloom, and if they were well known people might come from great distances away for the offered healing.

Generally the type of stone didn't matter, as they appear to be simple river stones or pebbles, but often the color seemed to be significant, with white as the most common, and black, green, and red also described. While color is the most common descriptive point there are specific examples in Scottish Charms and Amulets of certain types of stone used for certain purposes as well:

'Iron stone' (possibly hematite or iron ore): Cure all, held
Basalt: Used to heal horses
Jet: Curing diseases
Shale/coal, holed: Protecting animals from witchcraft
Fossilized shells: arthritis
Flint: General ailments
Amber: General healing, cure for snake bites, used for people and animals

Quartz: Heal all, victory, cures infertility

Trees and Herbs

Plants of all sorts play a vital role in folk magic and entire books have been written focused on this subject. For our purposes we will look only at a selection of trees and herbs that are strongly associated with the Other Crowd and are commonly used in Fairy Witchcraft.

Fairy Trees

Birch

Latin names: Betula pendula, Betula pubescens, Betula lent, Betula alba
Folk name: Lady of the Woods
Birch can be used to drive out negative spirits, particularly from animals or people, by hitting the afflicted person or animal with birch twigs. It was also an old custom to walk your property line at the Winter Solstice with a birch bough, beating the ground to drive away any malicious spirits (Mac Coitir, 2003). Brooms were often made using birch twigs, and can still be made this way to make use of the banishing qualities of the tree. In cases where the evil eye is suspected, a red ribbon can be tied around a birch to remove the curse. Birch is protective, especially of children and babies; an old Scottish tradition is to place a birch sprig above a baby's cradle, or to make the cradle itself from birch for protection (Mac Coitir, 2003). Although birch is used in our form of witchcraft it is generally considered a protection against fairies, and to hang birch over a doorway will keep fairies away from an area; this of course is why it is hung over cradles, to prevent the Fey Folk from taking the baby.

Birch oil can be used in cleansing baths to remove large amounts of negative energy. A few drops added to the bath water is sufficient. In a situation where the cleansing properties are desired, but a bath isn't feasible, the person's head might be dabbed with the oil or they might be lightly brushed or struck with birch twigs for the same effect.

Birch also has strong connections to love magic and is often used for that purpose. Giving a birch sprig to a lover is a symbol of devotion and the old Maypoles were often made of birch saplings (Mac Coitir, 2003). Birch in both the Ogham and Elder Futhark runes represents (among other things of course) new beginnings, birth, and new growth making its use in love and fertility magic logical.

In Fairy Witchcraft the birch belongs to the Queen of the Wind.

Blackthorn

Latin name: Prunus spinose

Blackthorn, like hawthorn, is both a tree of the fairies and one that can protect against them, and it is generally unwise to molest a lone thorn tree. Blackthorn provides sloes, which can be used to make gin and the wood is commonly used in making walking sticks and shillelaghs. Despite this pragmatic usefulness, blackthorn is often seen as an unlucky tree, strongly associated with fairies and witches (Mac Coitir, 2003). The blackthorn has its own fairy spirits, the lunantishees, who are known to punish anyone who harms the tree (Mac Coitir, 2003).

In Fairy Witchcraft the thorns from this tree are used in magic, particularly for cursing and binding. The wood of the blackthorn is the preferred material for the witch's staff or walking stick.

Elder

Latin name: Sambucus nigra

The elder was also seen as significant. This tree was associated with protection and also with the faeries (McNeill, 1956). It has long been a prohibition in many forms of witchcraft to burn elder wood; I personally only ever use the flowers and berries. The entire tree has a reputation for misfortune and places where it grows are said to be cursed (Mac Coitir, 2003). Several curses are associated with the use of elder including an especially cruel one to draw out the length of a woman's childbirth (Mac Coitir, 2003). The elder seems to have a contradictory nature, being used for healing and making musical instruments like flutes, but also used in cursing; it is said that striking a living thing with an elder twig will cause illness or death (Danaher, 1964). In contrast the bark of the elder is one of the seven herbs of power listed by Lady Wilde (Wilde, 1991). Elder in folklore is strongly tied to witches, fairies, and a female spirit called the 'Elder Mother' (Mac Coitir, 2003).

Elder is also used in protective charms against witches, with the person required to ask the tree first before taking any of its wood. This may reflect that often what can be used for ill can also protect against what it can cause.

Elm

Latin name: Ulmus campestris, Ulmus glabra

Folk name: Elven

Known to be a tree that is often associated with elves, it earned the folk name Elven (Cunningham, 1985). Elm is protective and is also associated with fertility; an old charm to cure impotence was to write the afflicted man's name on a twig of elm and hit him with it (Mac Coitir, 2003).

Hawthorn

Latin name: Crataegus monogyna

Folk names: Whitethorn, May tree, May bush

Both the blackthorn and hawthorn were dual natured, seen as both protective and also as fairy trees that could be dangerous (O Suilleabhain, 1967). The hawthorn is probably the most well known of the fairy trees, and a solitary hawthorn alone in a field was usually left alone, as it is believed that to damage or destroy such a tree would bring down the wrath of the Fair Folk on the person. It is considered terribly unlucky to bring hawthorn flowers inside or to burn the wood (Mac Coitir, 2003). Those who disrespect the tree are in effect disrespecting the Other Crowd themselves and that is never a good idea.

Hawthorns are sometimes used as clootie trees with rags representing prayers, offerings, and spells tied on the branches and around the trunk. The tree may also be planted for protective purposes near a home, and it is not uncommon for offerings of milk for the Good Neighbors to be poured out at the roots of a hawthorn.

The hawthorn has many associations with Beltane; some people celebrate the holiday in May when the hawthorn's flowers bloom. It may have been significant in part because of its flowers and berries, with the white flowers representing the hope of spring and its red berries the fulfillment of the harvest (Estyn Evans, 1957). Hawthorn is considered one of the seven herbs of great power by Lady Wilde, along with elder tree bark, ivy, vervain, eyebright, groundsel, and foxglove (Wilde, 1991).

Oak

Latin name: Quercus petraea, Quercus robur, Quercus alba

Oak has a strong association with the Fair Folk and it is said that oaks have their own spirits. Sacred fires are often made of oak and oak can be carried as a talisman. Drawing a circle around yourself with an oak stick or wand is said to be protective, especially against the Fey (Mac Coitir, 2003). Oak is also symbolic of physical strength and fertility and acorns are often used in magical charms for these purposes.

The oak in Fairy Witchcraft belongs to the Lord of the Wildwood.

Rowan

Latin name: Sorbus aucuparia

Folk names: Mountain ash, quicken

Rowan is a tree of contradictions, being both a fairy tree and also a protection against them. A very old protective charm against malicious witchcraft and fairy magic is to tie rowan twigs into a cross with red thread, as the saying goes: 'Rowan and red-thread put witches to their speed.' Rowan berries were also strung and worn as a necklace by some women in Scotland for protective purposes (Mac Coitir, 2003).

The rowan was seen as a lucky wood and was considered to be the best protection against negative magic; it is also considered by some to provide the berries that are the food of the aos sidhe (McNeill, 1956). Rowan planted by the front door of the home protects the house and rowan wood was preferred for making the sacred fires that cooked the little cakes for folk ceremonies (McNeill, 1956). On Beltane sprigs of rowan were hung above cradles, churns, and doorways to protect them from fairy influence (Wilde, 1991).

In Fairy Witchcraft the rowan belongs to the Lady of the Greenwood.

Willow

Latin names: Salix caprea, Salix cinerea, Salix sepulcralis, Salix alba

Willow is a tree of good luck. There are many folk beliefs around this tree that are similar to rowan – it is said to be protective against malicious magic and the evil eye and to guard milk from bad spirits (Mac Coitir, 2003). Unlike Rowan, however, it is considered inappropriate to burn willow, and some folklore prohibits bringing it into the house lest it prevent eggs from hatching (Mac Coitir, 2003). Willow is best gathered during the waxing moon when it is said it will remain flexible after drying, and in Fairy Witchcraft it is often used in healing charms because of its association with the moon, water, and its flexible nature. Interestingly, the tree itself does contain a compound that is used in modern medicine as a painkiller.

Yew

Latin names: Taxus baccata, Taxus baccata fastigiata

The yew was renowned for its long life and was one of the trees about which it was thought that trimming would bring bad luck (Danaher, 1964). In modern folklore the yew is associated with death, but this is not likely to have been how the ancients saw it as the modern view is largely based on the fact that yews are often found in growing in church graveyards. Its presence in graveyards was also blamed for its poisonous qualities as it was said the tree absorbed the emanations of the corpses buried around it (Mac Coitir, 2003). Despite these qualities, yew was also considered both lucky and protective and branches were used to ward off malicious magic and for divination (Mac Coitir, 2003).

In Fairy Witchcraft the Yew belongs to the Hunter.

Fairy Herbs

> *Similar to savin is the herb known as 'selago'. Care is taken to gather it without the use of iron, the right hand being passed for the purpose through the left sleeve of the tunic, as though the gatherer were in the act of committing a theft. The clothing too must be white, the feet bare and washed clean, and a sacrifice of bread and wine must be made before gathering it: it is carried also in a new napkin.*
>
> – Pliny the Elder

I think consideration should be given to the ritual Pliny describes in connection to harvesting selago, which is echoed by Lady Wilde in her book *Irish Charms, Mystic Cures & Superstitions* in relation to other herbs. This seems to reflect a genuinely older practice that herbs for magical use had to be gathered in a special ritualistic way, without the use of iron; all herbs in Fairy Witchcraft practice are gathered this way, although I don't worry so much about the color of my clothing or whether my feet are bare. I do make sure no iron is used and that an offering is left behind for the plant, and that the act is done with reverence

Clubmoss

Latin name: Huperzia selago
Folk name: Club-moss

> *Similar to savin is the herb known as 'selago'... The Druids of Gaul have pretended that this plant should be carried about the person as a preservative against accidents of all kinds, and that the smoke of it is extremely good for all maladies of the eyes.*
> – Pliny the Elder

Club-moss is a perennial evergreen herb that is found in Ireland, Britain, and in Europe (Huperzia Selago, 2013). Club-moss is recommended to protect the bearer from accidents, and Pliny connects it to healing of the eyes. Interestingly, as the first excerpt above from Pliny shows, even in pre-Christian times there was a prohibition against gathering club-moss with an iron tool, which is a common belief in later folklore as well. Gathering an herb with magical properties using iron is believed to destroy the plant's power; given that in the folk charm from the *Carmina Gadelica* given below, club-moss is used not only to protect against accidents, but also against fairies, who are also averse to iron, one might see a connection there as well.

Charm of the Club-moss
The club-moss is on my person,
No harm nor mishap can me befall;
No sprite shall slay me, no arrow shall wound me,
No fay nor dun water-nymph shall tear me.

Cowslip

Latin name: Primula veris

Folk names: Fairy cups, marsh marigold, key flower, Our Lady's keys (Cunningham, 1985; Grieve, 1995)

Cowslip, a type of primrose, grows in wet, marshy areas, it flowers from April to June and, because it is in the buttercup family, the yellow flowers resemble large buttercups (Foster & Duke, 2000). Care is needed in handling the plant, however, as it can be an irritant and may cause blistering (Foster & Duke, 2000).

Magically it can ward off unwanted visitors and reveal that which is hidden as well as making the possessor more attractive (Cunningham, 1985). It is also associated with the powers of success, victory, and overcoming obstacles. Finding, collecting and keeping this flower is especially potent against gossip and slander, but also acts as an overall blessing for the possessor.

Carmina Gadelica has a charm that mentions a plant it calls 'fairywort' – earnaid in Scottish Gaelic – that has always interested me. There is much debate as to which plant fairywort would be, with cowslip, flax, and foxglove being the leading suspects. I tend to favor cowslip as the most likely and so am proceeding under that association. Interestingly one online Scottish dictionary listed an alternate of earnaid as airneag, which means blackthorn sloe, although I am not strong enough in the language to have any certainty about that connection.

The Fairy Wort 162

I will pick the fairy wort,
With expectation from the fairy bower,
To overcome every oppression,
As long as it be fairy wort.
Fairy wort, fairy wort,
I envy the one who has you,
There is nothing the sun encircles,
But is to her a sure victory.

Pluck will I the honored plant
Plucked by the great Airmed, who knows all herbal wisdom,
To cast off me every tale of scandal and flippancy,
Ill-life, ill-love, ill-luck,
Hatred, falsity, fraud and vexation,
Till I go in the cold grave beneath the sod.

Foxglove

Latin name: Digitalis purpurea
Folk names: Fairy fingers, fairy petticoats, fairy thimbles, fairyweed (Cunningham, 1985)
Foxglove is strongly associated with the Fey Folk as its many folk names show. It is also an herb of witches and in some parts of Scotland it is called witches' thimbles instead of fairy thimbles (McNeil, 1956). Foxglove in small amounts has medicinal uses, but is deadly in large amounts. Foxglove is a traditional remedy for those suffering from elf shot (Mac Coitir, 2008).

Foxglove belongs to the Lord of the Wildwood in Fairy Witchcraft.

Ivy

Ground ivy is a plant that is commonly found in many areas and is often used for landscaping. It's a hardy plant that remains green even in winter, and is sometimes used for decoration during the winter holidays; the shape of the leaf gives the plant one of its folk names, which is 'catsfoot'.

Historically the entire plant was gathered in late spring for medicinal uses that included diuretics, indigestion, a mild stimulant, and externally as an astringent and treatment for tumors (Grieve, 1995; Foster & Duke, 2000). It can also be used in an infusion as a mouthwash for gargling to treat a sore throat and externally applied to open sores (Grieve, 1995). Great caution is needed with ivy, as there have been cases of severe allergic reactions in some people when the plant is consumed;

the plant is also toxic to horses (Foster & Duke, 2000). Ivy has a strong bitter taste and was used to clarify beer by the Saxon English before the widespread use of hops; however, the plant is toxic and can cause difficulty breathing in humans (Grieve, 1995; Foster & Duke, 2000).

Magically ivy is associated with fidelity and love, protection, and good luck (Cunningham, 1985). I personally associate it with binding things together, magically, and also with hiding or obscuring things based on ivy's ability to cover things. It can be useful in the magic of glamour or when you need to misdirect someone's perception, especially to protect yourself. Looking at its use in folk charms we can also say that magically it can be used for prosperity and increasing possessions.

This a charm to increase prosperity using ivy from the *Carmina Gadelica*. This is an interesting one because it specifies a time period 'a year and a day' that it seems the charm is meant to stay in effect. With that being the case I would recommend making this a seasonal tradition and refreshing the charm at the same time each year. Below is my own version:

The Tree-Entwining Ivy 158

I will pluck the tree-entwining ivy,
As Lady plucked with her gentle hand,
As the Powers of life have ordained,
To put milk in udder and gland,
With speckled fair female calves,
As was spoken in the prophecy,
On this foundation for a year and a day,
Through the hearts of the Gods of life,
and of all the Powers.

Rose

Latin name: Rosa

Roses planted near a home attract fairies (Cunningham, 1985). In

Fairy Witchcraft we use rose both for blessing and for very gentle cleansing. The flowers can be used in love magic and the stem and thorns can be used in cursing and protective magics.

In Fairy Witchcraft the rose belongs to the Lady of the Greenwood.

Rosemary

Latin name: Rosemarinus officinalis
Folk name: Elf leaf (Cunningham, 1985)
Magically Rosemary is used for protection, exorcism, purification, healing, and love (Cunningham, 1985). Rosemary can be added to bath water to purify or cleanse yourself and is burned to rid an area of negativity. It was historically burnt in sickrooms to cleanse out the lingering energy of the illness. A witch may also choose to burn rosemary before spells or other magical acts to cleanse the area. It is grown to attract the presence of fairy beings (Cunningham, 1985). Rosemary can also be worn to protect against enemies.

Yarrow

Latin name: Achillea millefolium
One of my favorite fairy herbs is yarrow, and it has a variety of magical uses. It is associated with love, beauty, protection, and healing. Its scientific name is achillea millefolium, from its association with the Greek epic hero Achilles; he was said to use it to treat injured soldiers on the battlefield. It is sown into clothing as a magical charm and worn to impart its qualities to the wearer (Wilde, 1991). In another folk charm ten yarrow leaves are plucked, one is given to the Fey as an offering and the other nine are placed in the person's sock for protection (Wilde, 1991). The plant can be found wild in fields and near roads growing about 3ft tall with clusters of tiny white flowers (Foster & Duke, 2000). Yarrow can also be grown in gardens and is easily dried by hanging.

There are several different folk charms that feature yarrow and can be used by modern Fairy Witches.

The Yarrow 163

I will pluck the yarrow fair,
That my face shall be more gentle,
That my lips shall be more warm,
That my speech shall be more chaste,
My speech will be the beams of the sun,
My lips will be the juice of the strawberry.
May I be an isle in the sea,
May I be a hill on the shore,
May I be a star in the waning of the moon,
May I be a staff to the weak,
I can wound every man,
No man can wound me.

The Yarrow 164

I will pluck the yarrow fair,
That more brave shall be my hand,
That more warm shall be my lips,
That more swift shall be my foot;
May I be an island at sea,
May I be a rock on land,
That I can afflict any man,
Yet no man can afflict me.

In spell #153, you would want to find the yarrow and then recite the charm while harvesting a small amount. Be careful while harvesting to do no unnecessary harm to the plant and take only what you need. Also when these charms talk about cattle and milk, I tend to see them in a non-pastoral setting as metaphors for abundance and plenty. The lines can stand as they are if you take this approach, or if you prefer you could adjust them

Spell of Counteracting 153

I will pluck the gracious yarrow
That Brighid plucked with her hand.
The gracious Lady of Healing
Came with her lovely face above me.
Bright Brighid came towards me,
With milk, with substance, with produce,
With female calves, with milk product.
In names of the Gods of life
Supply me with your abundance,
The blessings of the Lady of the well
To put milk in udder and gland,
With female calves, with progeny.
May you have the length of seven years
Without loss of calf, without loss of milk,
Without loss of means or of dear friends.

Incense Blends

All incense blends are basic recipes. Ground the herbs together in your mortar and pestle then add oils. Either burn on a specialized charcoal disc or mix in finely cut wood shavings/dust (I prefer apple) as a base.

Cleansing

Herbs: Peppermint, juniper, rosemary, rose, sage
Oils: Birch, rose, lemon

Blessing

Herbs: Oak, willow, hazel, elm, elder flower, apple, vervain, lavender, rose, and mistletoe
Oils: Pine, frankincense, and hyssop

Honoring the Fey

Herbs: Yarrow, rose, lavender, marigold, poppy, ginger,

dandelion leaf
Oils: Vanilla, and patchouli

Honoring Ancestors

Herbs: Mullein, rosemary, flax, Irish moss, copal, oak
Oils: Frankincense, myrrh, amber

For the Lady of the Greenwood

Herbs: Rose, witch hazel, willow, clover, mugwort
Oils: Amber and vanilla

For the Lord of the Wildwood

Herbs: Oak, maple, copal, patchouli, lemongrass
Oils: Dragon's blood and sweet patchouli

For the Queen of the Wind

Herb: Birch, nettle, mullein, flax, agrimony
Oils: Pomegranate and myrrh

For the Hunter

Herbs: Dandelion, fern, cloves, thistle, apple
Oils: Cinnamon and pine

Psychic Empowerment

Herbs: Mugwort, mullein, cedar, peppermint, poppy, copal
Oils: Sandalwood, frankincense, myrrh

Uncrossing

Herbs: Rue, hyssop, cinquefoil, devil's shoestring, frankincense, myrrh
Oils: Lemon and sage

Shield and Armor Incense

Herbs: Mullein, devil's shoestring, mandrake, galangal, blessed

thistle, agrimony
Oils: Black pepper, allspice, dragon's blood

Modern Experience

One of the strangest things that ever happened to me, Good Neighbor-wise, occurred while I was writing *Pagan Portals – Fairy Witchcraft*. My friend owns an occult store and I often will go and help her out there. One day while my friend was in a tarot reading and I was minding the counter I looked down and realized my wedding ring was gone. Right off my finger gone. I looked everywhere, even though it wasn't loose enough to fall off on its own. When my friend was done she helped me look. We could not find that ring anywhere. I was, suffice to say, freaking out and I had no idea how I was going to tell my husband – even for me saying, 'Fairies stole my wedding ring off my hand', sounds pretty extreme.

Fast forward nearly a year. I had a replacement ring. The book was written and about to be published. The store had been searched and cleaned and re-arranged and honestly the ring had been given up as a lost cause (pun intended).

And then one day when my friend was alone in the store she went back into her tarot reading room, which also has a small altar along the back wall, and there on the floor in front of the altar, sitting upright on its edge was my wedding ring.

Because sometimes they take things.

And sometimes they give things back.

Chapter 9

Magic

We gave ourselves up in old times to mythology, and saw the Gods everywhere. We talked to them face to face... Even today our country people speak with the dead and with some who perhaps have never died as we understand death; and even our educated people pass without great difficulty into the condition of quiet that is the condition of vision.
– W. B. Yeats, *Celtic Twilight*

A good many years ago a showman came to the town of Dingle and performed many tricks there. At one time he'd eat a dozen straws and then pull yards of ribbon from his throat. The strangest thing he showed was a game-cock that he used to harness to a great log of wood.

Men, women, and children were breaking their bones, running to see the cock, and he a small bird, drawing such a great weight of timber. One day, when the showman was driving the cock on the road toward Brandon Mountain, he met a man with a bundle of fresh grass on his back. The man was astonished to see crowds running after a cock dragging one straw behind him.

'You fool,' said the people, 'don't you see the cock drawing a log of timber, and it would fail any horse to draw the like of it?'

'Indeed, then, I do not. I see the cock dragging a straw behind him, and sure I've seen the like many a time in my own place.'

Hearing this, the showman knew that there was something in the grass, and going over to the man he asked what price was he asking for the bundle. The man didn't wish to sell the grass, but at last he parted with it for eighteen pence. The showman gave the grass to his boy and told him to go aside and drop it into the river. The boy did that, and when the bundle went down with the stream the man was as big a fool as another; he ran after the cock with the crowd.

That evening the same man was telling a friend how at first he saw the cock with a straw behind him, and then saw him drawing a great log of wood. 'Oh, you fool!' said the friend, 'there was a four-leafed shamrock in your bundle of grass; while you had the shamrock it kept every enchantment and devilment from you, and when you parted with it, you became as big a fool as the others.

– Curtin, 1895

Historically we know that the ancient Irish had many distinct types of magic workers, of which Druids and witches were only two. Generally, and in broad terms, witches were those who worked baneful magic; the word for witch in Irish, bantúathaid, is related to the word túath in its meaning of wicked or perverse, going against the right order. Druids were known to be supporters of the right order and community. Modern practitioners of Fairy Witchcraft blend these two historic threads as well as more modern folk magic practices to create their own magic.

Sympathetic magic, or using one thing to represent the thing you want to change or influence, is a major type of magic used in Fairy Witchcraft. To this end we may use a variety of methods, from drawing an image of something to using a small thing to represent a larger one, like using a business card in a prosperity spell to represent the business itself. We also do much with poppets. Poppet is simply an archaic word for a small figure of a person; poppets can be made of cloth, wax, clay, or salt dough. I like to choose the material based on how permanent I want the poppet to be, so that the ones I make for my family to use for healing and other such purposes are made of cloth, stuffed with the person's old clothes and hair, while those that are for strangers and are very temporary may be simple wax or salt dough. Once the poppet is made, preferably including an item from the person to increase the connection, I will ritually name the poppet after the person, and then it is ready to use. When I'm done with it, assuming I am, I un-name it and take it apart.

Another very common type of magic we use is the creation of charm bags. I am very fond of making charm bags for a variety of purposes. To make a charm bag I simply place an assortment of herbs and items that are focused on achieving my goal into a bag and then charge the bag with my intent. A money charm bag, for example, may contain pine needles, mullein, oak, cinnamon, bay leaves, and a few silver coins. A protection charm might consist of a black bag containing oak, thorns from a rose, agrimony, sage, and some nettles. The bag is then usually carried or placed in a way that is symbolic of your goal; planting a charm bag that you want to represent growing your prosperity is one example. I have a charm for travel protection that hangs from the rearview mirror of my car, to give another example.

Spoken charms are also often used, with the power of the witch's word being channeled through the spoken spell to create the effect they want. Candles are more often used for rituals and prayers, but may be used in magic sometimes as well. A Fairy Witch is not limited in what types of magic they use or what methods they prefer, although the general focus is on folk magic.

Although much of the magic we use is spontaneous and organic we also draw heavily on older folk magic that has been preserved. These often come down to us in the form of chants and spoken charms, occasionally with actions or herbal components. I'm going to include a variety of examples to give readers and idea of what I mean:

St. Gall's Incantations

There are a collection of healing charms that include some fairly overt pagan references found in the *Thesaurus Palaeohibernicus* grouped under the heading of St. Gall's Incantations. Below I'm including three of the originals and my own modified and updated versions because I find them very useful in my own practice.

St. Gall's Incantation #1

The first in the St. Gall's series is a healing charm for dealing with a 'thorn' which might apply to a thorn or splinter imbedded in the flesh. As with many such folk charms it mentions specific actions to be taken with the charm, in this case butter is to be used; the charm is chanted over the butter and then the butter is spread around – but not touching – the afflicted area.

Against a Thorn

Nothing higher than heaven, nothing deeper than sea. On account of the powerful speech said by Christ on the cross, remove from me the thorn, a thorn pointedly-cleaves, wounds, destroys, in me there is an opening on account of striking, an unlucky appearance, frightening, a fire springs, very fierce Goibniu's knowledge, Goibniu's attention, Goibniu's powerful attention overcomes it.

Put the charm on the butter not into the water and smear around the thorn, around its circumference and not on the cut nor on the affliction, and if there is no thorn in it will fall out the second spike from the front of his head.

Against a Thorn – Modern

Nothing is higher than the sky
nothing is deeper than the sea
by the power of the people of skill
remove from me the thorn, the biting thorn
very fierce the smith's skill,
The smith's attention,
The smith's powerful attention overcomes it!'

St. Gall's Incantation #2

The second charm in the St. Gall's series is directed specifically at healing diseases of the urinary tract, which I would say might include kidney issues or urinary tract infections.

Against Urinary Disease – Original

I am saved from sudden illness of urine, I am saved from salmon envy, I am saved from birds, skillful flocks, spell-workers.

Display this always where you habitually go to pour out: 'Publish to all nations, the end.'

Against Urinary Disease – Modern

Against urinary disease
I save myself from disease of the urine
Cunning birds will save us
Bird-flocks of witches will save us

This is always written in the bathroom: 'Spread the word to all nations.'

St. Gall's Incantation #4

The fourth charm in the St. Gall's series is a general healing charm that can be used for illnesses or injuries. It calls on the Irish pagan God Dian Cecht; however, if you prefer not to call on him you do have the option of modifying the charm to either call on another appropriate deity or one of the liminal Gods.

Against Various Ailments – Original

I save the dead-alive. Against belching, against javelin-cord, against unkind swelling, against iron wounds, against an edge fire burned, against a point a dog bites. Let him be sharply-red, three nuts withering, believe that three sinews are woven. I strike his illness, I overcome wounds lamenting of blood. Let it not be an endless swelling. Let him be healthy, pouring on I invoke the salve left by Dian Cecht with his family that what it is poured on be whole.

Set this always in your palm full of water while washing, and thou put it in your mouth, and use the two fingers that are next the little-finger in your mouth, each of them separate.

Against Various Ailments – Modern

I save those who are suffering.
Against flu and indigestion,
against wounds and injury,
against swellings and tumors,
against bleeding caused by iron,
against burns from fire,
against wounds from dogs,
against flesh that withers:
three nuts that give wisdom
three sinews that weave healing.
I strike against disease, I vanquish bleeding
let the illness not be chronic.
Let wholeness come to that where Diancecht's salve goes.
I put my trust in the salve which Diancecht left with his family
that it makes whole what it touches.

This next one is modified from Lacnunga CXXXIV-CXXXV and is meant to be used to cure elf shot, the sudden cramp, pain, or illness believed to be caused by an invisible fairy arrow. Elf shot is something that any Fairy Witch should be familiar with, both in how to use it and how to cure it. This chant is one basic method for curing it, and can be used for elf shot from a variety of sources including elves, dwarves, witches, and even deities.

For Elf-Shot, or any Sudden Stitch

Mix feverfew, nettle that grows out of a house, and plantain; boil in butter. Spread over the afflicted area and say:

Loud were they, loud, loud, when they rode over the mound,
they were fierce when they rode over the land.
Shield yourself now that you may escape this evil.

Out, little spear, if you are here!
Stood under linden, under a light shield,
where the mighty women readied their power,
and screaming they sent spears.
I will send back to them another,
a flying dart against them in return.
Out, little spear, if you are here!
A smith sat, he forged a knife,
little iron; strong wound.
Out, little spear, if you are here!
Six smiths sat, they made war spears.
Out, spear, not in, spear!
If a bit of iron is here,
Witch's work, it shall melt.
If you were shot in the skin, or were shot in flesh,
or were shot in the blood, or were shot in bone,
or were shot in a limb, may your life never be torn apart.
If it were dwarves' shot, or it were elves' shot,
or it were witch's shot, now I will help you.
This your remedy for dwarves' shot, this your remedy for elves' shot;
This your remedy for witch's shot; I will help you.
It fled there into the mountains...no rest did it have.
Be whole now! Gods help you!

Charm Against the Evil Eye

The *Carmina Gadelica* has a series of charms that all deal with the evil eye, that is the curse laid upon a person by another who wishes them ill or looks upon them with envy. This one is my personal favorite and I have modified it slightly to be more pagan; I love the imagery it presents and find it reminiscent of the Song of Amergin. Anyone who has read the works of the witch Sibyl Leek may recognize the middle portion of the charm, the 'power over' section, as she made use of this portion in an unhexing spell in one of her books, clearly drawing on the

Gadelica as a source. That same section has also appeared in a young adult novel by L. J. Smith called *The Power*; all of which could be seen as a testament to the power and flexibility of the *Carmina Gadelica* charms, as well as their intrinsic value.

Exorcism of the Evil Eye 141

I trample upon the evil eye,
As the duck tramples upon the lake,
As the swan tramples upon the water,
As the horse tramples upon the plain,
As the cow tramples upon the grass,
As the host tramples the sky,
As the host tramples the air.
Power of wind I have over it,
Power of wrath I have over it,
Power of fire I have over it,
Power of thunder I have over it,
Power of lightning I have over it,
Power of storms I have over it,
Power of moon I have over it,
Power of sun I have over it,
Power of stars I have over it,
Power of earth I have over it,
Power of sky and of the worlds I have over it,
Power of the sky and of the worlds I have over it.
A portion of it upon the grey stones,
A portion of it upon the steep hills,
A portion of it upon the fast falls,
A portion of it upon the fair meadows,
And a portion upon the great salt sea,
She herself is the best instrument to carry it,
The great salt sea,
is the best instrument to carry it.
In the names of the Three of Life,

In the names of the Gods of Skill,
In the names of all the Ancient Ones,
And of the Powers together.
– Excerpted from *By Land, Sea, and Sky* by the author

This next charm may be particularly useful in dealing with gossip and malicious rumors as well as unwanted romantic attentions. The charm references a thread 'going round you' so I would suggest using an actual physical thread or cord to wrap yourself or the person the charm is being said for. After saying the charm keep the thread somewhere safe. As always, alter any nouns or pronouns as needed if saying the charm for yourself.

Counteracting the Evil Eye 142

An evil eye covered you,
A mouth spoke of you,
A heart envied you,
A mind desired you.
Four have done you harm
Man and wife,
Youth and maiden;
Three will I send to thwart them,
I appeal to Danu,
Mother of the aos sidhe,
I appeal to Brighid,
Healer, Poet and Smith,
I appeal to Manannán,
God of wave and sea,
And I appeal to the Otherworld,
To all helpfully inclined spirits.
If it be a man that has done you harm,
With evil eye,
With evil wish,
With evil passion,

May you cast off each ill,
Every malignity,
Every malice,
Every harassment,
And may you be well for ever,
While this thread
Goes round you,
In honor of the Powers of Life,
And of the Gods above.
– Excerpted from *By Land, Sea, and Sky* by the author

Charm #146 is a cure for the evil eye. It is used to remove the negative energy that has been sent from a person. This is probably one of the best general charms to remove the evil eye.

Charm 146
I arise to make the charm,
Against the keen-eyed men,
Against the peering-eyed women,
Against the slim, slender, fairy-darts,
Against the swift arrows of fury.
Two made on you the withered eye,
Man and woman with venom and envy,
Three whom I will set against them,
Three gods of great power.
Four and twenty diseases in the constitution of man and beast,
Powers scrape them, Powers search them, Powers cleanse them,
From your blood, from your flesh, from your gentle bones,
From this day until your days on earth are done.

This is one I wrote to protect my home and family during a hurricane, although it can be used during any kind of storm.

Prayer of Protection Against Storms

Protect, O mighty Gods,
Myself and everything near me,
My family and my home,
May we be safe through the storm,
May we be safe through the storm
From every gust and gale,
From every flood and downpour,
From every tide and storm surge,
Through the day and darkest night,
Through the day and darkest night.
From every tree whose roots give way,
From every branch that breaks,
From every danger seen and unseen,
Shield us and keep us from harm
Oh, shield us and keep us from harm!

Blessing of the House 45

Bless this house,
From site to stay,
From beam to wall,
From end to end,
From ridge to basement,
From balk to roof-tree,
From foundation to summit,
Foundation and summit.
(Carmichael, 1900)

Cursing

Although sometimes seen as a controversial topic, there is ample evidence of cursing in every culture I have ever studied the folk magic of. Cursing might be used as a form of justice, such as we see in the use of satire, or as a punishment and often could only be removed by meeting specific conditions. In Fairy Witchcraft we see no moral issue with cursing if the witch feels it is justified and necessary[29].

Curse tablets are one type of curse that we find evidence for across the Celtic world. These lead or pewter tablets would be carved with a very specific description of who was being cursed and why, what the person wished to happen, and which Powers were being invoked (Green, 1997). The existing examples often seek to use the curse to exact justice in a situation, such as retribution for a theft. These curse tablets are usually written in Latin and Gaulish and are found at healing shrines and temples (Green, 1997). Curse tablets can still be used today, by writing down the curse and putting it into a swamp or lake, or beneath a walkway, although I'd recommend using wax.

Poppets are also seen in cursing magic just as in healing. One method used a poppet of wax or clay that would have pins or thorns driven into it (McNeill, 1956; Estyn Evans, 1957). The figure would be made to resemble the intended recipient of the curse, filled with sharp objects, and then placed in running water or burned (McNeill, 1956). This type of curse is intended to create a wasting illness or general ill health in the victim (Estyn Evans, 1957). In a similar type of cursing an ear of corn would be named after the person to be cursed and buried so that as the corn decayed the person would suffer (Wilde, 1991).

McNeill mentions the use of a witch-bone, a hollow deer bone with a bog oak ring around it through which blood was poured to ill-wish a person (McNeill, 1956). It was generally believed that to walk counterclockwise around a person or property could create a curse, particularly when combined with intent or a spoken curse. Finally, there is the practice of using stones to curse others. Saint Maodhog was said to have cursed two men by turning his sandals around to the left three times against them; and a very simple, but enduring belief was that a person could be cursed by turning a stone in your hand counterclockwise against them (O hOgain, 1999). One specific method is to hold a cursing stone in your left hand and turn it around three times counter clockwise against a person (O hOgain, 1999). Another is to use a spoken curse against someone while building a stone cairn against them, which Carmichael calls a cairn of malediction (Carmichael, 1900).

In Celtic culture there are many methods of cursing, and an equal number of protections and counter-curses. Cursing itself was seen as a serious action and a breach of social order, but could also offer power to the powerless. There was a deeply rooted belief that to set a curse without a good cause would bring negative repercussions on the curse caster, which can be seen in the beliefs around satire. In a modern setting using any of these curses should only be done with great caution and after great thought is given to the need and risk.

Norse cursing has its own distinct flavor that makes for an interesting subject to look into. Possibly one of the most well-known types of Norse curses, at least within Heathen groups, is the nidstang. A nidstang, or nithstong (scorn-post) is a 9ft pole carved with runes that curse a specific person and topped with a severed horse's head or skull (Pennick, 1993). The basic idea of such a pole was to disturb or enrage the landvaettir in such a way that they turned the luck of the target of the curse bad (Pennick, 1993). Nidstangs could also be used to desecrate an area, in which case they were called alfreka, meaning to drive away the elves, with the understanding that to drive away the landspirits was to make the area spiritually impotent (Pennick, 1993). Nidstangs were also combined with curse-runes, where certain runes such as thurisaz were carved a specific number of times in order to negatively affect the targeted person. In *Egil's Saga*, Egil places a curse upon the king and queen who have made him an outlaw by erecting a nidstang and reciting a verbal curse to deny the spirits of the land rest until they force the king and queen out of the country.

Modern digital nidstangs containing a written curse exist online and have been used for such diverse purposes as cursing negative groups that have co-opted heathen symbols to cursing the perpetrators of the 9/11 terrorist attacks. Such a digital curse would work in a different fashion from the traditional poles, unless the caster believes there are digital or virtual wights that can affect the person and aims at turning them against the target. I would say that this type of modern nidstang is aimed more at making a bold public statement or damaging the target's reputation.

Part of the ritual associated with the nidstang includes spoken or chanted curses and we also see these separately, sometimes used with the invocation of runes. In the Curse of Busla, for example, we see both types as Busla attempts to use witchcraft to save her condemned son by cursing the king, after confronting him as he slept. First she chants a long curse, which includes the verse:

Shall trolls and elves and tricking witches,
shall dwarfs and etins burn down thy mead-hall—
shall thurses hate thee and horses ride thee,
shall all straws stick thee, all storms stun thee:
and woe worth thee but my will thou doest
(Hollander, 1936)

When the king is still not willing to fully pardon her son, she continues with the final and most powerful verse:

Come here six fellows: say thou their names:
I shall show them to thee unshackled all.
But thou get them guessed as good me seemeth,
shall ravening hounds rive thee to pieces,
and thy soul sink to hell-fire!
(Hollander, 1936).

After reciting the curse she draws specific runes in a pattern. Only after this does the king relent and Busla removes the curse she has just laid on him.

Similar to this we see another type of curse that was spoken, but relied on verbally invoking specific runes. One version of this type of curse that I find particularly entertaining to study is the fretrunir, or farting curse. A father and son in Iceland were executed in 1656 after being convicted of using this curse against a pastor and a local girl in what is known as the Kirkjubol witch trial. Part of the chant that they used was said to be:

> *...which are to afflict your belly with great shitting and shooting pains, and all these may afflict your belly with very great farting. May your bones split asunder, may your guts burst, may your farting never stop, neither day nor night. May you become as weak as the fiend, Loki, who was snared by all the gods.*
> (www.worldsstrangest.com/mental-floss/the-mystical-farting-runes-of-iceland/)

Clearly the intent is not only to humiliate the person with excessive gas, but also to cause serious health problems relating to the stomach, intestines, and bowels. Another version from the Galdrbok includes the runes used and invokes an array of Heathen and Christian Powers, clearly with the same intent as the Kirkjubol example:

> *I write you eight áss-runes, nine naudh-runes, thirteen thurs-runes — that they will plague thy belly with bad shit and gas, and all of these will plague thy belly with great farting. May it loosen thee from thy place and burst thy guts; may thy farting never stop, neither day or night; thou wilt be as weak as the fiend Loki, who was bound by all the gods; in thy mightiest name Lord, God, Spirit, Shaper, Odhinn, Thorr, Saviour, Frey, Freyja, Oper, Satan, Beezlebub, helpers, mighty God, warding with the companions of Oteos, Mors, Notke, Vitales.*
> (Lawless, 2010)

There are also examples of rune staves used for cursing, generally by carving the runic symbol on an object such as a piece of wood or bone and then placing it in the path of the target. Several of these types of rune staves can be seen in the Museum of Icelandic Sorcery and Witchcraft, such as the killing rune, which is intended to kill livestock belonging to the target. Those who study runes in modern practice also have found that certain runes used on their own can be effective curses, generally aimed at disrupting a person's luck or negatively impacting things around them or their health.

Love Magic

Personally I'm not a fan of love magic, as I prefer my partner to be with me by choice. However, there is a long history of it in folk magic and it's really up to the individual practitioner to decide the ethics for themselves. Arguably we do a lot of non-magical things to try to win a partner too and some people may see magic as just another method to be used.

A brief skimming of the Strandagaldur (Icelandic Museum of Sorcery and Witchcraft) produces a rune stave designed to help a man win a girl's affections; he must carve the symbol on cheese and then get her to eat it. That particular rune stave, according to the museum, is from a centuries-old grimoire of Icelandic magic. Additionally the *Poetic Edda* tells us of two runes that could be used to win and keep a woman's affection:

> *That sixteenth I know, if I seek me some maid:*
> *to work my will with her:*
> *the white-armed woman's heart I bewitch,*
> *and toward me I turn her thoughts.*
> *That seventeenth I know, if the slender maid's love*
> *I have, and hold her to me:*
> *Thus I sing to her that she hardly will*
> *leave me for other man's love*
> (Hollander, 1962)

There was also a practice of carving runic love spells on staves or sticks in order to win a girl; although there is some speculation that these may simply be love letters, McLeod and Mees feel that the invocation of supernatural beings, such as trolls, places the staves solidly in the realm of love magic (McLeod & Mees, 2006). In *Egil's Saga* we see such a rune stave used with the intent to make a girl love a suitor, although instead it makes her sick. In another, more amusing, example a girl is given a drink with runes for love in it and apparently realizing this she gives the drink to a pig who then falls in love with the person who cast the spell (McLeod & Mees, 2006). In all of these cases the magic is intended to turn the woman's heart towards the man using the magic.

If we look at the Irish material, specifically the Brehon Laws and Senchus Mar, we find laws against a man using 'aipthi' (spoken or physical charms) to gain a wife. A quote from the *Senchus Mar* tells us:

> **A Woman to Whom Her companion Gives a Charm when Soliciting Her, so That He Brings Her to Lust**
> *i.e. when he is entreating her, it is then that he gives/utters the charms/spells to press his love upon her; i.e. bride price and éric-fine, according to the nature of the type of charm/spell; it was before entering the law of marriage that the charms/spells were given/uttered to her and it was in the law of marriage that they came to/against her (?)...and the smacht-fine applicable to the marriage contract from him for it, and bride price and honour-price and body-fine to her; and separation from him; or éric-fine, according to the nature of the type of charm/spell and her choice to her whether it is mutual separation that she will do or it is in the law of marriage that she will be.*
> (Borsje, 2012)

This is reinforced in the Brehon Laws where marriage through seduction by sorcery is listed as one of the acceptable reasons for a woman to divorce her husband (Kelly, 1988). It shows how seriously seduction by sorcery was taken that it was grounds for divorce for a woman, since the other reasons focused entirely on either failure of the man to provide her a child through assorted reasons or the man damaging her honor through slander or physical maiming. It also implies a belief that a man could effectively use magic charms or spells to seduce a girl into marriage against her own inclination.

In a tale that appears in various versions from the 8th through 12th centuries in Ireland we see a man going to Saint Brighid and requesting an 'epaid' (the singular form of aipthi, a spoken spell or physical charm) that will make his wife love him (Borsje, 2012). The saint provides what he has requested, either by having him sprinkle his wife with blessed water or by having him sain the house and bed with it when she is away, with the desired effect (Borsje, 2012). It is interesting to note that such actions and use of magic were clearly illegal in the law tracts, but this case is included in the story of the life of a saint. The result of this holy love magic for the man is a wife who loves him so much she cannot bear being parted from his side (Borsje, 2012).

There is also this from the *Carmina Gadelica*:

Love Charm 138

It is not love knowledge to you
To draw water through a reed,
But the love of him [her] you have chosen,
With his [her] warmth to draw to you.
Get up early on Sunday,
To the broad flat flag
Take with you Foxglove
And the Butterbur
Lift them on your shoulder
In a wooden shovel,
Get nine stems of ferns

Cut with an axe,
And three twigs of apple,
That have been found on the ground,
Burn them together on a fire,
And make them all into ashes.
Shake it over the heart of your lover,
Against the sting of the north wind,
And I will pledge, and warrant you,
That man [woman] will never leave you.

Modern Experience

As a witch it is important that we remember the power of our own words and spells. In order for anything we do magically to succeed we must truly believe it is going to succeed, but the flipside of that is understanding that magic is not a game. It has real world results and real world consequences.

When I was in high school I had a very wide range of friends, including several in their early 20s. One particular couple was married, but things had not been going well; at some point in an attempt to salvage the relationship they had decided to try having a child, but that wasn't working either. Finally they asked myself and a few of my other pagan friends if we could do a spell for them, and despite knowing the details we were young enough to think a baby was a good idea. So we did it. And sure enough she conceived. And equally sure enough as anyone with life experience could have predicted they were divorced before the ink was dry on the birth certificate.

That was the first time I understood that just because something seems like a good thing to do and you know you *can* do it, doesn't mean you should.

Now the flip side of that.

Many people don't like the idea of binding or banishing people, but sometimes such magic is a good thing. When I was 16 I was being stalked by a 26-year-old. It's a long story, but what matters is no adult would help me because he'd actually convinced people he was my boyfriend and that I was the one lying to avoid getting in trouble while saying things to me like we'd be better off dead together. And mind you I barely knew this man; I'd met him casually at a public social event once. He found out where I worked, where I lived, what my phone number was. I was utter convinced he was going to kill me. And so I banished him. With the small group I was working with at the time, I walked around our ritual circle with a broom, sweeping outwards and chanting: 'I am free, you are free, go away and leave me be.' And it worked, I never saw or heard from him again although I heard through the grapevine that he'd suddenly moved out of state.

And that was the first time I understood that sometimes what seems like a bad thing to do, isn't when it means ultimately making a choice between whose well-being matters more to me, and that sometimes one should take those actions that need to be taken.

Chapter 10

Dreaming and Meditations

Go not to the Elves for counsel, for they will say both no and yes.
Elves seldom give unguarded advice, for advice is a dangerous gift,
even from the wise to the wise, and all courses may run ill.
– J. R. R. Tolkien

'But Thomas, you must hold your tongue,
Whatever you may hear or see,
For if a word you should chance to speak,
You will never get back to your own country.'
– The Queen of Elfland in the Ballad of True Thomas

Dreams have long been understood as a way for different messages to reach us, not only from Gods but also from different spirits. The tricky thing with dreams is sorting out our own subconscious speaking from things outside us speaking. Learning how to discern one from the other is a slow process, but generally there are a few tips I use to separate out my own head from outside messages. Firstly I look at how I felt in the dream. There is – for me – always a feeling of awe or intensity that comes with this sort of communication in dreams that is absent in a regular dreams. I also look at the message itself; if it what I would expect or want to hear, I am pretty suspicious of it. The Gods and spirits don't, in my experience, show up to pat us on the back and say 'Atta boy' or tell us to do what we really want to do anyway. Of course in fairness most of my experience with dream communication is with angry land spirits who are trying to relay messages about how upset they are. It's not that dream communication will always be negative, far from it, but it will always have a purpose and that purpose isn't about feeding our egos, but about telling us something that the Power communicating with us feels we need to hear. I also find that dream messages are rarely straightforward; rather they often seem like riddles that have to be puzzled out. They can be highly symbolic, convoluted, or cryptic and usually require reflection to understand.

Intermediaries are any thing or other person who communicates a message to you. This can include everything, in my opinion, from casting lots to going to a seer. An intermediary is the middleman for the message. According to Tacitus, the ancient Germans divined the will of the Gods by casting lots, observing the movement of birds, and by watching special sacred horses. In seidhr the seidhrworker can act as an oracle to relay messages by going into a trance state; it may be that Irish practices like imbas forosnai and tarbh feis work along similar lines (although when seeking answers for yourself these may fall more into the direct communication category). In modern terms when we use Ogham, runes, or tarot for divination to know if an offering was accepted we are using an intermediary to communicate with the Gods. A person can train as a seer to interpret omens, lots of various sorts, and pass on messages to others as well. The thing to remember is that, just as with dreams, the messages received through intermediaries must be interpreted by you to be understood, and you are dealing with a message that has been relayed twice – once by the God to the intermediary and then again from the intermediary to you.

The final method I'd like to discuss here is direct communication. I personally think this method is more likely for people who do a lot of trancework or train for it, but the Gods can speak to anyone they want. This will be different for everyone, including everything from hearing it as a voice to seeing images or words, but is most likely to occur during trance or meditation[30]. Unlike in dreams you should have more awareness of what is going on, but as in dream communication there should be a sense of presence, of awe and intensity. Also, like with dreams, one of the ways I check the validity is whether I'm only hearing what I want to hear. Another way is to check, in the moment, to see if I can influence what is being said. If I can control the message or change what I'm being told then I know I'm just talking to myself. Now, that isn't to say you can't bargain, because you can – if a deity asks something from you that would be difficult or impossible, you can make a counter offer or refuse – but if you can directly influence the deity you think you are dealing with to say exactly what you want then it's your imagination.

Now the difficulties here are deciphering the meaning behind the message and being certain you know who the message is from. Neither of these is necessarily easy, which is why people used to train to be professional seers. For the modern pagan or heathen without access to a trusted expert opinion, discernment is key. Really take time to reflect on the message and what it could mean. Consider possibilities and look at the most logical meanings, and learn to trust your instincts.

Secondly, don't be afraid to question the source; just because they say they are deity X doesn't mean they are deity X. Over time you learn the 'feel' of different Gods by experiencing them in ritual and possibly through the various types of communication, but initially don't be afraid to question. Look at whether the deity is acting in a way that aligns with their mythology and whether the message aligns with the deity[31]. If something shows up wreathed in pink light, cuddling a bunny, with a message of forgiving your enemies and practicing nonviolence and tells you she's the Morrigan, I'd be highly suspicious of it. In the same vein if the deity doesn't give you a name, don't assume it must be a deity you are fond of or really like; sometimes we get messages from very unexpected places. This is especially important in dealing with the liminal Gods because we must rely on different forms of communication with them to form our understanding of them.

Many pagan religions believe in the importance of reciprocity, and this should include not only offerings and blessings, but also communication. We speak to them and they do answer, but we have to pay attention and be willing to listen. Our Gods are not omnipotent. They cannot make themselves heard if we won't hear them. And we are not perfect receivers, we mis-hear, misunderstand, misinterpret. Learning to communicate with the Gods and spirits is a process that requires effort, discernment, and openness. Land spirits are fond of using dreams to communicate with us, so we must learn to be aware of our dreams and how to translate them – keeping a dream journal is a really good idea. The Fair Folk may communicate directly, they certainly have the ability to do so, but they may also speak to us in dreams, through omens, or through actions like taking our things or causing us good or bad luck, and we have to be aware of that and know how to respond to it. And deities can do all of that and sometimes more. It takes effort to set up a structure to communicate with Gods and spirits, but it's worth the effort.

Guided Meditation to Meet your Fetch

Since your fetch is such a basic and important guide for you in your witchcraft, both spiritually and magically, one of the first things you should consider doing is reaching out and forming a strong connection to them. One way to do this is through a guided meditation, although don't be surprised if you find, once the lines of communication are open, that your fetch chooses to communicate with you through dreams and other methods more often. These are also exercises where you might consider casting a full circle in order to have a stronger connection to the Otherworld.

Find a time when you won't be disturbed, and sit comfortably. Either memorize the meditation, pre-record it and play it back for yourself, or have a friend read it to you.

Relax and breathe deeply…in and out…in…and out…

Feel the solid earth beneath you. Let your spirit move down, out, into the earth. Fill yourself with the energy that rests deep in the soil… When you feel empowered by this energy pull your spirit back up, out of the earth.

You find yourself in a wildwood, on a path that leads deeper into the shadowed trees. Walk down the path, breathing in the scent of the deep forest. The ground is hard beneath your feet and the leaves of the trees brush up against your arms as you walk, as if they were reaching out to you. Although you feel very safe in this ancient place there is a sense that someone or something is watching you as move deeper into the woods.

Up ahead you see light filtering in through the trees and you realize that you are approaching a clearing. Cautiously you move into the open space, leaving the darkness of the forest path behind. The clearing is sunlit and you relax as you walk out into the center, a slight breeze tickling your skin. Look around and observe your surroundings, the trees, the ground, the sounds of the forest. Take note of this place because this is where you will return when you need to seek out your fetch in the future.

As you are making note of where you are you hear a rustling in the underbrush. Turning towards it, an animal emerges. What is it? This is the animal form of your fetch.

The animal circles you, seeming to observe you the way you were just observing the clearing. Without warning it turns and disappears back into the deep forest, leaving you alone.

A moment later you hear rustling again, this time from a different direction and you turn to face this new sound. As your eyes search the shifting patterns of leaves and branches you see a figure stepping out from the trees. This figure is the human form of your fetch – take a moment to study this figure and familiarize yourself with them. When you feel ready greet them.

Your fetch replies, and you have an opportunity now to engage them in conversation. Ask your fetch whatever you want to, and be open to any messages they may have for you.

Your fetch may leave on its own when it is ready, or you may choose to thank it and say goodbye when you are ready. Allow your fetch to leave the clearing first. Only when they have disappeared from your sight should you head back towards the path that brought you to the clearing. Re-enter the trees and walk back down the path in the direction you came from. The way grows darker and darker until you can see nothing around you but blackness. The sounds of the forest fall away. You feel the Otherworld fading away and the mortal world returning.

Feel the solid earth beneath you. Let your spirit move down, out, into the earth. Fill yourself with the energy that rests deep in the soil… When you feel empowered by this energy pull your spirit back up, out of the earth.

Return to your body; feel yourself solidly back in mortal earth.

Relax and breathe deeply…in…and out…in and out…

Move slowly, reconnecting to your body, until you are ready to open your eyes.

Guided Meditation into the Sí

It is best before doing this meditation to go over proper manners and etiquette when dealing with the Good Neighbors.

Relax and breathe deeply…in and out…in…and out…

Feel the solid earth beneath you. Let your spirit move down, out, into the earth. Fill yourself with the energy that rests deep in the soil… When you feel empowered by this energy pull your spirit back up, out of the earth.

You find yourself sitting on the ground at twilight. Next to you is a staff of rowan carved with symbols. The earth is cool beneath you, but the air is still warm as darkness falls. A slight breeze carries the scent of grass and ripe berries. You hear the sounds of birds calling to each other as they settle in to roost for the night and the murmuring of water over rocks. Everything is covered in shadow, but you can see clearly. You are sitting in a field between an old forest and a river. At the other end of the field the shape of a hill rises up.

As you look at the hill something catches your eye, a twinkling light, like a firefly, but unmoving. Stand up, pick up the staff, and move towards the light...as you walk across the field towards the hill the light grows, flickering like firelight. You realize the light is coming from a door that opens up into the hill. Using the staff to help, climb up the hill to the door.

Looking in you see a magnificent chamber, set with a long table, decorated richly with gold and silver. The light is coming from an enormous fireplace at one end. The chamber is filled with Otherworldly people; some are sitting along the great table playing chess or fidchell, some are weaving and knitting, some are talking to each other. As you stand looking in, someone sees you and comes to the entrance.

This person will be your Guide in the Otherworld. Your Guide greets you warmly, 'Hello! Be welcome in this hall as a guest.'

Your Guide steps back and gestures for you to enter. Carefully place the rowan staff in the doorway to hold it open, and then enter the great room. Your Guide presents you with a token, an item to wear or carry while you are there to so everyone will know you are a guest. Your Guide will show you around and help you. You may ask questions, but be prepared to answer them as well. You may receive messages or gifts, but remember, things in Faery are not always what they seem.

(Allow everyone doing the meditation enough time to have individual experiences.)

You have experienced much within the Fairy Hill, but your Guide gently tells you it is time to leave. At the entrance you give your token back to your Guide before stepping out the door. You pick the staff back up and as you do the door closes and the doorway vanishes into the hill. You are standing alone on the fairy hill in the dark night. Carefully climb down the hill and walk back across the field. The night is silent now, and dark, and the wind is cold. Put down the staff and sit down, resting on the earth.

Feel the solid earth beneath you. Let your spirit move down, out, into the earth. Fill yourself with the energy that rests deep in the soil... When you feel empowered by this energy pull your spirit back up, out of the earth.

Return to your body; feel yourself solidly back in mortal earth.

Relax and breathe deeply...in...and out...in and out...

Move slowly, reconnecting to your body, until you are ready to open your eyes.

Modern Experience

I met my fairy familiar when I was 14.

I very quickly managed to – quite unintentionally – offend him and I didn't see him again after that for almost a decade. I'm actually pretty lucky that all he did in response to what I did (make a childish idle threat) was disappear for a decade. As an adult I have no illusions that I'd be so lucky again.

Fairy etiquette is a big deal because whether or not we care about, or know about it, it's essential to how the Gentry approach any interaction. There are things you can do and things you can't do, things you can talk about and things you can't talk about, and that is simply how things are whether or not it makes sense to us. They may pay back a loan with twice the value they borrowed, but should we give back a penny more than what was taken it will be a grave offense.

Chapter 11

Living Witchcraft

It's easy to believe in magic when you're young. Anything you couldn't explain was magic then. It didn't matter if it was science or a fairy tale. Electricity and elves were both infinitely mysterious and equally possible – elves probably more so.
– Charles de Lint

Sometimes, as is usual to-day in fairy-lore, it was a subterranean world entered through caverns, or hills, or mountains, and inhabited by many races and orders of invisible beings, such as demons, shades, fairies, or even gods. And the underground world of the Sidhe-folk, which cannot be separated from it, was divided into districts or kingdoms under different fairy kings and queens, just as the upper world of mortals. We already know how the Tuatha De Danann or Sidhe-folk, after their defeat by the Sons of Mil at the Battle of Tailte, retired to this underground world and took possession of its palaces beneath the green hills and vales of Ireland; and how from there, as gods of the harvest, they still continued to exercise authority over their conquerors, or marshalled their own invisible spirit-hosts in fairy warfare, and sometimes interfered in the wars of men.
– W. Y. Evans Wentz, 1911

Kids and Faith

There are certain questions that are commonly asked within the pagan community, and one that I see repeated at least once every few months is about raising children pagan. The exact phrasing of the question may change, but it's always expressed in two core ways: 'Should I raise my kids in my religion?' and, 'How do I teach my kids my beliefs?' In Fairy Witchcraft, where we deal with beings known to steal children, these questions take on extra weight, so they are worth considering here.

My answer to the first question is a simple: 'Yes. Of course you should raise your kids with your faith; if it's important to you why wouldn't you want to share it with them?' Now I'm obviously not talking about situations where there are legal reasons, such as a messy divorce, or extenuating circumstances, such as a pre-existing agreement with a non-pagan spouse, involved. But if you are actively practicing your religion and have children who you can include I really think you should, for several reasons.

First of all it will create valuable family traditions around holidays that your children can cherish even if they grow up to believe something totally different. This will also create opportunities for family bonding and spending time together that, sadly, in our modern lives we often don't have much of. Secondly, children generally like being included in things they know are important to you, at least in my experience. Thirdly it gives them a good understanding of your religion that will allow them later to make a decision about their own faith; related to that, if you keep what you do and believe secret you may inadvertently teach them that your religion is something to be ashamed of or not good enough.

It's entirely possible to raise your children in your religion without making it feel restrictive or forced, or teaching them that what you believe is the only option. I raise my daughters with my faith, but they are free to go to other people's religious services or to study other options. I've never understood the idea that we should not raise our kids with our own religion because it will somehow take away their ability to choose for themselves.

Finally, teaching your kids what you believe does, in theory, pass on the morals and guidelines for life that you have learned from your religion. Certainly this can be done in a secular way, but if you base your life on the seven Fairycraft virtues, for example, why wouldn't you want your kids to have that same guideline to live with? Also if you love your religion enough to practice it, why wouldn't you want to share that with your children and give them that same opportunity to enjoy it?

As to the second question, that one is easy – just include them in what you do and give direct answers to questions. I always give the girls the option of joining in with me if they want to. Rather than feeling forced or not wanting anything to do with it, my kids would have me doing ritual every night if I let them talk me into it! They love hearing stories about the Gods and Goddesses as well as the other spirits and our ancestors. They enjoy celebrating our holidays. If anything I have trouble keeping up with their interest, which is bottomless. I have never gone out of my way to teach them about my faith, I just include them when I celebrate and I answer their questions. The closest I've ever come to intentionally teaching them anything religious is buying the children's books to read to them. I don't think as parents we need to try to teach it if we are giving them living examples to follow and learn from.

This is perhaps especially essential in something like Fairy Witchcraft where children should know how to respectfully treat the Fair Folk and what is or is not safe to do. If you stop and think about it for a moment the folk traditions, the Fairy Faith itself, which is the core of our beliefs, has always been something passed on from birth. My own children have grown up seeing me honoring the Old Gods, the liminal Gods, the ancestors, and the Good People and they have a fairly good grasp of the concepts behind what we do.

Spiritual Devotion and Small Children

I remember the days, 20 years ago, 15 years ago, when spiritual devotion was an easy, flowing thing. If I wanted to stop and pray, or make an offering, or meditate on something I had the flexibility to do so. If I wanted to spontaneously drive out to a state park or to the ocean, I got in my car and went. If I was invited to attend an event or a group celebration I went. The only limitation I had was my work schedule. My focus when I prayed or conducted a ritual was to make it as perfect as possible. I had scripts to follow and high expectations.

And then, 12 years ago, I had my first child, and all that changed. My schedule wasn't my own anymore because there was no telling an infant to wait until I was done or finding that still meditative place in myself with a fussy toddler pulling at my hand. My previous approach to spirituality had been based around my own internal rhythms and patterns; what worked for me and when I felt pulled to do things. I had a very spontaneous spirituality, even in my set devotional work. When I planned things I had time to prep for rituals, to go over exactly what I was going to do until I was sure it could be executed perfectly. But all of that changed when children were involved.

There was a time when I chaffed a bit at the feeling of restriction, especially after my second child, who has several chronic medical issues, was born. The way I did things – the way I had done things for years and years at that point – suddenly had to be completely revised. It was a challenge, to be sure, but I believed from the beginning that it was vitally important that my children be included and that what I was doing be something they could also appreciate instead of something they would see taking my attention away from them.

We learned together how to form an organic approach to devotion and ritual. I had to accept that the idea of perfect prayers, recited with my full attention on worship, were right out the window; with small children you always have some small part of your attention on them and what they are doing.

My offerings became more creative and also simpler, and I grew to understand that the Gods and spirits want our best efforts, but our best efforts in that moment, not perfection. I re-read the *Carmina Gadelica*, seeing it not as a simple prayer book, but as a record of a living tradition practiced by people just like me, mothers praying their devotion within the daily round of feeding their families, bathing their babies, and worrying about the safety of those they loved.

I learned that it was better to try than not to do at all, even if the result was comical or rushed or interrupted. My devotional work became a study in perseverance, a type of devotion in its own way. If my morning prayers are interrupted by a hungry infant I sit down and nurse him and keep right on praying. If my Lúnasa ritual falls on an especially hot day then we celebrate inside so that my younger daughter can participate too without getting sick. We adapt, we work with what we have, and we give the Gods our best effort in that moment. Because I am sure the Gods and spirits – and I know for certain my ancestors – understand about hungry babies, and sick children, about life and human limitations.

My reward for adopting this approach is not only being able to continue my devotional practice no matter how chaotic my life may be on any given day, but more importantly, inspiring my children to want to do what I do. My oldest daughter came to me of her own accord and asked if we could start saying my night prayers together, so now we do them as a family. They look forward to each holiday as something fun they will participate in, and they are proud to be part of the traditions we celebrate. I look back at myself 20 years ago and I see someone who was free to totally devote themselves to their religion; I realize now that I still have that freedom if I choose to see my circumstances as a gift and not a burden.

When Your Ritual Goes Up in Flames

I conducted my first ritual when I was 12 years old. My friend had introduced me to neopaganism through Scott Cunningham's book *Wicca for the Solitary Practitioner* and I had gone on to read Buckland's *Complete Book of Witchcraft* and Sybil Leek's *Diary of a*

Witch. Now, months later, we had decided the time was right to conduct our first official moon ritual. I slept over at her house and in the middle of the night we snuck down to her finished basement, our arms full of purloined supplies, the correct pages of Cunningham's book dog-eared for reference. Unable to find enough candles we were using birthday candles pushed through upside down plastic planters, the thin flimsy kind you start seeds in, at the quarters. We set up our little altar and began our ritual with the unbridled enthusiasm of pre-teens. Holding the book close to our faces in the dim candlelight we cast our circle, invoked the Gods, and began the main body of our ritual. I can't remember exactly who noticed it first, but at some point one of us realized that our eastern quarter candle had burned down, through the plastic and set the carpet on fire. Almost immediately after this we realized the southern candle had done the same thing. Our circle was literally going up in flames. Chaos ensued, and our carefully made and blessed holy water was used to put out the fire. Thus ended my first ever ritual experience.

There are several valuable lessons in this story, not the least of which is the importance of fire safety and possibly adult supervision, but as I look back on it now I also see humor in it. I can laugh at myself, and I do. I also tell this story often in classes I teach to remind people that we all make mistakes, sometimes in spectacular fashion, but that no mistake should keep us from trying again.

Too often these days I see people encouraging a level of perfection in ritual that is unrealistic and leads to a shift in emphasis from experiencing a true connection to the divine to performing a flawless script. The former may include slip-ups and mistakes, but allows room for genuine experiential spirituality; the latter creates so much nervous tension about doing it right that often the entire point of the moment is missed. Or, put another way, I believe the focus in ritual should be on connecting to and honoring the Gods, not on putting on a flawless show. Of course the goal should be to do ritual well, whatever that means in your tradition, but there also needs to be an understanding that in any human endeavor you must expect the unexpected. Since my primary focus is the fairies/daoine sí/land spirits I tend to have quite a lot of chaos going on sometimes and have had my fair share of ritual mishaps. If you intend to practice Fairy Witchcraft then you had best brace yourself for the same.

So, what are some common things that can go wrong? And how do you deal with it when it happens?

Fire!

Believe it or not fire mishaps are fairly common, often the result of either lack of forethought (such as in my story) or overcrowding. Fire has a mind and spirit of its own as well and it isn't always going to do what you expect it to do. Always be sure to have water on hand and know where the closest fire extinguisher is. Also don't throw water on an oil fire, should you have one, as that will only spread the flames.

Mis-speaking

It happens to all of us, no matter who we are or how well we've prepared. You go to call the eastern quarter and say north instead. You're asked to call the ancestors at a ritual and flub your carefully prepared invocation. You are making an offering to a deity and halfway through the eloquent speech you spent so much time writing and memorizing your mind goes blank. You say Frigga when you mean Freya. You mispronounce Brighid or Cailleach. Or Samhain. The key here is not to let yourself get totally flustered – keep going and try to recover gracefully. If you accidently say thank you to the Fey, try to back off that as soon as possible, as politely as possible. If you happen to be in a situation, like a public ritual where you over hear someone else saying something foolish or inappropriate, decide if you will step back, step out, or intervene. I'm aware of an issue that happened at a local event's open ritual where someone attending stepped up and offered his eight-year-old daughter to the fairies, in jest, to the absolute horror of the ritual leaders who had to immediately try to take the offer back by making counter offerings. (Also – for the love of the green earth don't ever be that idiot, please).

Spilling Offerings

It will happen on occasion that as you go to make an offering it won't go where you intended. Mead bottles get knocked over, bumped into or otherwise end up spilling. Food offerings are dropped, slide off plates, or accidentally have something else set on top of them. The main problem here is that even if you could pick up a dropped offering or try to carry on with an otherwise ruined portion it's rather bad form to turn around and offer the Gods or Powers food or drink that's been spilled or is less than the best; in this case it's better to offer something new. I suggest keeping a secondary offering option under the altar. It can also happen that the Powers being offered to didn't like the original offering, which is why it ended up spilled and some quick divination is often helpful to ascertain whether it was the offering itself that needed to be changed or whether the offering was entirely unwanted. I will add though that sometimes the Good Neighbors will make things spill to indicate that they do want some of that given to them, so be aware of that possibility.

I Feel Like I'm Forgetting Something...

At some point all of us have those moments when, despite the best preparation, we realize mid-ritual we've forgotten an essential item or accidentally skipped over part of the ritual. I like to keep a box of spare items under the altar to cover possible needed items, and you can almost always go back to the skipped part of ritual and do it, even if it is out of order. Fairy Witchcraft ritual is really more of a general guideline that anything written in stone, so don't be afraid to be flexible if you need to be.

Miscellaneous Mayhem

There are endless ways that ritual can go wrong. Lighters stop working or offerings you're trying to burn won't catch. Incense won't light. If you are with another person or in a group someone else with a part in the ritual freezes, mis-speaks, or suddenly starts going in a random direction. The group energy is too high or too low. In most cases the best go-to solution is a group chant which helps keep everyone focused while the problem is mundanely addressed and gets everyone on the same page.

A subcategory of mayhem is the issue of children. If your group allows them in ritual or has them in the general area while ritual is going on its best to plan for the ritual itself to be short and sweet and be prepared for anything from tearful interruptions mid-invocation to stubborn insistence on participation. I can promise that no matter how often or clearly you explain what you are doing children are the definition of chaos. Sometimes this is good and adds a deeper element to the event, with children spontaneously singing happy birthday to the sun at Midwinter, for example, and other times not so much such as when my daughter who was nine at the time used her time to thank Freya for one of the blessings in her life to instead ask for the return of our missing pet cat. It's very important as a parent that you are ready to step in and quietly handle any child-related issue that might arise, even if that means removing yourself and the child from the ritual. If the child is not yours you can still step in when needed to curb the chaos as much as possible.

When to Stop

There are some cases when a mishap occurs that should stop the ritual. If anyone is physically hurt, stop. If any fire occurs that requires dousing or extinguishing with equipment, stop. If anyone attending the event becomes extremely upset, hysterical, irate, or otherwise out of control during ritual, stop. If something is said or done that is dangerous, stop and do some immediate damage control. Have an emergency plan for stopping ritual at any point quickly and efficiently. Also, there are situations when the ritual should be stopped, at least temporarily, and divination done, to assess whether continuing is a good idea. For example if you are using candles in glass holders and the glass cracks or your candle won't light, while there could always be a simple physical explanation, it could also be a sign that what you are doing isn't a good idea.

We should always try to make our rituals the best they can be, but we need to understand the inevitability of the imperfect. Too many times I have seen people at public rituals offered the chance to participate who refuse for fear of messing up. I believe the Gods value our efforts, flawed and human as they are, and that we not only rob ourselves of a chance to connect to those Powers beyond ourselves when we let fear control us but we also fail in such cases to fully offer to the Gods. I am not the best singer, but I sing from the heart and I believe that such an offering has great value. Not only am I giving something of myself but I am opening myself up to experiencing connection to the Gods and Powers in a way that can only happen through active practice, rather than passive observation.

Also, in my experience, the Powers have a sense of humor, and sometimes the best thing we can do is take a minute to have a good laugh at ourselves and then keep going. Ritual is rather like life in that way. Especially when dealing with and honoring the Fey you will find that expecting the unexpected is necessary. Things will rarely ever go as planned, and that's alright. Be prepared and learn to roll with what comes.

Modern Experience: What it Means to Me to be a Bantuaithech

There are many, many approaches to witchcraft and some are completely different from others, but it is true that the vast majority of witches in the Western world seem to follow what is generally termed a 'right-hand path' or benevolent witchcraft. This approach usually adheres to the same guidelines: a belief in a Westernized understanding of karma, following the Wiccan Rede, and belief in the rule of three. Because this is the most popular approach it can sometimes be seen in groups as the only acceptable approach, particularly with an emphasis on witchcraft that focuses on healing, blessing, protection, and a strong ethic of not causing harm.

However...

I'm a witch[32]. I have been a witch now for almost 25 years. My journey in witchcraft has been a complex one. I spent many years as a right-hand-path witch and then, to quote Pratchett and Gaiman's book *Good Omens,* I 'sauntered vaguely downwards' into dark witchcraft with a brief stopover in gray witchcraft.

I don't believe in karma[33], in the sense that what we do comes back to us in a reward/punishment system, or that being good makes good things happen. I do think that being a good person, however you define that, has value and should be strived for. But I don't think there is some universal power that metes out punishment or reward based on an arbitrary system of good or bad actions. One person's good action after all is often enough another person's bad, and so much depends on perspective.

I don't follow the Wiccan Rede, because I am not Wiccan, firstly, and secondly because I believe that sometimes 'harm' is good and necessary. Sometimes a small harm now prevents a greater harm later, or is being done for a larger purpose, such as the 'harm' done to my daughter when she had her cardiac procedure in order to correct a dangerous irregular heartbeat. Sometimes it's being done to protect something, like when I have to kill a hive of wasps that is above my garage (my husband is severely allergic). Sometimes it's simply a matter of deciding that the action is necessary, and taking it.

I don't believe in the rule of three, in any sense. I do believe that our mindset, be it positive or negative, affects our life, and that how we treat other people directly affects how other people, in a very general sense, treat us. If you are nice to people they are usually nice to you, if you are jerk they are generally a jerk in return. But life experience has shown me that bad things happen to good people and good things happen to bad people all the time. And that's not even getting into the stickety-wicket of who decides what is 'good' and 'bad' to begin with...

I have hexed. I have done bindings and banishings. I deal with spirits, both on friendly terms and commanding them, usually to leave a place. I am very pragmatic in my magic; I do what needs doing. And there has never been any terrible consequence to me from anything I have done although I will add here that I am very careful and I know what I am doing. The greatest consequence I have faced is the judgment and censure from some people within the pagan community for being open about the sort of witch that I am.

I think, sometimes, that paganism has spent so many decades trying to convince the rest of the world that we are all harmless and safe that any time someone comes along and says, 'No if it needs doing I'll do it, even if it's sad or unpleasant or hard,' there is an automatic response of immediately rejecting that idea. We don't want to own the dark witch anymore, or we want to make it a clear cut matter of 'good/light' and 'bad/dark'. We have bought into our own PR and we want our witchcraft safe and nice and palatable for the masses of non-pagans. We don't want the dark and scary as a serious practice, only as a sort of juvenile 'phase' that we say people will grow out of or as a side-show all-flash-no-substance joke. It's not easy to break out of that mindset, as a community. Heck it was hard for me. Everyone wants to be the hero in the story, not the pragmatist.

There are all sorts of witches in the world and that's exactly as it should be. We need the variety. Some are very gentle. Some are very loving. Some are very peaceful. Some are all of that, but if their back is against a wall they will defend themselves.

I am not that sort.

I was told once, in a visionary experience, that I needed to own the idea of being a badb, a bantúaithech, for lack of a better translation an 'old school witch'. Someone who isn't afraid of doing what needs doing. Who can heal or hex without hesitation. Who isn't afraid to go where other people truly do fear to tread. Who owns their own darkness and understands the balance that is needed between dark and light to preserve Firinne (truth/right order). The word badb itself when applied to a human means a witch of the dark and dangerous sort, the kind who shows up and gives an ill prophecy and then works magic to ensure it happens. A cursing-witch. The word bantúaithech[34] is related to the word túaithe and has strong negative connotations, being related to túaithbel meaning left-hand-wise, against the sun, to cursing, of working against the positive, and is also related through túath to the aos sidhe who witches were reputed to deal with and get much of their skill and knowledge from. So a badb or bantúaithech is a witch who works against the sun and who deals with the fairy folk, who curses and prophesies.

This was not a message I wanted to hear, nor one I was quick to embrace.

I really didn't want to be that person.

Because there is a comfort in acceptance. There is a comfort in staying weak, and avoiding confrontation, and letting other people handle the messy work. There is a comfort in being able to say, 'I am harmless and good and only ever help everyone.'

But you can't fight dán and a raven can't be a robin no matter how much it wishes it was.

So I have spent a lot of time learning to be a bantuaithech, an old school witch, and learning that you can still be kind and gentle even when you are the one who knows how to hex and does it when it needs doing. Learning that you can still be nice even when you are the one who isn't afraid to walk straight into the darkness and handle what you find there, and you are the one who does the things that generally seem to horrify so many other people. I had to learn that all those frightening connotations with the words badb and bantúaithech nonetheless represent the preservation of right-order, of fírinne – the dark witch doesn't curse for fun or maliciousness, but in the myths and stories she does so to bring back order when there is a great imbalance. She uses her own power to correct imbalances, often by bringing down important people – often kings or heroes – who have abused their power or greatly transgressed the social order. She is not a bad person, but she is the one who must do the dirty work in the stories in order to set things right . I had to learn not to fear using power when it needed to be used, especially in situations where those who were otherwise powerless needed to have someone act for them. I learned, ultimately, that sometimes the only way to preserve right-order is to go against it for a time.

I am that sort of witch, but it doesn't make me a bad person – if anything it has made me a better person because I understand the fear, and anger, and hatred that far too often drive other people. I embrace the darkness because I don't see it as frightening or dangerous, just as beautiful and empowering. I can empathize with suffering and being broken because I have been there. I appreciate the importance of being good and kind because I am so aware of the reality of the other side of that. I am kind not because I fear the consequences of not being kind – I don't – but because I know the value of kindness for its own sake.

But like Al Capone said: 'Don't mistake my kindness for weakness. I am kind to everyone, but when someone is unkind to me, weak is not what you are going to remember about me.'

Conclusion

Fairy Witchcraft is a religion and also a magical practice, but most importantly it is a worldview. It is a way of life. When you embrace the idea that all things have a spirit it changes how you interact with the world around you. When you understand that the Other Crowd are around us and can affect us it changes how you approach them and their places. When you have glimpsed the liminal Gods it changes how you understand who and what the Gods are.

Every day we have the choice to live our beliefs. Some of this is about really adopting the worldview of our religion; learning to look at the world around us through a lens that is at least colored with the cosmology of Fairy Witchcraft. We can also choose to live by the ethics that our religion teaches and strive to be an honorable person, as best we understand that concept, according to what our spirituality tells us that means. Strive to nurture the seven virtues that the Good People respect, and it will make you a better person overall. In this way we both look at the world and interact with the world from a place that is grounded in our religion. This is, ultimately, a natural thing and what most people raised within a religion do, but as people who are choosing now to come to this faith it can take some extra conscious effort to adopt this mindset. My children don't need to do this because they are growing up with our beliefs and values being taught and reinforced every day, but part of that as well is them seeing those beliefs and values modeled and lived by the adults around them and consciously restated.

Much of my daily practice is informal: placing a flower on my outdoor altar, pouring out a bit of my drink on the ground, pausing respectfully before entering a place with a strong spirit. Making an effort to connect to those spirits and respect them. And much of what I do every day is not for the Gods, but rather for the ancestors, house spirits, landvaettir, and huldufolk/daoine sí, which is truly the heart of Fairy Witchcraft.

If the big holy days are important to strengthening our relationship and reinforcing reciprocity with the Gods and spirits, then the daily practices are what really create and maintain those relationships in our lives. The daily practices are the lifeblood of our faith, the things that become habits which keep us always connected to the numinous even when we are not aware we are experiencing it. Daily spirituality isn't about grand gestures, but rather about small moments – and it's those small moments that really matter.

Fairy Witchcraft is not the same as the traditional folk beliefs of the Fairy Faith, although it is heavily rooted in them

Fairy Witchcraft is not the same as most other neopagan witchcraft traditions, although it is framed as one.

Fairy Witchcraft, like the Gods it honors, is liminal. It is something that is new and also old, something traditional and also innovative. Modern paganism is a constantly evolving landscape of new groups and practices, many of which try to meld older beliefs with modern religion. Fairy Witchcraft is one such new path that represents a way to bring the old Fairy Faith ways and beliefs forward into a modern neopagan context.

In many ways Fairy Witchcraft is very similar to other types of neopagan witchcraft; however, some of the basic tools used are different and it has a much stronger emphasis on practices associated with British Hedgewitchcraft or cunningcraft, such as crossing the hedge (spiritual journey work), partnering with spirits (in this case fairies), healing, making offerings, and connecting to the Otherworld in general.

Anyone may choose to follow the path of Fairy Witchcraft, but whether or not the fairies will respond is impossible to influence or predict. Some people spend their whole lives trying to connect with the fairies and never get any response while others would just as soon not have anything to do with them and yet are always surrounded by spirits. It is important though to have some kind of relationship with the world of Fairy in order to be a Fairy Witch because Fairy Witchcraft includes two main components. One is to include honoring the fairy folk in your practice and the other is to actively interact with them in your magics. The first is possible even without any responsiveness from the fairies but the second can never be achieved without a reciprocal relationship.

Fairy Witchcraft is generally a solitary practice. While it is possible to practice Fairy Witchcraft in a small group, it works best as a solitary effort because each person's connection to Fairy will be unique and experiential. Group work can be very challenging unless the group is very tight knit or experienced working together. Along with this though it should be noted that Fairy Witchcraft can be a family practice, something that is done as a family and is taught to children. While many other witchcraft paths have age restrictions, Fairy Witchcraft does not, believing that since the old Fairy Faith was practiced by people of all ages it is acceptable for it to be passed on in age appropriate ways to children.

Fairy Witchcraft is a modern faith that offers a way for pagans to connect deeply to the Fairy Faith of old. It seeks to revive some of the old practices of the fairy doctors and bean feasa, of the cunning folk and wise people, while looking to a neopagan religious framework. It is, at its heart, an experiential and wild path that pushes the witch to reach out to the Otherworld and take chances in order to create connections to Fairy; connections which involve risk balanced with wisdom. The path to Fairy is shrouded in mist and mystery, but it is there still, waiting to be found.

She's away with the fairies
She's flown off with the Folk
She's dancing in dreams

Of shadows and smoke
Leaping and lunging
Between that world and this
She's wandering wild
In moonlight and mist

Appendix A – Resources

Websites

Ashliman, D., (2009) *Fairy Gifts*. Retrieved May 24, 2012 from http://www.pitt.edu/~dash/type0503.html

Lawless, S., (2009). *Fairy Faiths*. Retrieved April 8, 2012 from http://Witchofforestgrove.com/2009/09/15/fairy-traditions/

Whittier, J. (2008) *Charms and Fairy Faith*. Retrieved April 8, 2012 from http://www.readbookonline.net/readOnLine/8364/

Yeats, W (1888). *Fairy and Folk Tales of the Irish Peasentry*. Retrieved May 24, 2012 from http://www.sacred-texts.com/neu/yeats/fip/index.htm

The myths of the *Ulster Cycle, Fenian Cycle*, and *Book of Invasions* http://www.maryjones.us/ctexts/index_irish.html

Movies

The Secret of Roan Inish, (1995) Sony Pictures
Ondine, (2010) Magnolia Home Entertainment
Into the West (2011) Echo Bridge Home Entertainment
The Secret of Kells, (2010) New Video Group
Fairy Faith (2001) Wellspring Media
The Secret World of Arietty (2012) Buena Vista
The Spiderwick Chronicles (2008) Paramount
Labyrinth (1986) Sony Pictures
Pan's Labyrinth (2007) New Line Home Video
The Lord of the Rings (2002) New Line
The Hobbit (2012) New Line
Hellboy II The Golden Army (2008) Universal Studios
The Dark (2006) Sony Pictures

Appendix B – Glossary of Terms

Alfar – Supernatural beings in Norse and Germanic belief that have their own world, are not Gods, are offered to, can influence our world, especially weather, and can affect people for good or ill

Aos sí – ACE SHEE – people of the fairy hills

Banshee – BAHNshee – literally 'fairy woman', a spirit that is associated with a particular family and appears, wailing, before someone dies; previously also the Washer at the Ford, a fairy who would appear in rivers washing the clothes of those about to die

Bean Feasa – Bahn fahsa – 'wise woman'

Cailleach – KAY-llyuch – witch, hag, crone Goddess

Daoine sí – THEE-nuh SHEE – people of the fairy hills

Elfshot – Small invisible arrows used to pierce people and animals, which cause illness

Elflocks – Inexplicable tangles in hair or people and animals that appear overnight

Etins – Malicious spirits

Fairy – Elfland, Fairyland, the Otherworld

Fairy – A being of the Otherworld or land spirit

Fairy Doctor – a person who has learned how to deal with malignant witchcraft and fairy magics

Fey – Otherworldly or supernatural

Huldufolk – Literally 'hidden people'

Otherworld – A world similar to, but different from our own, which has more magic and is where many Fey beings come from

Sí – SHEE – Fairy hill, hollow hill, also an adjective that means 'of fairy'

Bibliography

Allen, D., and Hatfield, G., (2004). *Medicinal Plants in Folk Tradition: An Ethnobotany of Britain & Ireland*

The Ballad of Tam Lin (nd) Retrieved from http://www.sacred-texts.com/neu/eng/child/ch039.htm

Bauschatz, P., (1982) *The Well and the Tree: World and Time in Early Germanic Culture*

Bedell, J. (2006). *Hildur Queen of the Elves and Other Icelandic Legends*

Berk, A., and Spytma, W., (2002) *Penance, Power, and Pursuit, On the Trail of the Wild Hunt*

Blain, J., (2000) *Wights and Ancestors*

Borsje, J., (2010). *Rules and Legislations on Love Charms in Early Medieval Ireland*

Briggs, K., (1967) *The Fairies in Tradition and Literature*

Briggs, K., (1976) *A Dictionary of Fairies*

Briggs, K., (1978) *The Vanishing People: Fairy Lore and Legends*

Briggs, K., (1978) *An Encyclopedia of Fairies*

Bord, J., (1997) *Fairies: Real Encounters with Little People*

Callow, E., (1882) *The Phynodderre and Other Legends of the Isle of Man*

Campbell, J., (2005) *The Gaelic Otherworld*

Carmichael, A., (1900) *Carmina Gadelica*

Chadwick, N., (1935) *Imbas Forosnai*

Chambers, R., (1842) *Popular Rhymes, Fireside Stories, and Amusements of Scotland*

Cunningham, S., (1985) *Cunningham's Encyclopedia of Magical Herbs*

Curtin, J., (1895) *Tales of the Fairies and of the Ghost World*

Daimler, M., (2010) *By Land, Sea, and Sky*

Daimler, M., (2012) *A Child's Eye View of the Fairy Faith*

Daimler, M., (2014) *Pagan Portals: Fairy Witchcraft*

Danaher, K., (1972) *The Year in Ireland*

Danaher, K., (1964) *Irish Customs and Beliefs*

DeVries, L., (2010) Red Clover., http://medicinalherbinfo.org/herbs/RedClover.html

Egil's Saga

Ellis Davidson, H., (1988) *Myths and Symbols in Pagan Europe*

Ellis Davidson, H., (1989) *The Seer in Celtic and Other Traditions*

Estyn Evans, E., (1957) *Irish Folk Ways*

Evans, D., (2005) Matronae. Retrieved from http://www.celtnet.org.uk/gods_m/matronae.html

Evans-Wentz, W. Y., (1911) *The Fairy Faith in Celtic Countries*

Evert Hopman, E., (2011) *Scottish Herbs and Fairy Lore*

Foster, S., and Duke, J., (2000) *Eastern/Central Medicinal Plants and Herbs*

Fraser Black, G., (1894) *Scottish Charms and Amulets*

Freeman, P., (2008) *War, Women, and Druids*

Froud, B., and Lee, A., (2002) *Faeries*

Froud, B., (1998) *Good Faeries, Bad Faeries*

Gray, E., (1983) *Cath Maige Tuired*

Green, M., (1997) *The World of the Druids*

Green, M., (1992) *Dictionary of Celtic Myth and Legend*

Gregory, L., (1988) *A Treasury of Irish Myth, Legend & Folklore*

Grieve, M., (1971) *A Modern Herbal*

Grimm, J., (1982) *Teutonic Mythology, volume 1*

Grimm, J., (1883) *Teutonic Mythology, volume 3*

Gruber, B., (2007) *Iceland: Searching for Elves and Hidden People*

Guerber, H., (1908) *Myths of the Norsemen*

Gundarsson, K (2007) *Elves, Wights, and Trolls*

Hall, A., (2005) Getting Shot of Elves: Healing, Witchcraft and Fairies in the Scottish Witchcraft Trials. Folklore Vol. 116, No. 1 (Apr., 2005)

Hall, A., (2007) *Elves in Anglo-Saxon England*

Hall, A., (2004) *The Meaning of Elf and Elves in Medieval England,* Retrieved from http://www.alarichall.org.uk/ahphdful.pdf

Hall, A., (2011). *The Contemporary Evidence for Early Medieval Witchcraft-Beliefs*. Retrieved from www.academia.edu/1528964/The_Contemporary_Evidence_for_Early_Medieval_Witchcraft-Beliefs

Heimskringla

Hodge, W., (n.d.) *Waelburga and the Rites of May*. Retrieved from www.friggasweb.org/walburga.html

Hollander, L., (1936) *Old Norse Poems*

Huperzia Selago (2013) Online Atlas of the British & Irish Flora www.brc.ac.uk/plantatlas/index.php?q=node/2831

Hyde, D., (1890) *Beside the Fire*

JCHAS (2010) Journal of the Cork Historical and Archaeological Society

Jolly, K., (1996) *Popular Religion in Late Saxon England: Elf Charms in Context*

Jones, M., (2003) *The Wild Hunt*. Retrieved from www.maryjones.us/jce/wildhunt.html

Kirk, R., (2006) *The Secret Commonwealth of Elves, Fauns and Fairies*

Lawless, S., (2010) *The Ethics of Malevolence*

Lecouteux, C., (1999) *Phantom Armies of the Night: The Wild Hunt and the Ghostly Processions of the Undead*

Lecouteux, C., (1992) *Witches, Werewolves, and Fairies*

Lecouteux, C., (2000) *The Tradition of Household Spirits*

Lendering, J., (2013) *Matres, Matronae, or Mothers*. Retrieved from www.livius.org/man-md/matronae/matronae.html

Lenihan and Green (2004) *Meeting the Other Crowd*

Lindow, J., (2002) *Norse Mythology: A Guide to the Gods, Heroes, Rituals, and Beliefs*

Locke, T., (2013). *The Fairy Doctor*. Retrieved from www.irishabroad.com/blogs/PostView.aspx?pid=4404

MacAlister, R., (1941) *Lebor Gabala Erenn*

Mac Coitir, N., (2003) *Irish Trees: Myths, Legends, & Folklore*

Mac Coitir, N., (2008) *Irish Wild Plants: Myths, Legends, & Folklore*

MacDonald, L., (1993) People of the Mounds. Dalriada Magazine

MacGillivray, Deborah. (2000). The Cait Sí. Retrieved from http://deborahmacgillivray.co.uk/scotlore_caitsí.htm

MacKillop, J., (1998) *A Dictionary of Celtic Mythology*

Mac Liommóir, M., (1984). *Faery Nights Oícheanta Sí*

Magic and Religious Cures (2014). *Ask About Ireland.* Retrieved from www.askaboutireland.ie/reading-room/history-heritage/folklore-of-ireland/folklore-in-ireland/healers-and-healing/magic-and-religious-cures/

Martin, M., (2012) *A Description of the Western Isles of Scotland*

Matthews, C., and J., (2005) *The Elemental Encyclopedia of Magical Creatures*

Matthews, J., (1997) *The Druid Source Book*

Matthews, J., (1999) *Celtic Seers Sourcebook*

McNeill, F., (1956) *The Silver Bough, volume 1*

McNeill, F., (1959) *The Silver Bough, volume 2*

McNeill, F., (1961) *The Silver Bough, volume 3*

Merseburg Incantation. www.pitt.edu/~dash/merseburg.html

Meyers, K., (1906) *The Triads of Ireland*

Miller, J., (2004) *Magic and Witchcraft in Scotland*

Narvaez, P., (1997) *The Good People: New Fairylore Essays*

Nenonen, R., (2014) *Finnish Myth*

O Crualaoich, G., (2005) Reading the Bean Feasa. Folklore Vol. 116, No. 1 (Apr., 2005)

O Crualaoich, G., (2003) *The Book of The Cailleach*

O Donaill, N., (1977) *Focloir Gaeilge-Bearla*

O Dubhain, S., (2010) *Celtic Karma*

O hOgain, D., (1991) *Myth, Legend, and Romance*

O hOgain, D., (1995) *Irish Superstitions*

O hOgain, D., (1999) *The Sacred Isle*

O Suilleabhain, S., (1967) *Nosanna agus Piseoga na nGael*

O Tuathail, S., (1993) *The Excellence of Ancient word: Druid Rhetoric*

from Ancient Irish Tales
www.dil.ie/
Old Farmer's Almanac (2012)
www.almanac.com/calendar/date/2012-08-17
Our Troth, vol. 1 (2006)
Paine, A., (2006) *The Healing Power of Celtic Plants*
Parkinson, D., (2013) *Phantom Black Dogs*
www.mysteriousbritain.co.uk/folklore/phantom-black-dogs.html
Paxson, D., (2008) *Trance-portation*
Paxson, D., (2012) *The Way of the Oracle*
Pennick, N., (1993) *Runic Magic: The History and Practice of Ancient Runic Traditions*
Plant Life (2012) White Clover
Pliny the Elder, *Natural History*, 1st century CE
www.maryjones.us/ctexts/classical_pliny.html#22
Pocs, E., (1999) *Between the Living and the Dead*
Rolleston, T., (1911) *Myths and Legends of the Celtic Race*
Ross, A., (1970) *Pagan Celts*
Rowan Laurie, E., (2012) *A Circle of Stones*
Scherker, A., (2013) *Protecting Elves from Highway Construction is a Thing in Iceland*
Schreiwer, R., (2013) *The 12 Nights of Wonnetdanz*. Retrieved from http://urglaawe.blogspot.com/2013/04/twelve-nights-of-wonnetdanz.html
Sikes, W., (1880) *British Goblins: Welsh Folk-lore, Fairy Mythology, Legends and Traditions*
Sjoedsedt, M., (2000) *Celtic Gods and Heroes*
Soderlind, R., (2013) *Elves in Modern Iceland*
Stokes, W., (1901) *Thesaurus Palaeohibernicus: A Collection of Old-Irish Glosses, Scolia, Prose, and Verse*
Tichy, O., (2010) *Bosworth-Toller Anglo-Saxon Dictionary*
Towrie, S., (2013) *The Wild Hunt*
Viking Answer Lady (n.d.) Sacred Space in Viking Law and

Religion

Walsh, B (2002) *The Secret Commonwealth and the Fairy Belief Complex*

Wedin, W., (1998) *The Sí, the Tuatha de Danaan, and the Fairies in Yeats's Early Works*

White, C., (2005) *A History of Irish Fairies*

Wilby, E., (2005) *Cunning Folk and Familiar Spirits*

Wilde, L. (1991) *Irish Cures, Mystic Charms & Superstition*

Yeats, W., (1962) *The Celtic Twilight*

Yeats, W., (1998) *Fairy and Folktales of Ireland*

Yeats, W., (1888) *Fairy and Folk Tales of the Irish Peasantry*

End Notes

1. A more in-depth article I wrote on this subject, which overlaps this material somewhat, appears in Lughnasa/ Samhain 2014 issue of the peer reviewed CR journal Air n-Aithesc.
2. Caillí is generally translated as witches from Irish, but can also mean old women, nuns, or hag. It is also the name of a Goddess who is associated with the winter in Cork, Ireland, and parts of Scotland.
3. Mna feasa simply means wise women.
4. Elf shot is a small invisible arrow that is a primary weapon of the fairies. It causes invisibly wounds that result in sudden pain, cramping, or a pinching sensation in people and a wasting sickness in livestock.
5. A geasa (plural geis) is a taboo that if broken brings extreme bad luck and death. Magical work in a Celtic cultural context means understanding what geis are and how to deal with them, and it is likely that any Fairy Witch will likely end up with geis of their own over time.
6. Never use an herb medicinally unless you have been trained to do so or have experience with herbs. Many herbs can be dangerous if misused, even ones that are commonly found in teas, and many can interact with other herbs and medications in dangerous ways.
7. Generally in this book I will use a lower case 'f' fairy when I mean the being and a capital 'F' Fairy when I mean the place.
8. The word fetch is also used to describe the ghostly apparition of a living person who appears as an omen of that person's impending death, and so the fetch has something of a dire reputation. I might surmise that such appearances were attempts by the fetch to warn the person, rather than to bring about their doom.

9. People in the southern hemisphere will have to tailor directional motion to fit their environment so that these motions hold true to the concepts behind the actions. They should not simply be done by rote, but should be done in accordance with the spirit behind them. The same is obviously true for celebrating holidays and the timing of the holy days.
10. Fairy Witchcraft is not the only group or tradition that uses the septogram as a symbol, just like Wiccans aren't the only ones who use the pentagram, I know of at least two others who use it, a Druidic group and the Otherkin. So just be aware that it is not a symbol in any way exclusive to Fairy Witchcraft.
11. Genus locii are spirits of place, usually personifications of a specific area or embodiment of that place's soul.
12. I honestly do not know where I got this idea from, but it had been with me for as long as I can remember and I have found many other modern Fairy Workers who share the same prohibition.
13. This intensity of emotion is one reason why it is so unwise to anger the Fair Folk, because their enmity knows neither compassion nor mercy, but is a pure anger. We often perceive it as cruelty because it is unfettered in its intensity.
14. I know of at least one case within the past few years where a woman who offended the Fair Folk by filling a place they considered theirs with wrought iron was physically shoved off a retaining wall and broke her arm
15. The Other Crowd dislike unclean things including dirty water and urine.
16. There is a very old superstition about giving the gift of a knife, or any blade – to do so will sever the friendship. This is a very basic sympathetic magic principle, the idea that to give a blade will cut the connection between the two people.
17. Only some fairies, however, as the color red itself is a fairy color. Leprechauns originally were described clad all in red,

many dangerous Otherworldly figures in Irish mythology appear wearing all red, and fairy animals are often described as white with red ears.

18. Seelie is a Scots word that means blessed, lucky; wight means being, creature
19. Daemon – '(in ancient Greek belief) A divinity or supernatural being of a nature between gods and humans.' www.google.com/search?q=definition+daemon&oq=definition+daemon&aqs=chrome.0.69i57j0l3j69i62l2.6419j0&sourceid=chrome&ie=UTF-8
20. The folk beliefs vary across Ireland in ways that can be contradictory, so that the tree that should never be cut and brought inside in one area, lest it draw the Fair Folk, is the same one recommended elsewhere to protect against them. Similarly one area might believe that keeping dirty water in the home draws fairies and grants them entrance while another area believes this water drives them away. This can make it difficult to say almost anything with absolute certainty as there are nearly always exceptions. Studying these beliefs, and more importantly putting them into practice means understanding these contradictions and choosing which beliefs to apply in your own life.
21. The Fairy Rade or Fairy Ride is a concept seen in many cultures of a procession of higher ranking fairies who ride out together, often at specific times of year like Samhain and Midsummer. Crossing paths with a Fairy Rade is dangerous, although we can see examples in stories such as the tale of Tam Lin where a mortal is recovered from the fairies after being won back during a Rade. The Fairy Rade sometimes is similar to or confused with the Wild Hunt.
22. Some modern spirit workers and traditional witches do choose to ride with the Wild Hunt. I won't say I've never done it, but I also won't encourage other people to try it. There is always a danger with the Hunt that you won't come back.

23. This may tie into the idea seen on the continent of the Wild Hunt as spirits who travel the air and can take people. There is much crossover, as we previously discussed between the Wild Hunt and the fairies and in certain areas, especially Ireland and the Orkneys, it is likely that the Wild Hunt and the Fairy Host are one and the same.
24. This section appears in part in *Pagan Portals: Fairy Witchcraft*.
25. This prayer is one of my own, but is an amalgam of several traditional prayers.
26. A poem from the Finn Cycle in Old Irish often called Summer has Gone.
27. This is the same dedication ritual that appears in *Pagan Portals: Fairy Witchcraft*. It is the only dedication ritual used in this tradition.
28. This passage also appears in my earlier book *Where the Hawthorn Grows*.
29. Our approach to cursing may best be said to follow the Wheaton Law, i.e. 'Don't be a dick.' If you have no other recourse, if you've exhausted other avenues of response, if it's really truly necessary then do it. But what I tell people is if you wouldn't physically fight the other person over the issue then you shouldn't magically fight them over it either. Cursing should be a last resort in desperate situations.
30. I'm not going to discuss possession work here; that's a whole different category. I do suggest Diana Paxson's book *The Essential Guide to Possession, Depossession, and Divine Relationships* as a good guide book on the subject as well as Filan and Kaldera's book *Drawing Down the Spirits: The Traditions and Techniques of Spirit Possession*.
31. This is extremely difficult with Odin due to the scope of his mythology and variety of his by-names and personalities.
32. I've discussed in previous blogs that I am both a witch and a Druid. I see the first as a personal practice, a skill, and the second as a role within the community. In my life they

provide balance and dovetail nicely with each other, and both work within my Irish Reconstructionist Polytheism.

33. Okay that's a bit of hyperbole on my part, but it's complicated. I don't believe that what we do creates some kind of energetic rubber band effect that snaps back and hits us, but I do believe in the Hindu and Buddhist ideas of karma.
34. To clarify a point: the word bantúaithech is Old Irish and is the word used in the myths to describe female magic users, generally translated as 'witch'. Be Chullie and Dianann are referred to this way in the Cath Maige Tuired when Lugh asks what power they will bring to the fight (they promise to enchant the trees and stones and earth to appear as a great army by the way), and a further list of ten women of the Tuatha De Danann is given and described this way in the Banshenchus. The word, however, did not survive into modern Irish. There is a similar term, tuathánach, which means rustic or country dweller and tuathbheartach means evil-doing. Interestingly túathgeinte, meaning the Good Folk did survive as tuathghinte in modern Irish. Similarly badb, meaning a witch, is Old or middle Irish; in modern Irish babdbh when applied to a human means a scold and only has vague connotations of cursing.